D1286794

The
SQUAD

The
SQUAD

The US Government's Secret Alliance With Organized Crime

Michael Milan

Shapolsky Publishers, Inc.
New York

For additional information contact:
Shapolsky Publishers, Inc.
136 West 22nd Street
New York, NY 10011

First Edition 1989

9 8 7 6 5 4 3 2 1

Library of Congress Cataloging-in-Publication Data is available:

L. C. card number 89–10929

Milan, Michael
    The Squad: the secret alliance between organized crime and the U. S. government.

ISBN 0–944007–52–X

Manufactured in the United States of America

A Shapolsky/Shadow Lawn Press Book

Dedication

To the police officers of our cities: the real strength of our country.

To the "Good People," as they like to be called, for showing their patriotic duty by saving hundreds of thousands of American lives in World War II.

And to my Greek doll who weathered the storm.

Contents

Introduction

You can call me Michael Milan. Everybody else does, or something close to it. Milan's not my real name. Officially I have no real name—just the names they called me when they sent me out on jobs. Mike Milan was only one of them. It's the one we'll use in this story. I've used a hundred names on the job, none of them my own. The people who know me—the people that I once reported to—even they didn't want to know my real name. They sent me orders with my serial number in the upper right-hand corner: 80762546. That number was a code, and it always meant that someone who I'd never met was supposed to die. By my hand. The people who gave me these assignments always referred to them as "foreclosing a loan," "delivering a package," or "terminating someone's employment." "Killing" was something the bad guys did. We were supposed to be the good guys. I wasn't the only person executing the contracts. I worked with others and they didn't have real names either. They only had their serial numbers and the names they picked up along the way.

My story takes place over the span of forty years when I was a member of an undercover squad—J. Edgar Hoover's private Squad. It was a top-secret operations unit that did jobs so dirty even the other intelligence services were afraid of it. The Squad operated on the fly out of the Departments of Justice and Treasury from 1947 to 1971, and for all that time we were more rumor than fact. We were the boogey men that FBI recruits talked about when they were brought up from Virginia. We were the guys in the black fedoras and behind the sunglasses that made files disappear from locked offices between five in the evening and nine the next morning.

The Squad itself no longer exists as a unit. It faded away as the Old Man was falling from power; it died when he died. This story is about the Squad and about the kinds of jobs the Squad specialized in: executions. The Squad was set up by Mr. Hoover personally. He recruited each one of us individually. He picked us out of the Families, out of the OSS, or out of local police forces. He figured us to be specially trained for undercover work because we came from the streets. His own agents, the guys who came out of law school, couldn't do what we did. Besides, the Old Man always said that he would never put regular FBI agents undercover because he was afraid they might get corrupted. We were different. He knew exactly what we were. He pulled us in one by one, told his bodyguards to leave the room, and made his decisions right on the spot. He either liked you or he didn't, but you knew where you stood. He looked us right in the eye, told us to stand up straight and keep our hands out of our pockets. And then he ordered up exactly what he wanted. He knew our backgrounds and he made sure that we knew that he knew. He pulled out these grey file folders and read from them right into our faces like he was reciting chapter and verse: names, AKAs, dates, warrants, convictions, dispositions, time served, warrants outstanding, cases still open. He put the round in the piece and the pieces in our hands. He was the best cop I ever knew.

Mr. Hoover had decided that the courts of the United States did not properly administer justice the way he thought they should. Whether he was right or wrong is for history to say. Personally, I know he was right. All that matters now is that there were certain cases that never hit the courts. They never *could* hit the courts. Maybe the cases were too sensitive or Mr. Hoover felt that the courts would never dispense the justice he wanted. Many times, these were cases that involved national security or that couldn't be prosecuted because there was no evidence. In these cases the guilty people walked away. Mr. Hoover had a way to deal with that. He found ways to make the guilty parties disappear. He devised what could only be called an execution squad made up of no more than ten men at any one time, none of whom ever went to any FBI academy or took a civil-service exam. None of the men were supposed to be seen by regular FBI agents. He called us the Unknowns. We always worked in the background, finding the people the Bureau couldn't and turning them into John Does on hundreds of Medical Examiners' reports for over forty years. Some people we turned into informants—although I hate that word—who were used to pursue cases through regular channels. Sometimes we were there and gone before the regular Bureau agents ever got to the scene. We would do our work and plant the necessary evidence for the FBI to follow. How we got the evidence wasn't important, just so that it held up in court. If it didn't, we'd have to go back to work. Sometimes the regular agents never even got to the scene because there was nothing left for them to do. No blood, no bodies, no questions. People just disappeared. Loans were foreclosed. The packages—as ordered—were delivered.

We rarely sat together at meetings. Most of the time we just got our orders directly from Mr. H. We never acted on our own. Mr. Hoover still believed in justice, even though some people might say this was no justice at all. For the ugliest and most difficult of cases, Mr. H. had a special routine. When he was satisfied and had consulted with those he trusted, he would sit down at a table by himself and eat his supper. Then afterwards, by the turning over of glasses, one by one, he would decide whether a man was to live or to die. This became a tradition over the years.

We were a kind of necessary evil because our ways were evil. I don't apologize for that because we had to be worse than *they* were. As a member of the FBI execution squad, and of the OSS before that, I can say today that there was only one way to deal with the people who wanted to cross us and that was to be worse than them. If you ask me what I was—what I have to live with even today—I was a professional killer. I dealt with both sides, the government and the Families, but I didn't cross the line. Most people don't know that in those times when our country was threatened, the Family, *La Familia,* as we called it after World War II, or the "Good People," which is how they refer to themselves, put aside all their differences with Uncle Sam or even local authorities. In fact, and this is unknown to the government to this day, about twenty years ago when they sent me to find out who was killing migrant workers in California, a button man from the Family out of Chicago came along and assisted me. Mr. H. didn't want to know who assisted me. He didn't care. He was satisfied that the job he asked me to do got done and nobody asked any questions. That was the type of alliance J. Edgar Hoover had with the Families.

The government had its ways of doing things and the Family had its ways. In the government offices, it's called "policy." Among the Good People, it's called "the right thing." And we all were taught that the Families' ways aren't the right ways, but even the Families did what was necessary to protect their country. When it comes down to it, we're all still Americans when somebody shoots at us. Whether that person wears a Swastika around his arm and carries a Mauser or smokes a thin cigar and carries an Uzi, he still threatens all of us. What we did on the Squad was right no matter what anyone says. We operated in our own way but we got the job done at a time when the free world was very vulnerable. History will show that we were necessary.

If people who read this story want to sit in judgment of me or of the Squad, they should know that what happened in Germany and Europe, what happened in Eastern Europe after the World War, and what's happening today in Cambodia and Iran and other countries where dictators can put a whole population before a firing squad or in prison camps, *can* happen here. Do you think that before *Kristallnacht*, the night of broken glass, most Jews in Germany believed that a whole country would turn against them? They knew that the Nazis hated them, but the Jews considered themselves Germans. They owned businesses, they worked in the great banking houses of Europe, they taught in the universities, they fought for the Kaiser's army in the Great War, they had money and influence, and they had friends in the government. When Germany suffered, they suffered. They were as loyal to their country as Jews in America are to this country. And yet, on November 9, 1938, their whole world turned against them.

All of that can happen here. I've seen it happen again and again with my own eyes. I was one of the earliest Department of Justice men ever ordered to infiltrate the Ku Klux Klan. It was in 1953, and Mr. Hoover sent me down there himself as a deep cover operative because President Eisenhower couldn't afford to step on any Southern senators' toes by having an FBI investigation stirring up the dirty laundry in their states. What I saw, what I *did*, showed me that it was happening here. We eventually got our men inside the Klan, and eventually people like Martin Luther King, who was a hero and a patriot even though Mr. Hoover didn't like him personally, made sure that the whole world knew what was happening in the South.

I saw the same events take place in California ten years years later when the farmers began executing the Mexican labor organizers. It was like the 1930s all over again, only this time the victims were Mexicans instead of American farmers from the Dust Bowl. The big farm owners hired motorcycle gangs to terrorize the workers and kill local police and sheriffs' officers. The gangs—years later sociologists began calling them Satanic cults, but they were just a bunch of thugs who only understood violence and murder—bragged that they weren't afraid to die. We caught one of them and performed a "live autopsy" on him. That was our way. That was Mr. Hoover's way. We kept him alive during the autopsy so we could tape-record his screams. Then we sent him back to his friends along with the tape. The killings stopped. The gangs said they weren't afraid to die, but we taught them the *way* they were going to die if we caught them.

Now it's happening all over again with the drug cartels and rival gangs of pushers that shoot kids on street corners. Some people say it's like the syndicates during Prohibition, but I know that it's not. I grew up on the Lower East Side during the Twenties and I worked the neighborhood crap games for Benny Siegel and Meyer Lansky. Meyer and Benny didn't murder women and children. Lucky Luciano didn't push narcotics in school yards and turn children into killers. Maybe they weren't heroes, but when FDR, J. Edgar Hoover, and Tom Dewey realized that the Nazis and Facists had spies all over the New York waterfront, they turned to Lansky, Luciano, and Frank Costello for help. And when the time came to send our boys into Sicily and behind the lines in Europe, General Donovan asked the Families to send their soldiers into the war. That was how the OSS worked, and it never stopped working that way even after it became the CIA. You can ask Fidel Castro about that because when the CIA needed some heat to put the hit on him, they turned to button men from the Families to do the job.

You look around today and see that the drug syndicates run the cities. Your own kid can go to school one morning and come home in the afternoon with a vial of crack. And one week later he might be robbing money out of your wallet to pay some pusher. And that same pusher will take money from your kid and use it to hire a shooter to blow some rookie cop's brains all over the front seat of his police car. If Mr. Hoover was still alive and giving orders to the Squad none of this would be happening. History was on our side. Now I'm not so sure. If the Squad was working today as we used to, you would see many more dope dealers pushing up flowers instead of pushing crack. When we were a unit, law enforcement agencies all over the country owed us a great debt of gratitude, even though they didn't know it. We saved them the trouble of finding evidence that some million-dollar mouthpiece would get thrown the hell out of court. We saved them from watching while sniveling judges found technicalities to let sex fiends back out on the streets to cut open defenseless women in dark hallways. The Families needed the cops to keep the peace. When a cop was killed, we found the rat who did it and dealt with him in our own way. The cops didn't care. A dead rat is a dead rat no matter who kills him. Mr. Hoover understood that. That's why he sent the Squad in to the the dirty work.

Maybe the truth is tough to swallow, but it's still the truth and it bears repeating so it will sink in. There was an execution squad. It was run personally by Mr. Hoover, who set it up without the official knowledge of the FBI. You won't find it anywhere in the records. There were no FBI agents on the Squad. All of us were handpicked individually without the knowledge of anyone else in the Bureau, although through the years, I have come to realize that there were people in the FBI who knew *what* we were even if they didn't know *who* we were.

If you ask me, I would say look around and you'll see that right now that the FBI execution squad is still needed because there are people and organizations actively working to take away our freedoms. They use drugs to trap our children and turn them into addicts. They are the South American generals who use our fear of Communism to bribe us with phony intelligence so that they can bring drugs into our country. They were the Asian drug importers who blackmailed us with our past deeds because they believed that the American justice system was as corrupt as theirs. I admit that we played into their hands at first. We turned our backs while we let them bring heroin into our cities. We thought we needed them, and maybe at the time we did. But now we know what they are and what they did. And even if it seems as if our regular law enforcement system is going to be overwhelmed in this new war we are fighting, I can assure you that it won't. I believe that somewhere there are people who still remember the Squad, although it's been dormant for almost twenty years. It still exists in the minds of the people who knew what it did. These few people who remember may be very old now, but they have friends and associates.

If you read somewhere that a drug dealer has simply disappeared or that a former Nazi war criminal is gone from his house one morning, the chances were that he had learned the painful truth about the Squad. If a cop killer turned himself in at the local police station because he was more afraid of what would happen to him if he didn't than of going to jail for life, maybe he learned the hard way what you're only reading about. I admit that our way wasn't the legal way. But Mr. Hoover told us—and we believed him—that the legal way wasn't always the best way.

I'm old now and the years have taken their toll. You can't kill people, one after the other, year after year, the way I've done and not hear the screams or see the faces in your dreams. I'll wake up in the middle of the night in a cold sweat and hear the click of a hammer in the darkness or the pop of a gunshot through a silencer coming at me out of a nightmare. I tell myself over and over again that I did the right thing. When I have to justify it to myself in the hours before dawn when nobody else in the house is awake, I say that Michael Milan was a professional killer who, with other professional killers and upon the orders and the express approval of the head of the FBI, the chief law enforcement officer in the federal government, defended his country. Maybe Michael Milan is an anachronism, a man after his time right now. But he was very much a man of his time when we started. And so were all the members of the Squad. What we did was good, even though we used the ways of evil. I don't ask anyone to forgive me or the Squad. But I believe that we were in our own way directly responsible for whatever good life Americans lead today. You may not like to hear that, but it's true.

Years ago, I told parts of this story to Steve Kendell, a writer-producer in Hollywood. He called it a piece of American history that must be told and asked me to write a book about it. But at that time, there were too many members of the Squad and people from the OSS still alive. I finally began writing my story a few years ago because I believe that Kendell was right, but I put it in my desk drawer and locked it up. Now Bill Casey, one of the last of all the agents in the special group of the OSS, is dead. General "Wild Bill" Donovan, the man who ran the OSS and who I worked for personally, died years ago; Lyndon Johnson, who played a part in this story, is dead, and, of course, the Old Man has been gone for about seventeen years. And on the other side of the line, it's the same thing. Mr. "F.C.," Frank Costello, who knew Hoover well and worked with him on many occasions, is dead. Meyer Lansky, who I worked for and who played a major role in helping to win the World War, died about ten years ago. It's now OK to tell the story.

I've still played it safe by changing the names of the ordinary people who are still alive. I used the real names for people like Mr. Hoover, Mr. Costello, Meyer Lansky, Bugsy Siegel, Sam Koenig, and Tommy Ryan. They're all public people and a lot has been written about them already. I also used the real names of Presidents Roosevelt, Truman, Eisenhower, Kennedy, Johnson, Nixon, and Ford. I worked for all of them and even helped keep President Ford alive so I might as well use their real names. But other names, names like Johnny Santos, who has hung onto life for all these years; Gerard Brinkman, whose family is still in Texas; Augie Russo, who I think might still live in the old neighborhood; the Rosario brothers and "Four Eyes" Littman, who couldn't be satisfied with the money they were getting and had to grab for more, are not real names. These people are real—the names are not.

I should begin by telling you about myself so that this story makes some sense. First of all, I'm Jewish. I was born on the Lower East Side of Manhattan in 1924. All I heard about when I was growing up was that the Jews all over Europe were getting beaten up and killed. Why didn't they fight back, we asked ourselves? Kill a few of them. Kill all of them. Even as a kid you get to thinking it's me against them, and the only way to stay alive is to be meaner, tougher, and faster than everybody else. I never lost that attitude even though it got me into as many scrapes as it got me out of.

Because I was a Jew, it also meant that I could never be a made member of the Family even though I did Family business.

That's important because the story I'm telling is about a guy who has to walk along a tightrope between the dons on the one side and the federal government on the other without compromising either side's information. If I was a made man or a sworn police officer, I couldn't have done it without winding up stashed into the back of a car trunk with my head stuffed down into the middle of my intestines. But I was neither and that's what kept them guessing and me alive. I didn't understand all of that when I was a kid, but I followed the rules that Mr. Costello and Mr. Hoover laid down. When I got older and couldn't scrub the blood I'd spilled off my hands anymore, only then did I understand how dangerous the game had been. I had learned that neither side ever really trusted the other, but they worked together so that each could do its own business. The Families want to keep on making money from things the government should allow them to do but is too stupid to figure out. The cops, who are more afraid of nuts than of crooks, just want to stay alive. When I understood that, I knew I should've been scared more times than I was.

The Lower East Side was a pretty rough neighborhood when I was growing up, and you learned when you were very young to use your hands to defend yourself or you didn't go out of your house much. I was getting into fights with other kids as early as I can remember. Maybe I had a chip on my shoulder, I don't know. I do know that I got a lot of bloody noses and black eyes from kids much bigger than myself, but I gave them as good as they gave me. My father finally told me, "If you like to fight so much, get into the ring." So I did. I boxed amateur over at Grand Street when I was twelve and won my weight division. When I went into the Navy, which was where the OSS put me, I won the U.S. Navy welterweight championship. I had to knock out three palookas in the same night to do that.

Maybe I took to fighting too easily. Maybe people would say that Mike Milan used his hands too much. But when you're a kid and you splatter somebody's nose, you figure, what the hell, it'll grow back. When you fight a guy in the ring, it's business as well as blood. He's in there for the same reason you are, and after the two of you slug it out until you can't stand up anymore, you understand you've been through the same thing together. You both faced your fears and tried to beat the other guy's brains out to make the fear stop eating at you. At the end of it, you and him wind up being pals for life. I also didn't take seriously the time in the drunk tank down at the Williamsburg Police precinct when I cut open a singing canary's belly for the Lucchese Family. I was a pug with a nasty attitude back then. I could use my hands and I wasn't afraid of spilling blood. After the hit, I acted like a real tough guy about it. I'd made my bones. I was in it as deep as any of Tommy Lucchese's button men and I felt like a big shot.

I got my start in the rackets early by running the skim for Meyer Lansky and Benny Siegel off the local crap games. It was Mr. Lansky who bankrolled my first fight even though it didn't make my father too happy. But what could he say? Mr. Lansky was one of his biggest customers at the clothing store. I learned pretty quick from Meyer Lansky that the secret to doing business was making the right connections and keeping your word. If you said you were going to do something, you did it and you took the rap for it if things didn't go right. That was called being "stand-up." If the other guy fucked you, then you fucked him. Only you fucked him worse. That's called being smart. But just going around fucking everybody is not how to do business.

Mr. Lansky taught me that you had to reach accommodations with people. You had sitdowns and worked out your differences. If money had to change hands, then so much the better because most people will do anything for money. Mr. Lansky had a way of figuring out what the other guy really wanted out of a deal—he liked to say if you could make the other guy think he was getting what he wanted, then you could take anything for yourself. Whenever he came to a sitdown, Mr. Lansky always had his percentage figured out in advance. He kept it all in his head, too. "Never put anything on paper," he said to me once. "That way they never know what you got." Now that he's dead, I'm putting it on paper. After all these years, the truth about the Squad can be told because Mr. Lansky, Mr. Costello, and Mr. Hoover were all heroes in their own ways. I don't claim to be a hero. I only claim to have walked with heroes.

I already told you that I made my bones in the Lucchese family in 1944 just before I went into the Navy. They were holding this rat in the drunk tank down at the old Lower East Side precinct house beneath the Williamsburg Bridge. We always called it the Williamsburg Precinct. The cops tossed me into the lockup with the rest of the drunks, slapped me around a little just to make it all look like it was on the up-and-up, slipped a knife into my pocket, and then disappeared. I pulled out this flask of booze that was really one of the most powerful Mickies you ever saw and passed it around. It worked fast. It had to because Mr. Lucchese and some of his associates dropped in to see how I did the job. I woke the rat up first, so he would know what he was getting. When he saw Lucchese staring at him through the bars, he pissed down his leg. Then I cut him. They let me out of the lockup, packed me into a car, and we ditched the knife in the East River. The drunks slept through the whole thing.

It was the same story during the war when I had to rub out people for Captain Roscoe McCall. I'd make the hit and walk away like I hadn't really been there in the first place. But after I went down to Atlanta for Mr. Hoover to turn up informants who'd testify against the Ku Klux Klan, I saw a different kind of fighting. I met up with lugs who hated people in the same way the Nazis did. These were Americans, people who's parents had come over on the boat just like mine did, but people who would look at a black or a Jew and say, "You don't have a right to be alive." It makes you sick inside to see how deep-down ugly people can be. Mr. Hoover wanted me to get an informant from the Klan who would turn state's evidence against his buddies. I had to join them, fight alongside them, carry a baseball bat and bust windows in little wooden Baptist churches and unprotected synagogues. I had to beat up a rabbi. Atlanta changed me. It made me see things in a different way. For the first time, I understood that innocent people could be hurt. For the first time I saw how weak and defenseless people really were on the inside, even the biggest and toughest of them. After Atlanta, I could feel pain in myself and others, and hitting people was no longer a street pug's game.

I've worked as a fight manager and promoter. I used to put together exhibition cards for local arenas and match up some of the old timers with kids trying to break in. I can tell you a lot about the prize-fight racket, but that's not what this book is about. I've also been a car dealer, selling limos to the foreign embassies. That was my cover for the Squad and what helped to pay my bills. Whenever

Mr. H. asked me, I could recite to him which country's UN mission bought what car and where he could find it parked if he wanted to plant a bug on it. Sometimes we even put the bugs on right in the shop. Free-of-charge, compliments of the Squad. There was a time when I really needed the dough to start a family, and selling cars was the only steady work I had.

The most lucrative work I had was as a kind of private investigator for the boys high up in the *Fortune 500s* who wanted jobs done but couldn't get the police to do them on the up-and-up. I can't mention their names or talk about them much in this story because most of them are still alive and don't like it when people talk about them out of school. But I can tell you this: put aside your fairy tales when you read the financial pages. The real news never hits the *Wall Street Journal.* You'll read about some of it in this story.

Here's the main thing you should know about me: I always wanted to be an actor like Jimmy Cagney. I had the looks, I had the attitude, and I could think on my feet. I used my wits to figure out what I had to do to get through any situation, and I knew I had the talent because I could act out the part. I could pretend to be brave when my knees were shaking; pretend I wanted some girl to like me when I only wanted to get some information out of her; pretend I was a homicide dick when I was really going over the police intelligence files to make secret hits for Mr. Hoover. Lots of guys stood away from me because they thought I was tougher and meaner than I actually was. It was always a performance. Acting helped me get what I wanted when I was a kid, and it saved my life when I worked on the Squad. I wanted to go to Hollywood and be in the movies. I had the chance, too, but Mr. Hoover put the kaybosh on it. Jack Warner himself said to me, "Mike, stay out here and work on the lot. You'll make it. I can always pick'em." Mr. Hoover must have felt that he couldn't cut me loose. He said, "Mike, this is not for you," and that was that. He called Mr. Warner and I was back selling cars in Brooklyn. I don't squawk about it anymore. I acted for real just to stay alive.

So when you read in this story where I can handle myself pretty good, you should not think I'm just bragging or that I'm Superman. I learned what to do on the streets. I'm a prize fighter. I know how to hit somebody the right way so that every punch hurts. I was fast on my feet in those days and I was a body puncher. I could bring down guys who were much bigger than me because while they were swinging roundhouse punches at my head, I was ducking and putting everything I had behind uppercuts right under their rib cages. If you think that won't take the breath out of somebody fast then you've never felt a good body shot. Besides, if you know how to throw a jab the right way, you can break somebody's nose and have him seeing stars before he even sees you move.

I'll start my story at Mitchell Field out on Long Island. It's an old military base where I've been going these past few years to work out at the gym, punch the bag, and shoot baskets. But the story really began many years ago on the Lower East Side, during the time of the Great Depression when I was twelve and made a bet with Meyer Lansky on a Yankee game. I won a buck off Meyer that day, but he shoved a twensky in my pocket. I wanted that twensky. Who wouldn't? Money meant everything during the Depression. But I handed it right back to Mr. Lansky and bought his respect with his own money. I figured that it was smarter to impress the most important man in the neighborhood than to pocket a twensky. The money would soon be gone, but first impressions can last forever.

By impressing Mr. Lansky, I caught the attention of Sam Koenig, the local ward leader. Mr. Lansky and Mr. Koenig walked together. Between them they shared great power. I know they picked me out of the gang when I was only a kid. It wasn't because of who I was but what I did. I knew who Mr. Lansky was, even though I pretended to my papa that I didn't, and I showed him I wouldn't grab for the short money. That told Meyer Lansky that here was another person who, like him, could figure out a percentage and give up the short odds to play the long ones. I have stayed alive for all these years in the Families and on the Squad by playing by that same rule.

Many years after that day, just before Sam Koenig died, he cried in my arms. He was only a skeleton clinging to the tail edge of his life. His gaunt, dying man's head was propped up on the pillow—yellow skin against white cotton—his mouth was wide open and gasping for air. He told me how he had offered my name to the Lucchese Family. He had offered my name to the officers in the OSS who needed triggermen to work military bases on the East Coast. He told me how he had gone to Frank Costello after the War and asked him to extend his protection and friendship to me. And he told me about Mr. Hoover and how he had intervened with the Old Man on my behalf. With his own honor at stake he had put my name forward. He asked me, "Was it wrong, Mendel, for me to have played God with your life?" I told him that I was the wrong person to ask. Now I look at the end of my years and I want to ask the same question about the lives of others. Maybe Sam Koenig will tell me the answer when I see him again. But I'm getting ahead of myself.

My story will probably shock you. I haven't pulled any punches except for changing some of the names as you already know. But, I'm telling the story as it was and why it was. You and history can be my judges. If you ask me whether I killed people, I would say yes. If you asked me how many, I would say more than I can even remember. If you ask me whether I killed anybody in the name of the Squad without express orders from the top, I would say that after I made my bones, only one. Even then I received my orders to kill him after the fact. That was just to make it right with the Old Man who gave me his judgment before he died.

What I did for the other side, for the Families? That doesn't matter. This story isn't about the Families—it's about the Squad. And, besides, nobody ever got nothing from the Families that they weren't supposed to get. That's all I'm going to say about that. What matters is that I never crossed the line. The line was there—both sides knew it was there—both sides respected it. What we did was for our country, and that stands above all lines. I figure it this way: God knew what we were doing. He let us attend to His business in our own way while He looked in the other direction. Now, in my sleep I see the faces of those who's hands I've taken and held. I see the faces of people who's hands I still want to take, but know now that I never will. I now accept one thing I couldn't understand when I started: each person's life has a weight, no matter how small. When you take that life, you take that weight upon yourself. You alter your balance sheet in the Book of Life. That's what Cain learned when he took the life of Abel, his brother. That's what I learned too late. I have to settle my accounts now. God will settle up His accounts with me soon enough.

Mitchell Field

I'm working the heavy bag in the gym over at Mitchell Field. I'm back in my own world again. Throwing punches in flurries while I'm ducking and weaving, putting combinations together that don't give a man time to think. Make him blink his eyes 'cause the left stays square in his face. I move in, punching on the bag. I clinch and steady it. Catch a breath. Keep my head low. Then I move out, punching off the bag even faster. Can't let him come after me. Can't let him get started. Play peek-a-boo, crouch, snap a jab, jab, jab. Double up on the jab. Triple up on the jab. Snap it.

I like the way a punch feels when you connect with it. And I like throwing the short stinging jabs that make a man's face burn red and puffs up his eyes. Or connecting with a hooking uppercut dug right under his diaphragm that sucks out all the air and locks him up so he can't move, or a straight overhand right that lands flush on his nose and flattens it out in five directions at once. When you throw a good punch, you throw it right from the dead center of your fear with the weight of your whole body behind it. You use your leg muscles and drive your fist with the swing of your shoulders. You make your contact right on your knuckles and punch through his face like you're taking his head clean off. All fighters hit from fear. They feed on fear. Fear is what keeps us alive.

Maybe I'm feeling too good. Maybe I think I look like the kid I was fifty years ago when I wanted to be a movie star. Maybe all the weight I lost has taken off the years as well. I say it's 1944 again and I'm fighting some piece of pork in the Navy championships. I skip to my left and dig a quick, hard uppercut into the bag and push off with two high left jabs. I'm up on the balls of my feet, dancing away, making him work if he wants me. Then I'm low and in tight, fighting out of a crouch and playing peek-a-boo behind my gloves with the cement-foot palooka lumbering after me, measuring my head for his one lucky shot of the night. He wants my pretty face spread all over the canvas. I pull my head back and drop my hands. I flash him my Jimmy Cagney grin before I slip away.

Take the poke, you fuck. You're goin' through the ropes.

Swish. His wild right goes sailing over my head like he's in slo-mo. So I set him up again with two high jabs that split his lip. Bam, bam. The gorilla's head snaps back.

Where'd they come from, you sonofabitch?

I fake a looping right with my shoulder more than my hand and he pulls his head back. Then I fire a left hook straight up under his chest cavity with everything I got. I feel the oomph of that punch all the way across my back, down the backs of my legs, and straight to my ankles. The gorilla's whole midsection seizes up. He gasps for air. I know he's ready. I push off the hook with a high double jab just as he drops his hands. Bam, bam. The jabs sting his eyes so they water right up. Then I smother him with as many rights and lefts as I can throw in one minute flat. My arms work like pistons driving into the heavy sand. I keep throwing my punches as the sweat runs through my sweat band like it's a teabag. I keep throwing 'em until I'm out of air and near gasping. Then I throw two more just to push off the bag. Even when a man's knees buckle and he's going down you still bury him with all the punches you can throw until they pull you off. Make them pull you off. Make them scream. Make them throw themselves in front of you, but never stop hitting.

Now I'm starting up again with a deuce of spring-loaded lefts—the fastest left hand in the world is what they called 'em forty years ago—but just before I go sliding back to 1944 and the USO party that always used to follow the fights, I see this black Marine out of the corner of my eye. He's big like a heavyweight, mean like a prize fighter, and his eyes follow every move I make. I circle around the bag to get a better look at him, but I bob in and out so he don't know I'm giving him the once over too. He's watching me like a scout so I give him something to look at while I flash face cards in my mind, looking for a match with his. Dance for the man, I say to myself, and I do the Ali shuffle out of a peek-a-boo. I see the Marine's head bob when my head bobs, his fists clench when I throw a punch, and his hips move when I go up on my toes. It's like he's clocking me for somebody else. Now he walks up and stands directly alongside the heavy bag.

"Tom Seamus," the Marine says, referring to a fighter I used to manage years ago. "Irish Tom Seamus out of Boston. Didn't you used to manage him? Whatever happened to that kid?"

This Marine is tall and thick-framed, maybe six-three or four, about thirty-five years old, and he has hands like a pair of wrecking balls. One good shot from either hand would bust somebody's head right in half. He's got a prize-fighter's stance, legs spread apart so he can move either way, fists slightly clenched, and arms bent at the elbows. I can see that he's used to having his hands bandaged and curled up inside gloves.

"Couldn't get him any fights outside of Boston," I say between breaths. "He put on a lot of weight and got slow-footed. Finally got a job with his brother loadin' bananas or something." I point to the Marine's balled-up fists. "You still get in the ring?" He has a shaved head the way many career Marines do and a thin mustache that sits almost directly on his lip. His eyes are bloodshot enough to tell me he likes to drink, and the unmistakable twist of his flat nose tells me that he's broken it more than once. He may be big, but he's been hit by someone just as big and powerful as he is. It's hot in the gym and I can see large beads of sweat breaking out all over his forehead. But most of all, I can't take my eyes off the polished double bars on his shoulders.

"Once in awhile," he says with a gleaming killer's smile that I never want to see facing me in a ring. "I'm just up from Pensacola where some of your old friends asked me to stop in and say hello," he says in a voice loud enough for everyone in the gym to hear. Then he lowers his voice. "There a place we can talk?"

"How about some coffee, Captain?" I ask him.

He tells me to suit up and meet in him in the commissary across the quadrangle from the gym. It's not an invitation, though, not the way he keeps his voice level and flat and breaks it off when he's finished. He's not asking; he's giving me an order. Sonofagun, I'm getting an order. But there's something about his attitude that tells me he's more than just a career officer. Career officers never stare at enlisted men—they look through them like they're invisible. This guy's staring at me like he's taking surveillance pictures of everything I do. His eye's widen when he says Pensacola because he wants to see what I do. But this a game I've played before with cops and feds, especially when they talk about friends of mine from a place where I don't have no friends. I don't ask him who the friends are supposed to be and he doesn't give me any names. So now we both know that I know that I don't have any friends in Pensacola, but I'm gonna go ahead and play his game anyway. And he's all smiles and I'm all smiles, but when I'm alone in the locker room I make sure that my .45 is loaded and strapped nice and tight to my ankle. I ain't gonna whack out no Marine captain in the middle of an commissary in broad daylight, but I ain't gonna be no sitting schmuck either.

So I'm sitting across from this guy at a table in the very rear of the room when a waiter brings over a bowl of strawberries and puts it in front of me. The Marine says nothing. Now he's all business and not smiling anymore.

"I got the right fruit?" He asks in a low voice while I just blink my eyes once in response.

It's been years since anybody used the fruit code. I had thought it died along with J. Edgar Hoover and Mr. C., but I was in for more surprises. The Marine puts his clenched fist on the table and slides away his hand. There on the table in front of him is a Krugerrand, shining even in the recessed lighting of the commissary. The strawberries, the gold coin—probably even freshly minted, I figure as I look at it—who's around that still remembers the Squad? It's got to be ancient history, I'm saying to myself over and over as I look at that coin. When the Old Man died they just shoved it under the rug and quietly shredded all of the records.

Then the Marine slides the coin across the table so it sits right in front of me. I'm still not saying a word. I don't know where this guy's from but he ain't no Sicilian—he's either a fed or KGB. And if's KGB, he's got maybe two minutes before I pop 'em. I raise my knee real slowly while I reach down for my ankle holster. Maybe I'm just scratching my leg. Maybe I'm tightening a shoelace. Could be doing anything as far as he's concerned. But he stares right at the spot where my hand was and waits until I stop moving. Maybe he's showing me professional courtesy or maybe he wants to see if I'm dumb enough to pull a rod right in the middle of an officers' mess.

"Mike, the Enforcer," he finally says, nodding his head at the table where the Krugerrand sits. "It's a contract."

Now my head's really spinning. This is 1987 and the Squad's been dead for fifteen years. I'm only a disabled vet nowadays and a sports promoter who stages exhibition cards with tank fighters at the Nassau Coliseum. Who's this guy working for? He's bigger than Larry Holmes and using a code that was retired while he was still saluting DIs in boot camp. He very slowly reaches inside his shirt pocket for what looks like a white envelope while he keeps his other hand square on the table. At least he knows the drill. Gotta give somebody credit for that. He pulls the envelope out of his pocket and puts it on the table. He's got nothing else in his hands. Now he breaks the seal on the envelope and takes out a computer printout. I can see the serial number even from across the table: 80762546. A blast from the past. Then he hands the printout over to me.

"Believe me, Mike, I thought the old days were dead and gone," he says. "But your serial number is still active."

I don't say a word because I'm not supposed to. I just look down the printout for the names of the people whose executions have been ordered by someone who is obviously in a very high position at the Department of Justice. But I can tell you, I'm not liking this one little bit.

"I didn't want to be the courier on this one," the Marine says after a pause. "I thought we were supposed to be playing it by the book. But I guess I'm wrong."

I know all of the names, of course. *Caporegime,* underboss, John "Johnny White Roses" Rosario, his brother Billy Rosario, and Jake "Four Eyes" Littman. All of them belonged to the Johnny "The Skinner" Santos crew, the *borgatta* down in New Orleans. I ran gold out of the States with the Rosarios over twenty-five years ago for the CIA when we were setting up the Indochina pipeline. Now I'm getting real nervous. Anybody who even knew about the Squad in the Department of Justice knew that Families were off-limits. That was a line we never crossed—it was part of the deal.

I couldn't help remembering, as I looked at the strawberries and the gold coin on the table and at the flimsy piece of paper in my hand, how I got into this business in the first place. Although I didn't know it at the time, it was at my first meeting with Frank Costello, the Boss of all Bosses, the head of the Commission. I was only a kid, fresh out of the Navy, still feeling my oats because we won the war, and strutting around the Lower East Side like I owned the place. How could I have known then that among my friends and benefactors Meyer Lansky and Sam Koenig, their associate *cappo de tutti cappi* Frank Costello, and their ally, FBI Director J. Edgar Hoover, my fate had been sealed. In 1947 my life was plotted out by four people who had made and broken the lives of thousands of people. But I knew none of that. It was revealed to me slowly over the course of the next forty years in hundreds of places I was ordered to visit where I executed contracts on people who had received judgments of death.

The Marine was still sitting there, sweating through his collar and along his armpits, looking at me closely as if he could read my mind. What was he thinking? In his mind, was I just an old hood from the streets who would do a quick job for a few bucks that nobody else would touch? Was he sent to find a fall guy who would take the rap for another botched CIA enterprise? Was he thinking that someday soon he would hand somebody else a contract on my life? Was he even a Marine?

It had been twelve years since anybody had asked me to do a hit. Since that time I'd walked away from it. I'd walked away from the world of amateur spymasters and secret governments and presidents of corporations who bought and sold the lives of people who might someday get in their way. When I worked for Mr. Hoover, I believed I was on the side of justice, even if it meant bending the rules of justice when the fit wasn't right. But the one thing I'd wanted, I'd finally got. I'd walked away with my life. Now some guy wearing a Marine captain's uniform had just pushed a gold coin across the table and handed me a contract on lives of people I'd known since I was a kid. No matter how hard I tried, I couldn't keep my mind from going back to that one day forty years earlier when I'd first met Frank Costello and this whole business started.

Boss of All Bosses

It was 1947 and I had been out of the Navy for two years, my chest still popping buttons 'cause we'd won the war. At first I just knocked around the streets, picking up action here and there and letting friends of friends know I was back in town and looking for work. I sold used cars off the books for a local gas station owner I knew from before the war. It was a legit cover for putting new paint and plates on the buggies his friends had snatched for their out-of-town heists. I made unannounced visits to merchants in the rag business who were not paying their vig to my clients on time. And I settled disputes between the boys from Little Italy and the few Jewish businessmen who still stayed on the Lower East Side. Today you'd call me a financial consultant. They paid me for keeping the peace. I'd been working indirectly for one of Frank Costello's underbosses at the time, but I didn't know it.

I had never met Frank Costello, but I'd certainly seen him and heard about him from people I knew. He had a reputation for hardly ever speaking to anyone in public. Mostly he spoke with his hands and his eyes. He would point. He would make a fist and shake it at someone. He would turn his thumbs down. To make a comment, sometimes he would shrug his shoulders and grunt from deep inside his belly. And when he spoke in words, he growled like it hurt him to breathe. Or he hissed in a whisper that was like a knife.

"You don't talk to Frank Costello," old Sam Koenig once told me years before as Mr. C.'s limousine pulled up to the curb. It was a warm spring day and the first time I'd ever seen Mr. C. in person. "You don't even look at him unless he looks at you." I was twelve years old then and had just started collecting the skim from Meyer Lansky's crap games. I kept a good count and was always on time with my deliveries. Mr. Lansky had told me that he was going to move me up in the organization. Sam Koenig and I were watching Frank Costello get out of a car in front of Pollack's fruit stand on

Essex Street. Mr. Costello was a round man with short arms and legs, and he needed the help of his two button men just to make the step down from the car's running board. A small crowd had gathered, but they pretended nothing was happening. Frank Costello shaded his eyes with his hat brim as he pushed his way along the sidewalk. He stopped in front of us, paused just long enough to look Koenig directly in the eyes, and then swaggered up to the fruit bins. He motioned quickly with his hands at the crates of fruit, making two's and three's with his fingers over each fruit as if he was putting a hex on 'em or something. Then he inspected each paper bag as Pollack handed them over. Mr. Costello dug around in a bag of apples, pulled out an orange, held it up to his face, handed it back to Pollack, and looked over at Koenig who seemed to nod before turning away. Frank Costello went back to his car without looking back in our direction and drove off towards Delancey Street. That was the only time I saw him in person before we had our first meeting.

Now it was early November and the weather had just turned chilly. I was twenty-three. My life was about to change because Frank Costello wanted a sitdown. I didn't know why he wanted to see me, but I wasn't worried because the message was delivered with a basket of strawberries. Strawberries were my favorite fruit and the button man who brought them, a pal named Augie from my Grand Street Boys Club days, knew it. It was the Family's way of saying you're not in any trouble. The heads of the syndicates always sent messages with fruit or flowers because it was their way of throwing cops or Feds off the scent. Augie didn't even have to say anything. He just handed me the strawberries and motioned to a car in the street. Then he rolled his eyes all the way back and nodded big. That told me it was either Mr. C. or somebody close to him.

We drove back to my place where I got dressed for the occasion. I knew it was important and asked Augie to do me a favor and wait while I put on my special white-on-white linen shirt and searched for my best ruby cufflinks, the ones that sent red sparkles on the ceiling when they caught the light. I picked out my new black suit and wore a gray fedora with a little feather in the band. Anything less would have been a sign of disrespect. I was spending a lot of time in front of the mirror and knew that Augie was getting restless. He grunted a few times and paced real loud outside my bedroom door while I straightened my tie just right and slicked down my hair. I was proud of the way I looked and still wanted the chance to go out to Hollywood and show my stuff. I knew I was taking too long getting dressed, but I wanted to get a good crease in the tie. I strutted back and forth in front of the mirror like Jimmy Cagney in *The Roaring Twenties,* until I could hear Augie's shuffling in the next room getting louder and louder.

"I have to pat you down before we get into the car, Mike," Augie said when I came out of the bedroom. We'd had our share of street fights in the past, and I could tell he was a little scared about challenging me. "No insult, you understand. It's the house rules." He held out his hands and I turned around. He ran his hands around my wrists, under my arms, around my chest, and all the way down my legs to the ankles. He was looking for a knife as well as a gun. "They might pat you down again when we get there just to make sure I did my job."

I shrugged my shoulders and let him know without speaking that I understood. More than a few of the old dons had been rubbed out by messengers who'd been well paid for a one-in-a-million hit. I really wanted to know where this guy was taking me, but it was against the rules to ask. Also, to ask would have been a sign of cowardice or at least a lack of trust—something that a Sicilian would take very personally. From the minute he handed me his basket of strawberries, I knew that I was being watched very carefully. Whatever this was, it had to be important.

We drove very leisurely across Houston Street towards Delancey, letting the trucks pass us and staying close to the curb. The wheelman didn't want to draw any attention or wind up in any scrapes. And when we pulled up in front of Marshioni's soda fountain, I knew that Mr. Costello had chosen the place to make our meeting as private as possible. This was not one of his regular stops. The car pulled up short and I waited for Augie to open the door. I knew all the rules: make no moves on your own, let them take you where you're supposed to go, and keep your fucking mouth shut.

On the street in front of Marshioni's there was nothing out of the ordinary. I saw two of Mr. Costello's men wearing overcoats with the collars turned up, their hands stuck in their pockets like they were wrapped around the handles of ice cold revolvers. Two older men were playing bocce ball near the corner like they were still on a farm in the old country. One of them looked up to see who was getting the treatment. It was "Tommy Ryan" Eboli, an old *caporegime* from Prohibition days. He was allowed to break the rules.

"You're coming up in the world, young man," Mr. Eboli said, and I suddenly felt unprotected. I didn't know Tommy Ryan and I could have sworn he didn't know me. Or maybe he didn't have to. He only had to know that anybody who gets limoed up to meet the Boss of all Bosses is going somewhere in the world. He was right. I didn't know what was in store for me, but I knew things were changing quickly. The driver opened the door to Marshioni's and my button-man friend motioned for me to sit at the counter. He left. I waited. My mouth was dry and I would've loved to put away a strawberry ice cream soda, but the kid behind the counter didn't come over. He had his orders, too, I figured, so I just sat there counting the paper napkins in the metal holder. I really wanted a soda.

Out of the corner of my eye, I saw the door to the back room slowly open. I didn't turn around to face it, but cocked my head slightly so I could keep it in view while I pretended I was playing with the napkins. One of Mr. Costello's men peeked around the door, saw where I was sitting, and ducked back inside. Then a different man came out and walked toward me, making sure that no one was looking at him. He stood behind my stool and grunted, making a sound like was clearing his throat. When he caught my eye, he motioned with his head toward the back room. I got up, and he followed me to the back.

The room was darkened, with only daylight coming through a wire-screened window with a frosted-glass pane. Through the shadows I could see that there were three men all standing around a table, but no Frank Costello. They motioned for me to sit, and I did, glancing around the room quickly to see the men's faces and what they were doing with their hands. You can't ever let button men see that you're watching their hands because then they get edgy. I put my own hands on the table and waited without trying to shift around in my chair too much. Another test. If I was too nervous, they would tell that to their boss. On the other hand, I couldn't be too cocky and look as if I didn't have a care in the world because they would tell their boss that I had no brains. Nobody who sits down the with the biggest boss in the city can be cocky. I figured I had to show that I was a little nervous because that was a sign of respect. It meant I was being careful around people I had to be careful around.

I had grown up in Marshioni's but had never been in the back room before. I also realized while I was sitting there that Mr. Costello must have known that it was part of my neighborhood—not his—and had set our meeting there as a sign for me to interpret. He expected me to understand that. That was an even greater sign of respect. Now I knew why he was the Big Boss. I really was coming up in the world.

The rear door opened, throwing a bright shaft of afternoon light into the darkened room. My eyes didn't adjust in time to see Mr. Costello swagger through the doorway. I only saw his outline standing over the table as the door closed behind him. I stood up and took his outstretched his hand.

"*Bongiorno, padrone*," I said as I held his hand and looked down.

He motioned for me to sit and then pointed to one of his men who hustled out of the room. He said nothing, but looked me up and down as if he was inspecting me or something. I knew that the suit I put on was the right thing to have worn for the occasion. Mr. Costello's man returned with two small cups of thick, black Sicilian coffee and put them down in front of us. I waited until Mr. C. picked up his cup and held it out over the middle of the table. I did the same with mine, but kept it lower than his.

"*Salude*," he said and slurped his coffee. I waited until he drank and then put the hot, steaming cup to my lips. The coffee burned the insides of my mouth and I felt my eyes tear, but I took a slow drink as if I felt nothing. Mr. C. put his cup down and leaned forward across the table. "You have friends among the Good People, and they have told me what you did in the war and what you are doing now." His voice was almost a whisper, harsh and broken as if it was hurting him to speak. He nodded, giving himself approval for what he had just said. "But everything you have done is in the past. It has only brought you to this table. From now on you will be judged by what you will do for me. It is your future we talk about now." He paused again. His lips moved, but he made no sound.

Frank Costello took another long swallow from his coffee cup. He drained it dry, put it back on its dish, and pushed it across the table towards the man who had brought it. Then he waved it away with a gesture that meant there would be no second helping. He looked at me again. "I am going to ask you to do something for me. If you are successful, I will ask you to do other things."

One of Mr. Costello's men handed him a small bag of oranges which he turned upside down so that they all rolled across the table. "When you have done what I ask you to do, you will buy some fruit," he whispered, pointing with the edge of his finger out the window to Pollack's fruit stand a few blocks away. "If the fruit you put in one bag is of all the same kind, I will know that you have succeeded. If you mix the fruit in any way, I will know that you have not succeeded."

Now he leaned forward across the table, rested all of his weight on his elbow, and pointed his little finger directly at me. The ring on it was only inches away from my nose. His breath was thick and you could hear the rumbling of congestion deep in his chest. He was a man who had chained up his emotions, but you knew that his dark, heavy Sicilian blood raged inside of him. He lived, like all of us, between a controlled fury and a grinding fear. "You and I, we will never talk. But people who know you and who you trust will tell you what I want." He took a deep breath and grabbed me by the shiny lapel of my black sharkskin jacket, pulling me in even closer so that no one else could hear us. "Very soon now, someone I send to you will you show you a line between our side and their side. He will say that you must walk that line. Walk it, Michael my Enforcer, but never cross it." Then he sat back in his chair and wiped his dripping mouth. Without another word, he drew his finger through the air between us, signalling the end of our sitdown. Then he looked away quickly and got up. The meeting was over. I would see him plenty of times after that, but I would never speak to him again.

Augie waited in the room until his boss had left. "You hungry, Mike?" he asked. Hungry? I coulda pissed right down the leg of my new black suit. "You wanna drive over to Ratner's or something? Maybe we have a little *abboccamento* with someone the boss thinks you should meet. You tell me what to eat there, huh?" he said.

I just wanted a fuckin' soda, but I knew this guy had more business with me. "Yeah," I said. "What the hell, we'll get some blintzes."

"That's right, *blinsiz*," he laughed, haw-hawing as if I'd told him he'd have to wear a skirt and bra to his next hit. "We'll eat blinsiz." So we left Marshioni's in the same car that we came in but with a different wheelman.

He said nothing as we drove down to Delancey again where we made a left toward the Williamsburg Bridge. We made a U-turn across Delancey and parked around the corner from the restaurant. As we got out of the car, Augie pointed his finger at the wheelman and then motioned to the curb. He was telling him to wait for us. That meant we were still on company time.

Ratner's wasn't crowded at that time in the afternoon. The regulars who ate lunch there had gone and it was still too early for the regulars who ate dinner. In fact, there were more waiters than customers and not one of them was under seventy. They were all stooped over and shuffling back and forth like old men in a rest home on their way to the bathrooms. Augie motioned to the waiter nearest us that he was going to a small table in the back of the place far away from the door and facing the front. There was a man in a pinstripe suit already sitting there reading a newspaper. He must have been waiting for us to arrive.

The waiter looked at the man sitting down and back at us. Then, as he slowly handed us the menus, Augie waved them away and barked, "Just bring us blin-*siz* and coffee and leave us alone." The waiter kept on nodding as Augie gave him orders, tucked the menus back under his arm, and then through his thick glasses, looked directly at me with a blank expression that seemed to be asking:

—*Nu, Mendel, bischt einer Mensch?*

He didn't stay long enough to find out whether I was going to act like a *mensch* or not. Instead, he shuffled off to the kitchen to order the blintzes. Augie and I walked to the table where he sat down and motioned for me to do the same. The person who was already sitting there said nothing. He didn't even look up from his paper.

"Blin-*siz*," Augie said to himself like he was trying out the word in his mouth so he could remember how to say it later. "Blin-*sis*. Hey, these better be good Mikey 'cause you're one of us now."

The waiter came back with pickles, water, and a basket of bread. He plopped them in front of Augie with a thud, making sure that some of the water splashed on the tablecloth. It was a Jewish waiter's typical reprimand. Augie turned to him with a slow glare. "Didn't I tell you to just bring the food and leave us alone?"

Again the waiter looked at me like I was to blame. I leaned over to Augie. "Probably doesn't speak English," I said. "Wouldn't understand what we're talking about."

Augie nodded. It made sense. He motioned to the man in the suit sitting across from us. "Mr. C. wants you to meet someone, Mikey," he whispered. "His name is not important. Just listen to what he says and do what he tells you to do."

The man in pinstripes put down his paper and looked at me. "We want you to talk to someone for us. The man's name is David Balin and he runs a small brokerage house down on Rector Street called Murphy Simpson and Associates." He paused to let me get all these my names in my head. Then he continued: "The Murphy Simpson company has been doing business with the other Families for years. We just want them to work for us exclusively. If that means we have problems with the other Families, we can take care of that ourselves."

"I don't have to tell you that you never write anything down, right?" Augie interrupted. "It all stays in your head. Names, dates, phone numbers, figures, everything. The boss wants nothing in writing. That way when you tell the cops you don't remember nothing, the DA can't shove some piece of paper in your face and hang you on your own handwriting." I already knew about that from Meyer Lansky.

The man in pinstripes continued. "The person we are all working for has a number of businesses that are completely legitimate. He wants investors for them. He wants a brokerage house that he controls to manage issues of public stock, find underwriters for it, handle our employer's own accounts, and that sort of thing. He needs to trust the people that handle his money." This guy had to be a lawyer, I said to myself. Why was I here? I didn't know what the fuck he was talking about. "Needless to say," he said anyway, "we're looking for a brokerage house small enough and private enough where our business can get special attention. Eventually, we might want to become partners with that brokerage house. Eventually. But we want a partnership option at the outset in case we want to exercise it in the near future." I still didn't know what he was talking about.

"That's where you come in, Mikey," Augie said, holding a dripping sour pickle in his fingers and looking for the best end of it to bite. He closed his eyes and chomped off the tip like it was a cigar. Then he put it down as Pinstripes handed him a brown envelope. He talked and chewed his pickle at the same time. "We want you to take this to Balin, push it under his nose and . . ." Pinstripes shifted in his chair, nervous and jumpy. He cleared his throat and glared and Augie shut up.

"Mr. Balin, who has represented the company ever since Murphy Simpson died, has done business with some of our associates but never with—" he paused, and I got his meaning, ". . . but never *directly* with us. We've spoken to him through lawyers, but now we feel it's time for a more straightforward approach. Someone he's never seen before. Someone young who won't attract a lot of attention. A war veteran, like yourself, who isn't really associated with the rest of the company."

It was all clearing up. No one knew me outside of the neighborhood and I had never been in any real scrapes with the cops. Mr. C. didn't want to send his muscle down to the Street because they'd be spotted before they even got out of the car.

"The trick is to get you inside his office without kicking down his door or announcing that you're there on behalf of our company," Pinstripes said, picking up his newspaper and showing me a want ad. "This was in yesterday's *Wall Street Journal.*" I started reading the ad. "You can read it for yourself on the way down," Pinstripes sniped, grabbing up the paper. "It simply says that Murphy Simpson and Associates is looking for a young man—preferably a veteran— to train as a runner and eventually as a salesman. That's you." I preened.

"You walk in there, Mikey, like some honest Joe Dogface answering the ad. You don't have any experience, but you're a war veteran and you're willing to learn, get it?" Augie said. "So the old broad outside Balin's door thinks you're a real looker that she wants to see in the office every day. So she says to her boss that there's a, a . . ." He turned to Pinstripes, who said: "A bright young man?" "That's it," Augie agreed. "A bright young man. She says to her boss: 'There's a bright young man out here who's answering our ad.' He lets you into his office, you go in, you take this envelope out of your pocket, and put it on his desk. You tell him you're our delivery boy and that this is his last chance to stay in business. He reads what's inside and he'll get a partner that'll make him a lot of money. He refuses and he's out of business for good. You don't argue with him. You don't even have a conversation with him. You give him the envelope, turn around, and scram."

The waiter walked up with a plate of cheese blintzes and sour cream. Augie paused while the waiter put the food down. Then he continued. "We coulda given this to anyone, Mike, but Mr. C. wants you to do it. You know, he wants you to get broken in on the up-and-up side of things." Augie looked down at the plate of cheese blintzes and sour cream. "We'll eat and then we'll all drive down there in the same car." He picked up a blintz and looked it over like it had just fallen out from under a car. He took a bite. "Blin-*siz*," he said slowly, as he chewed.

We ate, finished our coffee, and got in the car. We reached Rector Street where we parked a half a block away from the building. Augie handed me the envelope and patted me on the shoulder.

"He's up on the fifth floor," he said, and pointed to one of the hundreds of windows in the buildings in front of us. "Do it just like we told you. Don't threaten him in any way and don't you even put a finger on him. We'll wait here."

I walked up the street and turned into the wide, polished-glass entrance of a tall limestone building. The walls were all marble on the inside and I could hear my steps echoing on the tile. Everything was shiny like some museum painting, reflecting the pretty yellow light from the overheads. It reminded me at first of the inside of a school, except it was much bigger. I looked along the walls for the numbers of all the offices upstairs—the building directory—and found Murphy Simpson, 503. Balin was in 503A. I followed the signs to the elevators that stopped at the fifth floor and stepped into one that was filling up with a small group of people. I waited for the elevator man to close the metal cross-hatched doors before I looked around at who was in there with me. Suddenly there was a woosh and a jerk. The elevator started and stopped and the man was yanking open the cross-hatched doors again. We were on three. I didn't even have time to get a good look at the secretaries who were in the car with me. If I had been on my own time, I would've had the names and numbers of those cuties before the elevator reached the next floor. And I would've shown them some good times, too. The elevator man called out my floor and I stepped off the ride.

Balin's place was around the corner from the elevator. It was an office with very big, very wide, thick glass double doors with heavy brass handles. I opened them a crack and could hear the clack of typewriters, ringing telephones, and the loud ticking of the tape machine from inside. It sounded like an East Side bookie joint. I opened the door all the way and saw two or three guys at desks. They were wearing shirts and open vests, and one of them had his sleeves rolled up and was smoking a cigarette. It was hot inside, even though the windows were open and the fans were blowing. I could see the words MR. DAVID BALIN painted in gold on a glass door all the way in back.

I walked up to the woman sitting at a desk in front of the glass door. She made like she didn't even want look up at me, but I could tell she was peeking. The other girls were giving me the once-over, too. A couple of the real young ones were giggling. I loved it. Girls always looked at me like I was something they wanted to take home from a store. It's been that way all my life. If you understand that about yourself, you can always get what you want. Movie actors know it, too, and I knew I had what it took. That was one reason why I always wanted to be an actor. I knew I had the stuff.

I smiled my "we won the war" smile until she finally looked up at me. She smiled back, pointed to another desk in a far corner of the room, and said, real bored, "If you're here about the job." There were these two guys—Joe-college types—standing in front of a polished wooden bench against a wall next to the desk and some eighty-year-old grandma was yelling at them to use pens instead of pencils for filling out the job application sheet. One of them was a blond and the other looked like an Irish carrot top. Then they took their papers and went to empty chairs on opposite sides of the room. I better work fast, I figured, or I was going to be there all afternoon.

I like to think of myself as a guy who can scan all the angles right away and come up with a plan. You always start by deciding what you want and then work backwards. That ability saved my ass more than once in the OSS when I had to think my way out of tight situations. As I looked at the two other guys in the office looking for a job ahead of me, I knew I had to get them out of the way and show Balin that I could walk right into his office anytime I wanted. Getting them out of the way without causing a ruckus was the trick. Then I had an idea.

"Do you know where the bathroom is?" I asked the secretary in front of Balin's door.

Without looking up, she pointed with her pencil to the main doors and said almost like one word: "Out those doors and to your left then three doors on your right."

"Thanks," I mumbled and walked out to see how many people were in the halls and in the bathrooms and then to count the shitstalls in the men's room. The halls were deserted at that end of the building. All the people from the elevator seemed to be heading down the other hallway. At least I would have the privacy I needed. I also noticed that there were three stalls in the men's room. That should be enough, I thought, even if another person was on the can. I had to work fast because I knew I didn't have much time to bring everything off.

I slid back into Murphy Simpson and Associates and leaned over next to the blond guy who was looking for the runner job.

"Do you have a girlfriend outside?" I whispered in his ear.

"Me?" he whispered back. "No. Why?"

"There's a skirt out there who stopped me on the way back from the can. She says she's looking for you."

"How do you know it's me?" he whispered again. "Did she ask for me by name?"

This guy was getting to be a pain in my ass. "No," I said. "She just said tell the blond guy on the bench in there that she has to talk to you for a second. She said it's important. As far as I'm concerned I just did you a favor. I really don't care what you do because she's a looker and I'll go talk to her myself if you're too busy." I got up to leave when the kid tugged at my arm.

"No, it's OK," he said. "Please show me where she is."

"She's just outside," I said. I pushed open the door and he and I stepped out into the hall. "That's funny," I said to myself but loud enough so that he would hear. "She was just here. Maybe she went around the corner to wait." And I pointed in the direction of the bathroom. I followed him around the corner, making sure that there was no one in the hall, and when he turned around to look at me, I belted him right in the stomach. He doubled up and I hit 'em a good shot to the side of the head where he wouldn't be cut open and bleed all over the floor and me. He went down in a heap. I helped him to his feet and got him into one of the shitstalls in the bathroom. I sat him on the toilet, closed the stall, straightened myself out in the mirror, and went back to the office.

The carrot-top was still sitting on his seat; he hadn't been called in yet. It worked the first time without a hitch so I did it again and it worked out just as well. As soon as carrot-top poked his head around the hall and turned around to complain, "Is this a fraternity prank?" I hit him so hard in the stomach that he passed out cold right there in the hall. I had to drag him into the men's room, sit him on the next toilet, and hit him again. I heard blondy groaning from the first stall. If he got up and staggered back into the office, it could throw a monkey wrench into my plan. So I made sure carrot-top wasn't going anywhere and then I went back to blondy and belted him especially hard across the top of his head with my fist and he went back to dreamland where he was gonna stay for the next two days if nobody bothered him. Now with the two of them out of the way, I had my clear shot at Balin. I took off my jacket in front of the mirror and washed up. Then I slicked back my hair and straightened my tie. I didn't want to look all messed up when I stood across from Balin. Then I went back to the office where the old bat was looking around like somebody had lifted her keys. She wasn't sure anything was missing, she kept on telling the other girls, but she could have *sworn* that there were three boys here and now there were none. And Mr. Balin had wanted to interview them this afternoon. He told her they just *had* to hire someone and now she was gonna catch hell from the boss.

"They had to go ma'am," I said, walking up to her desk.

"Both of them?" she asked.

"One of them said he had another job interview and the other said his girlfriend was waiting for him. They said it was taking too long. But I really want the job, ma'am," I said. "I can wait here for the rest of the day if you think I have a chance."

"Hmmph," she snorted, turning up her nose. "I think there are too many jobs available these days," she complained, and handed me an application form to fill out. "Just start filling this out, young man, and I'll tell Mr. Balin that you're the only one out here. You can finish your form after you talk to Mr. Balin. You walk right over to that desk," she said pointing to the desk in front of Balin's office, "and wait. It will only take a minute." Before I even got to the desk I could hear Balin's buzzer on the other side of the door.

"Oh, all right. OK. I'll see him and get it over with," I heard Balin say. Then the intercom on the desk in front of me went off.

"Send the young man in, please," the intercom said.

"Excuse me, Mr. . . . ?" The secretary asked.

"Milan, ma'am."

"Mr. Milan. This way please." The secretary stood, opened the door, and showed me inside.

I looked around the office: big windows that opened up on the little people walking along the street below; thick, brown-leather couches and chairs that smelled like the inside of a new car, and a giant color photograph of some guy in a white sailboat on bright blue water. Nice life. I could get a hard-on for this, I thought, and sat down without being asked. I figured I'd just make myself at home and push the guy a little and maybe I could get him to tell me how I could get into a classy setup like his. I knew if I got him to sign on the dotted line instead of just dropping off the envelope and standin' there like a deaf-mute, the boys'd think I had something special. Besides, I wanted to know why this creep rated so high. What did he have in the brains department that I didn't?

David Balin was sitting behind his desk, staring at a thick ledger book and copying numbers into it from a long piece of paper tape. He looked over at me, scowled that I was sitting down, stood up, and stuck out his hand. I carefully took it in mine, measuring my grip around his knuckles, and shook it firmer than I had to. I could feel Balin cringe as I applied pressure, then I let go quickly. I took the envelope out of my pocket and put it on his desk.

"Mr. Mi-*LAN*?" Balin said as he opened the envelope and saw the name of Mr. C.'s company on the agreement.

"I'll make this short and sweet, Mr. Balin," I said. "I'm only here to deliver a message and walk out." Balin turned to reach for the phone, but I grabbed his hand before he could move it and wrapped my fingers around his knuckles. I had him locked in a vice grip and squeezed the knuckles against one another with a grinding motion. I felt him tense up along his entire arm. I also saw the grimace seize up his face. "I can crush it as easily as I can let it go, Mr. Balin. It doesn't matter to me at all. But just so that you know why they call it 'knucklebreaking.' " I steadied the pressure but didn't release his hand. Then I went into my pitch. "They told me to tell you that theirs is a straight deal. Their company is a hundred percent on the up-and-up and you'll make a lot of money if you go along. You've already worked with some of their people so this is just the same thing you've been doing before. I don't know how the deal is supposed to work because they didn't tell me. They only said to tell you that you'd make a lot of money and so would they. If you don't go along with them, you won't stay in business much longer."

"Is that a threat, *Mister* Milan?" He said through clenched teeth.

"It's what they told me to tell you, Mr. Balin," I assured him, so nobody could say I made a threat. That's all I gotta say. I think it's a good deal because who wants to lose his business?"

"OK," he said. "Let me go."

"No phone calls?"

"Only a simple question," he said, real snotty. I released his hand. "What am I supposed to do with this?" he asked, pointing at the agreements like they could give him the clap. I was supposed to keep my mouth shut, but since he asked me a direct question, I figured the polite thing was to answer it.

"I leave them on your desk. You can tell me what you're gonna do if you want. Or you don't have to say a thing. All I'm supposed to do is put those in front of you and say: 'Mr. Balin, my friends are making one last offer. If you accept it, you'll make a lot of money. If you don't, then you won't be in business much longer.' That's it,

Mr. Balin. The agreements are there. Somebody else will be talking to you soon, I guarantee it."

"Wait just a goddamn minute," he said. "Mrs. Flynn told me there were other job applicants out there. But now she tells me that you're all alone. What happened to the others?"

"They're in the can," I told him. "They'll be there for awhile."

"You did this in the middle of a business day?" he asked as if he figured I dragged the two guys out by their hair while everybody just stood around and watched. "Just like that?"

"Just like that, Mr. Balin." I said. Why spoil it for him? The Families have always used what people feared most about them to their best advantage. You don't even have to lift a finger if someone already believes you can move a mountain. "It's only a matter of time before you'll have to go to the can yourself," I told him. "If you get my meaning." I could see that he did. I could see in his eyes he had already given up. It was a look I had seen plenty of times in the ring just before a fighter got his beating. You could always see it in the eyes first. "Mr. Balin," I said, seizing the advantage that I knew was there, "if you got something they want, they're gonna get it in the end no matter what else happens. You can either make your money while they make theirs or watch them make theirs while you get nothing. Either way, they're gonna get it. I'm outta line for sayin' this, but if you sign those papers now and give 'em back to me, you won't have to see any of us again. You'll come out ahead and I'll look really good. I just done you a favor."

He looked down at the papers. "It doesn't much matter what's in here does it?" he asked.

"I don't know, sir," I answered, sincere and nice. "I really don't."

He picked up his pen and signed the papers with a quick couple of strokes.

"Now get the fuck out of here," he said. "I feel crummy enough."

I yanked the papers off his desk before he had any more time to think about what he was doing. All I knew was this was going to look great. I folded them up and put them in my suit pocket, left his office, and grabbed the elevator for the lobby. The elevator man and the broads in the car with me never knew why I was smiling like a jerk all the way down to the first floor. I almost ran through the lobby and out into the street. I looked down the block. There they were, Augie and Pinstripes sitting in the car like a couple of Wall Street swells who'd just made a mint. They had, but they didn't know it yet.

"What took ya so long, Mike?" Augie asked as I climbed in the car. "We thought he had a gun on ya." And he laughed.

"He was ready," I said, handing him the papers. "I figured it was better to seal the deal on the spot."

"You talked to him?" Pinstripes asked. "I thought we said..."

"Holy fucking shit, look at this," Augie said to Pinstripes as he opened the papers. "The cocksucker signed."

"I've been pushing him for weeks," Pinstripes said as he stared at the signature.

"How'd ya do it, Mikey?" Augie asked, belching pickles.

"He just wanted to talk," I answered. "So I talked to him. Anyway, he figured that a sap who could walk straight into his private office was not the kind of person he could get rid of so easy. So he took my advice and signed up with us."

"I dunno, Mikey," Augie said. "But I guess it's OK."

The wheelman started the car. We drove back to my neighborhood where they left me off in front of Pollack's. As I got out of the car, Augie called out to me: "We already got the papers, Mike, so you don't have to do nothin' else. You know what I mean?"

I didn't answer him. I walked up to the fruit bins and motioned to old man Pollack to fill up a small bag with oranges. He did—all oranges—and held out the bag for me to inspect. I nodded, he nodded, and I turned to see Augie and Pinstripes smiling at me from the car. Then I handed over the oranges to Augie and said, "Now the job is done." Augie didn't answer either. He took the bag of oranges and put them on the seat beside him. The car pulled away from the curb with a screech and headed west towards Little Italy.

The Old Man

On the Lower East Side, people used to say that when Roosevelt had a problem he couldn't solve, he turned to God. If the problem had to do with the Lower East Side, God would tell him to talk to Sam Koenig.

Sam Koenig was the *macher*, the *ganzer macher*, the center of life in the neighborhood. He wasn't important because of how much he knew. It was *who* he knew that counted, and how he could get people he knew to do what he wanted. So when I found out many years later that it was Sam Koenig who had put Costello and J. Edgar Hoover onto me from the very start, I wasn't surprised. But if you had told me then, even in 1948 when I was just two years out of the Navy, that Koenig had steered me into the Special Group, you could have knocked me right over.

Koenig seemed to know everybody, and when he put the fix in, it wasn't because he expected something in return the next day. That wasn't it at all. He was a man who built up a vault of favors. Everybody owed him and he knew how to exchange favor for favor, even putting people together whose paths might never cross. That's how he built himself one of the most powerful neighborhood political machines in the country. He put judges on the bench, sent congressmen to Washington, and got you out of hot water with the cops. If your nephew was laid off and needed a job with the city, you saw Sam. And if some paper-pushing son of a bitch was putting the bite on you for a chunk of dough under the table, you saw Sam.

His word went all the way to the top. When Roosevelt needed votes from New York, he went to the Republican Sam Koenig. And in 1942, when Captain Roscoe McFall, who was running an OSS operation out of a hotel room in midtown, needed local muscle to cut a deal with Charlie Luciano to put some boys he could trust on the docks, he also went to Sam. Luciano was spending the war stamping license plates up at Dannamora so Koenig talked to Meyer

Lansky and Frank Costello about setting up a meeting with him. Meyer, especially, thought he could get Luciano sprung when things cooled down after the war. Koenig got Governor Dewey to bring Lucky downstate to Sing Sing where he could enjoy some of the comforts of home. And he also got Dewey to grant him a pardon as his cut for letting his button men organize the docks. What nobody knew except Meyer and Frank was that Luciano had his own men in the OSS underground units sent to Sicily in advance of General Patton. By the time our troops entered Palermo, Lucky's men had organized the entire island and were diverting U.S. fuel supplies into the European black market.

When I was drafted out of Seward Park High School in 1944, it was Sam Koenig who put me in the OSS operation he'd set up with Luciano, Lansky, and Costello in 1942. I worked undercover at Navy bases up and down the east coast until the end of the war. And that was how I came to Hoover's attention. So you could say that it was Sam who put me into the Squad, and years later before he died, he admitted that he had spoken to Hoover about using me for some special jobs.

Just like any of the celebrities Ed Sullivan wrote about in his column, J. Edgar Hoover was a man of mystery to a Lower East Side kid like me. I knew that he liked to stay at the Carlyle up on Madison Avenue whenever he came to town. He didn't mind being seen at a swanky place like that, especially when he stepped out at night with the local politicians and the show dames they hung around with. He liked it when he saw his picture in the papers the next day. What I didn't know was on that afternoon in 1948 while I was looking at his picture on page one of the Daily News was that Hoover was in town looking for people to beef up an operation he was running strictly on the q.t.

Like most afternoons, I was eating lunch at one of the rear tables in Ratner's. And like most afternoons, I was alone, reading the results of the horse races the day before. Because I had to make my collections from the East Side book around dinnertime, I always liked to know who had made out on the day's action and who had taken beatings. As usual, I sat facing the front so I could keep an eye on the door while I read the papers.

I noticed these two guys come in who I made to be cops right away. They stood up too straight for local torpedoes and their shoes were shined up real bright like they had marched in a lot of parades. I made like I was just part of the local scenery, but I knew they were looking right at me. I was glad I wasn't carrying a gun. One of them walked over to one of the waiters and whispered something in his ear. Then they followed him to a table and sat down.

So far so good, I said to myself. If they were cops looking for me, they would have come right over. Cops don't stand on ceremony. If they were button men from somebody's family, I'd know soon enough. Either way, I was going to finish what I was eating and cut out the back. Then my waiter comes up to the table and drops a dish right in front of me.

"Your dessert," he says without looking at me.

"What dessert?" I asked him, just a little jumpy that he had walked up to me without catching my eye first.

"Your strawberry shortcake," he mumbled, motioning with his head to the two men at the front table. "Happy birthday."

Now I look up toward the front and the two guys are looking back directly at me. Then I looked at the shortcake and I got hungry all over again. One of the men nodded, waiting for me to nod back, and stood up. OK, I figured, strawberries are strawberries so they must be carrying a message from Mr. C.

"Mike Milan?" the taller of the two men asked as he stood over my table, raising his voice at the end of my name like he was going to put the collar on me as soon as I said yes. I didn't like the tone of that "Mike Milan" at all.

"Someone would like to see you," he continued.

"Who?" I asked. I figured since they weren't button men from one of the Families, all the rules were off. And if they were cops, they flashed no warrants so I didn't have to go nowhere with nobody.

The shorter guy swept the room with his eyes like he was George Raft checking for screws before telling John Garfield that they were busting out of stir that night. "Somebody big."

"That don't tell me nothing," I said. "Somebody big can be anybody. Besides, I got appointments."

"They'll keep," the taller man said. "The Old Man won't." And he sat down at the table and leaned over so nobody else could hear us even if they were listening. "We sent you the strawberries like we're supposed to. You're supposed to know that we're OK."

"Yeah," I said, laughing just a little. "But they were supposed to be fresh strawberries."

"In the middle of winter?"

"If they ain't fresh, I got to think about it," I said as I dug my fork into the shortcake. "You guys wanna tell me anything else?"

The shorter guy was getting nervous.

"You're supposed to see the fucking strawberries and say you'll go to a meeting. That's what they told us and that's what you're supposed to do." Then he turned to his partner. "If he don't come, the Old Man will pop a fucking vein, and it's gonna be our necks." Then he turned back to me. "You gonna come along or do I gotta tell my boss that you're a no-show? He's not gonna like that."

I got up. "Can I bring my cake?" I asked.

"And you can eat it, too," the taller of the two men said as they took me outside to one of those new slant-back Cadillacs that were selling for over two grand in the showrooms. The taller guy slid behind the wheel while the shorter of the two got in the back seat alongside me. Then we pulled away from the curb and headed west along Delancey Street. We turned right at the Bowery and headed uptown toward twenty-third street where we caught Madison Avenue and took it north until we parked across the street from the Carlyle. It was a ritzy joint alright, I said to myself, but even if Mr. C. liked to stay there from time to time, he never liked to hob nob in public. Must be something big.

The two guys took me past the tuxedo at the front desk and into the elevator where they whispered the floor to a Spanish kid in a Phillip Morris outfit. The kid slammed his gates shut, pushed the lever over, and we pretended like we were alone while the car was pulled up the shaft with a swish. In a flash the kid stopped the car, pulled the two gates back and sung out the floor number. We walked out into the dark green hall and made a left turn. So, this was where the rich people stayed when they came to New York. It was so quiet and the lights were so weak and dim, I felt like I was walking the last mile.

We turned a corner and stopped at the first door. The tall guy knocked three times, then twice, and the door swung open to reveal two guys in shirtsleeves wearing shoulder holsters with .38s tucked inside. One of the men was sitting on a couch in a far corner listening to the radio and holding a coffee cup. They both stared at me like they were comparing my face to the hundreds of Wanted posters pasted up in the post office. They were just like cops. Cops never take their eyes off you. They make you feel like you're standing in a department store window everytime you talk to them. These guys were the same way. Button men from the Family are different. They never look at you until you do something funny. They know how to show a guy respect. Cops and feds don't show respect to nobody.

A tall guy motioned me inside the room and the guy on the couch stood up. "Tell the Chief that Mike Milan is here," the tall guy said to no one in particular. The man with the cup looked at me even harder through his two narrow slits for eyes like he was taking a mug shot for his files. Then he gave me one last sizing up and down like a prizefighter who was going to start throwing punches. Finally, he lit a cigarette and leaned forward, his elbows on his knees as he blew a cloud of smoke toward the door.

"Hurry up and quit posin'," the tall guy said again. "The Chief ain't got all day."

Then the man on the couch got up, walked over to a door to an adjoining room, knocked, and stuck his head inside.

"Milan is here, sir," he said in a low voice like he was a secretary.

"Send him in," a voice growled from behind the door.

The tall guy jerked his thumb toward the door in the rear and I followed it. I still didn't know who was in there waiting for me, but I figured that, without nobody telling me otherwise, I was under Mr. C.'s protection and nothing could happen to me except that he didn't know about it. And if anybody was so stupid as to try to pull something off, Mr. C. would make him wish he hadn't. So, even though you might think I was a little careless in just taking this guy's word and all, that's the way things used to get done.

I walked through the living room of the hotel apartment and into what turned out to be the bedroom. And waiting in there, sitting at a small writing desk by the window and glaring at me beneath his thick bulldog eyebrows as I walked through the doorway, was J. Edgar Hoover in the flesh. He was wearing a fresh-pressed white dress shirt with extra long collars and a flap-over breast pocket, a wide brown tie with polka-dots, and thick brown suspenders with leather turnbuckles. His pleated pants, which were a lighter shade of brown than the tie, were baggy, like he'd been sitting in them all day, but still held a military crease all the way down from his waist to his cuffs.

I'd seen his picture in the papers a thousand times since I was a kid, but it was nothing like seeing him sitting there looking at me right in the eyes. Nothing at all.

"Do you know who I am?" he asked, standing up. But before I could answer, he waved the man at the door out of the room and motioned him to close it behind him. Now just the two of us were in the room together.

"Yes," I answered. "Sir." After a pause that took too long. I was still a snot-nosed kid, still too stupid to give other people their due, still thinking that I was the same invincible Navy middleweight champ who had the fastest left jab in the entire service. He hrumphed, satisfied that I had added the "sir," but unsatisfied that it took long enough for me to figure out that that's what I was supposed to do. Then he took a file folder off the top of the writing desk behind him and opened it, looking down at it as he spoke.

"Michael Milan," he began, almost as if he had committed my file to his memory. "Born, New York City, 1925; graduated Seward Park High School, 1943; served in the Office of Strategic Services attached to the Navy 1944 to 1946, trained as an ordinance technician; earned seaman first class rating, military serial number . . ." He stopped and looked at me." This is all stuff we know." Then he flipped a few pages over in the folder and began again.

"Arrested, 1937, NYPD, charged with possession of stolen property, charges dropped; arrested again, 1943, NYPD, drunk and disorderly and possible accomplice to homicide *in a police lockup!*" He looked up at this, maybe for emphasis, and gave me a long, hard stare. Then he continued like was reading from the pulpit: "Known associates, 1938, Meyer Lansky, Benjamin Siegel, Charles Luciano, Frank Costello; 1943, Tomasso Lucchese; 1947, Frank Costello again . . ." He paused a second time. "This is all stuff most people don't know. Should I go on?"

I stood there as dumb as a stone. The man was unsmiling, his heavily jowled chin resting against his chest, but he didn't look as if he was going to put me away or nothing. He just stood there, waiting for me to say something, but knowing there was nothing I really could say. If he had the evidence to back up what I knew was true, he had me dead to rights. But I had the feeling this wasn't just a roust. Why bring in the head of the FBI on a roust? Then I figured, maybe they want to turn me into a snitch. But when they want to turn you, they beat the shit out of you first just to let you know what you can look forward to in stir. No, I said to myself, this was something else.

Hoover flipped over a few more pages in the file, eyeballing them like he was checking a racing form, and looked directly at me again. "Nine, November 1944, USS Ranger, Aircraft carrier berthed at Brooklyn Navy Yard, report of a missing seaman, report of a Hellcat Torpedo Bomber that fell overboard." He raised his voice as if he was asking a question. "And a seaman Milan is the crewman nearest to the accident. Three, January 1945, Quanset Point Naval Air Station, Marine drill sergeant Brumer found dead from an overdose of morphine, and there is a seaman Milan implicated in that incident as well. Should we talk about Fort Dix, where I don't know what the hell a swabbie named Milan was doing assigned to an Army processing center, but I guess in the Navy anything is possible?"

What was I supposed to say—that those were all assignments? That I had to admit to homicides because the cases were all classified as military operations? I toughed it out.

"I don't know what those military records mean, sir," I said. "I was assigned to all those bases and I happened to be acquainted with the personnel involved in the accidents. The Navy has classified all of them as accidents."

"I know what the Navy has classified, *Mr.* Milan," he said, stressing the Mr. as if he didn't believe it himself. "But can I ask you a question, strictly off the record?" And as if to make the point, he turned around to the desk and flipped the file folder closed.

"Do you know how many Nazis our troops let sneak into this country at the end of the war?"

I knew there were a lot because of all the forged identification papers that kept turning up in discharge records that I had investigated down at Jacksonville Naval Air Station before I was discharged myself.

"Do you know how many Soviet agents are operating in this country out of the United Nations?"

You didn't have to be a genius to figure that one out. There were Russian spies all over the place, and everyone knew it.

"Sit down for a second," Hoover said and pointed to one of the easy chairs in front of the far window. He got up from behind the desk and sat down directly across from me. "I'm not going to play any games with you. I know who you are, what you did during the war, and what you're doing now. I'm not going to threaten you or ask you to rat out anyone in the Families."

The fact that he used the term "Families" told me more about Hoover than anything else could have revealed.

"I'll be direct," he said, opening another file on the table beside his chair. "I want you to do for me what you're doing for Frank. Only when you work for me, you'll be working just like you did in the war. This time it'll be for Uncle Sam instead of the Family. Same assignments, same group."

I didn't say anything, and he didn't expect me to say anything. I just shut up and let him do the talking. Besides, I figured, if I said anything to incriminate myself, I might just wind up in the slammer, or worse, in the chair.

"Your reputation—what you've done up to now—has brought you here," Hoover said in a way that reminded me too much of what Mr. C. had said to me the year before. "But now we wipe the slate clean, and whatever you do from now on determines how long you'll stay." He paused and leaned forward on his elbows.

"I'm looking for fellows I can trust," he continued, but this time in a friendlier tone. "I can't use the boys in the Bureau because what I need to do isn't really Bureau business. I need guys like you who aren't afraid to get a bloody nose once in awhile and go out on a limb with no one backing you up."

Hoover was trying to get his message across without telling me exactly what he wanted. Finally he blurted it out. "Lookit, I need guys who can pull jobs when I need them pulled. Kick in a few doors and get me evidence against Nazis that G2 and the boys in Washington forgot to check. Slap some creep around so he talks about a crooked judge that's setting a foreign Communist Party worker loose with only a rap on the knuckles. And I need a squad of men who know how to pull the trigger and bury the body so it don't turn up floating in a canal the next day for a bunch of flatfoots to poke their billy clubs at." He paused to let the full impact of what he was saying sink in. Then he started up again.

"The courts are letting too many people off the hook for crimes that ten years ago would have landed them in the can. I don't mean you boys and your friends; I mean the dope pushers and cop killers. There's a whole new breed coming into this country these days, and it's us against them. There are plenty of foreign agents who got into this country after the war and neither the courts nor the immigration people can touch them. And these people were killers during the war. They ran the camps or shot our POWs down in ditches. We gotta let them know that we know who they are. And we gotta be worse than they are. I need some triggermen who can get in, do the hit, and get out. Cops can't do it. Only guys from the Families and the wartime field personnel can. You're both."

I could see the picture he had painted. As the chief of the Bureau, his hands were tied. He had to stick to the letter of the law no matter what he did. But if he had his own private group of button men, he could point to a sap and the guy would get hit. The Bureau covers up the evidence, and nobody's the wiser.

But the old boy was no fool. At least with me, he knew who he was recruiting for the job. "In the position you're in," he said. "You'll be in the know about certain things people you deal with would pay a lot to find out. It's just like the war," he said. "Loose lips . . ."

"You can trust me, Mr. Hoover," I said. I had earned my reputation of never giving up a trust while I was in the OSS. Looking back on that day and knowing what I know now, I didn't realize the importance of what he was saying. I was a triggerman and I was being hired by a new boss; that was all. But Mr. Hoover wasn't looking for palookas. He was looking for guys who could think as well as they could follow orders, and guys who would keep their mouths shut no matter what.

"I believe I can, but I want to make it clear. What you do for me, you do for me. What you do for Frank Costello is something else. I don't ever want to know," he said, opening his hands and pushing them out straight as if he was pushing the rest of his Sunday dinner across the table after he'd eaten too much.

I only managed to stare back as he spoke. At first, I really didn't believe what I thought I was hearing, but it sank in real fast. For years, we'd always wondered what the FBI boys would do if they ever got their hands on information from the inside. Now, the head of the FBI was telling me that he didn't want to know. He didn't expect me to rat out Mr. C. or any of the other bosses. He was letting them have what was theirs so not to upset the balance.

I also realized that Hoover never once asked me if I agreed to his deal. It was as if he never even considered that I had a choice. At first I thought he figured that if he said, "This is what must be done," I would just have to go along. Then I thought that maybe he figured to blackmail me. After all, he knew that I was running jobs for Mr. C., and it would only take one phony witness to say that he saw me pull the trigger and I'd get my one-way ticket to Death Row at Greenhaven. But that wasn't it either. Somehow, Mr. Hoover knew that I was stand-up. That I would do the right thing because I'd done it in the service.

"You're not going to know the identities of the other man in this unit," he said. "For the present, you'll work alone. In the future, you may work in teams, but I doubt it." He told me that my Navy records would be changed. I would become a wounded war veteran and receive medical benefits for the rest of my life. "That way, nobody can trace why you're being paid," he said. "At least in the beginning. Later on we may make other changes. Your Navy discharge may become an Army discharge. No two records will ever check, but you'll keep getting your payments as if you're disabled."

Then he told me that if I ever got married, they'd be able to pay me Social Security through my wife if they wanted. "Just like you're a dead man," Hoover said with just a hint of a smile, as if he were enjoying a private joke that nobody else would ever share. "When the time comes, the checks will be paid to your wife's name and if anybody ever asks how Michael Milan is paid, we'll just list him as Beneficiary Deceased or Disabled. It is the perfect cover."

There was still a big question that I didn't dare ask. I was supposed to be a cop. A fed. I was working for the family and I was being told to work for the FBI. But the jobs were the same. The question was on the edge of my tongue. How do you ask the chief of the FBI what you say to your *padrone*, the Boss of all Bosses who sits at the head of the commission? What do you say to the man who sent you out to earn your bones and before whose eyes you swore to uphold the law of *omerta*? Was I supposed to tell Mr. C. that I worked for J. Edgar Hoover? I was on a tightrope and Hoover knew it.

From that time on, my presence in the family would no longer be as it was. I would be an outsider in their world and an outsider in Hoover's world. I would be able to trust no one even though both sides would trust me. Hoover had done all of this by bringing me to this meeting. He had used the code to gain my trust. How had he known about the code? That was a secret known only to people in the Family. But that question was too dangerous to ask. Even then I knew it was a subject not to be opened. I only asked the obvious question.

"Since you say you know what I do, what do you expect me to tell my friends and the friends of their friends?"

"Work for your friends the way you see fit," he answered. "I won't ask you about it, and I don't want to know about it. Someday you may be surprised to learn more about your friends and their families than you know now. But, I believe Mr. Costello once told you about a line that you must not cross. Now it is even more important that you know where that line is and who your friends are on either side of it. I'll put it as bluntly as I can. If you use what you learn from me to profit on the other side of the line, than *both* sides will stand away from you because you cannot be trusted. But you're still very young. Maybe too young for this. You only have to know that the person who stood up for you before Frank Costello is standing up for you now. This meeting is over. It never took place. And now I don't know you. You will be sent for if needed." And with that he turned around and dismissed me from his presence as if he were some swami in the desert.

I didn't tell Frank Costello about my meeting with J. Edgar Hoover, of course, but somehow during those early years I could feel that he knew. Maybe it was the way he ushered me into his presence or maybe it was the guarded way he spoke about the feds and the FBI agents who were always tailing him. It wasn't until many years later when I had received the same set of instructions from Hoover and Mr. C. that I saw the two of them in the same place at the same time. It was in Grand Central Station before Mr. C. officially retired and before The Chin was to take his pot shot at him. I had just walked away from J. Edgar Hoover when I saw Frank Costello in front of me. I turned around and there was the Old Man. I turned back and there was Mr. C. They saw each other and I saw both of them. Then they turned and walked in opposite directions. That was how I knew that they were working together and had been for many years. And that was how they told me that they trusted me enough to let me see them together in the same place.

Twenty years after that day, I read in a book somewhere that Mr. Hoover and Mr. Costello had met many times in private and that they even owned a racetrack down in Florida. But I didn't have to read it in any book. Sam Koenig, the man who stood up for me to Meyer, to Frank, and to the Old Man, the man who had turned my life in this direction because he and Meyer Lansky had made a judgment about me while I was still a punk rolling boxcars at the Chrystie Street crap games, had told me all about it.

When he was a dying old man, Sam Koenig confided all of it to me, even the little details about the judges who stole from the victims of crime, the fathers who sold their daughters to storekeepers for a night's worth of food, and the mothers who had begged him with their bodies to keep their sons out of jail. It was Sam Koenig, the old man who used to sit on the fruit crate in front of Pollack's, who moved people around like pieces on a checkerboard. You would never know it to look at him, but he had the ability to pick people out from a crowd, point his finger, and set them in motion. That was how it was done in those days. And for me, by the time I was twenty-three, Sam Koenig had moved me so far in that I would never get out for the rest of my life.

Ludlow Street

It wasn't long before I heard from Mr. Hoover again. In one of the many different patterns of concealment that would be repeated over and over again for the next thirty years, the Old Man had me pinched by the New York City cops. I was walking down Ludlow Street on the last day of February and feeling my oats when they sped around the corner out of nowhere and pulled up alongside me in a squad car, screeching their tires along the curb louder than a cat fight in an alley at night. Then before the car even stopped, they jumped out of both doors like they were going to beat the shit out of me. Right in front of my friends, they grabbed me by the arms, spun me around, slammed me against the fender, patted me down real good, slapped the cuffs on, and tossed me into the back seat like a sack of mail. They said they were picking me up on a gambling rap and threw in possession of stolen property for good measure. Then they drove me down to the Centre Street lockup and threw me in the tank without getting my fingerprints or anything. That's how I knew something was fishy about the collar.

I didn't get to make my phone call after I was arrested. And I was surprised that none of the local bulls on Mr. C.'s Centre Street list didn't pass the word along to any of the *capos* or underbosses who were playing cards and drinking their anisette just around the corner. That first night while I was rotting in the tank, I figured I must have really done something wrong because no one came down to spring me. At breakfast the next morning, though, I knew this was a setup because I wasn't given my tray with the other stiffs. Two of the screws led me out of the tank and down the hall to the visitor's room where they gave me my own tray and left me alone.

This didn't make any sense, I told myself. Maybe they were giving me poisoned eggs or something. But, when I picked up the metal hospital-tray cover, I found a small numbered key on the plate right beside the food. The tag on the key read LaGuardia Arrivals Terminal, March 1. And the number on the key was 242. I memorized the date, place, and number and shoved the key down into my athletic shorts. Then I took a couple of forkfuls of the yellow water they called scrambled eggs. Compared to the dinner of my mama's flanken I'd eaten two nights ago, this was horseshit, and I couldn't have kept it down even if I'd wanted to.

The screws waited outside the cage until they made sure I wasn't shoveling this slop into my mouth anymore and then rattled on the wire mesh window to tell me then were coming back. They were obviously part of whatever syndicate Hoover was building right under the noses of the New York City cops. However, since Mr. C. was able to get the same kind of service from the turnkeys at Centre Street, I suspected that something had to be up between the two of them. It stands to reason that two big bosses shouldn't be using exactly the same organization of people unless one boss is winking at the other. This, of course, had to have been the case between Mr. C. and Mr. H., but I didn't know it for sure at that time.

The screws muscled me back to the tank where I got the fish eyes from the other stiffs who'd been picked up and thrown in there with me. Why did I rate the special treatment, they must have been wondering? How come I got taken out of the tank while they were eating? I had been asking myself the same question until I realized that the Old Man was using the last place anyone would expect as his way to pass me my drop, my dough, and my orders for the first job. If this was how he was going to send me all my orders, I had better stake out a soft cot because I was going to be spending a lot of nights locked up in the pokey.

Before I got to feeling too sorry for myself, a new pair of screws turned up to put me in prison shackles and drag me off to what I thought would be my arraignment. Instead they took me to an interrogation room in the precinct where a red-faced, beer-belly, donkey detective stuck his mug into mine and kept screaming about some gambling operation I was supposed to be running. I told him he'd have to fuck himself upside down in the middle of Times Square to get me to tell him anything. He grabbed me by my collar and shook me so hard I thought my teeth would rattle out. I even bit my tongue between my front teeth and it started bleeding. The cop smiled when he saw the blood in my mouth.

"Take a picture of it, screw," I said. "Because when I'm outta these irons I'm gonna shove your fuckin' head up your fuckin' ass so far it comes out your mouth."

"Fuckin' kike, I'mna beat the living shit outta you," the cop said and made like he was going to hit me a good one when another cop came in and pulled him off. He slammed him against the wall and put his mouth inches away from the cop's face.

"Shanahan," he said. "Don't fuck this one up. 'Cause then I'll be the one coming after you." He grabbed Shanahan's tie, twisted his collar hard against his neck, and pinned him against the wall of the interrogation room. Then he looked over his shoulder at me.

"We're gonna let you walk outta here, boyo," he said. "But if you blab what y've seen to anyone, you'll be on crutches for the rest of ya life. And it won't be me that's puttin' ya on them, I promise ya that."

I sat myself down and waited for the second cop to take the cuffs and leg irons off. Shanahan just glared like he was on fire. After I was out of the harness, the cop motioned for me to remain where I was and pushed Shanahan out of the room.

"I expect y've gotten what ya were sent here fer," he said with a long, all-too-knowing look at me over the top of his large, red clown's nose that was covered with the peeling-away skin of a heavy drinker. He smelled of liquor, his nose was running like a faucet, and his eyes were glassy and bloodshot.

"Ya mind that ya steer 'way clear of Shanahan," he warned, jerking his head at the closed door. " 'Cause he'll beat ya ta death and get a wink from the boyos upstairs. And don't be thinkin' that he'll wind up floatin' in the East River afterwards neither," he continued with a shake of his head. "Business deals is business deals, and there won't be no fallin' outs over a few dead kikes." He stood me up and straightened out the wrinkles in my jacket and lapels. "The rules is this—and I'm repeatin' 'em just in case no one ever told ye. When y'er inside this lockup, yer ass is *ours*. Ya do what y'er told when y'er told and ya damn well shut up about it. If Shanahan slaps yer face, ya stand there and take the slappin'. What ya don't do when someone asks you a civil question—just for the sake of keeping this on the up-and-up—is shoot off yer mouth. Yer answer is, 'I don't know nothing about that, *OFFICER*.' That way *Detective* Shanahan says to his sergeant, 'I questioned the suspect and he had no knowledge of no crimes.' "

It was beginning to sink into my thick skull. Everybody had to do his job to keep his job. It was a lesson I would never forget.

"Now, Mr. Michael Milan, boyo," he continued, emphasizing every word so I wouldn't misunderstand his intention, "I won't repeat this to the people you work for if you don't repeat it to the people I work for. If y'er gettin' me meanin'."

"I'm sorry if I've caused any trouble, *OFFICER*," I said. "But I don't know what you're talking about. I certainly don't know about any crimes and there's nothing I have to complain about."

"Don't let it never be said that Jewboys don't learn real fast," the cop said, smiling that he'd gotten his point across and relieved that his intervention had prevented bad blood from rising up and spilling over on both sides of the line. "Now ye'd best be gettin' on yer way before Shanahan drinks down the fifth of scotch he has in his desk drawer and gets crazy all over again."

I was signed out of the lockup and released. I caught a cab on Centre Street and took it straight to LaGuardia without even stopping back at the house and explaining my unscheduled overnight to my mother. She, like a lot of other people over the years, would have to wait until a job was done before I could talk about where I had been.

It was getting on toward afternoon by the time the cab reached the airport, and the crowd at LaGuardia was already gathering for the afternoon flights to Washington and Boston. To them, I was just another passenger blending into the flow as I made my way through the arrivals terminal to the luggage lockers. As I walked, I felt in the pocket of my athletic shorts for the locker key I'd stashed there for safekeeping, drawing one or two stares from blue-haired old biddies who must have been wondering what some unshaved kid in rumpled clothes was doing playing with himself at the airport. Don't get too excited, ladies, it sure ain't you I'm thinking about, I said to myself as I hurried through the crowd.

I had found the key by the time I had reached the luggage lockers and waited a few minutes until a mob of arrivals passed by. Nobody stopped over at the lockers. I looked for locker number 242, put the key in the lock, and turned it. I found a lawyer's leather briefcase on the floor of the locker. I pulled it out, stuck it under my arm like a businessman on the way to a meeting, looked around to see whether I was being watched, and carried it into the men's room where I could take my time and see what was inside while I sat in the privacy of the can. I even waited a couple of minutes before opening it to make sure that I wasn't followed. There were two envelopes inside the briefcase—one containing two-and-a-half grand in tens, twenties, and fifties and the other containing plane tickets for the night flight to New Orleans—a reservation to the Fairmont Hotel just outside the French Quarter, a street map of the city, a newspaper clipping about the organized gambling and whorehouse operations that had made New Orleans famous ever since I could remember, three carefully typed eyes-only memos from the director of the New Orleans field office of the FBI to Bureau Chief Hoover in Washington, and a telephone number on which someone had handwritten "your eyes only." Without anybody having to spell it out, I knew it was a special direct phone line to report the end of my assignment. That was how we did it in the OSS.

There were no obvious orders for me in the briefcase so I guessed I was to figure out what I was supposed to do from what was in the memos. It also looked like Mr. Hoover wanted me to use the information about the New Orleans gambling syndicate to help me in the operation. My instincts told me that he wanted me to recruit local muscle for any jobs I had to pull. I personally didn't know anybody down that way, but at least the newspaper article would send me to the right address.

The eyes-only memos were about an investigation into a theft of what the head of the field office down there—an agent named Rizzoli—called "low-level" military secrets. If it was such low level, I thought as I sat there on the hard toilet seat, how come the FBI or the Army couldn't clean up the mess itself? And how come Mr. H. wanted me to make the acquaintance of the local syndicate? If this had been an OSS operation, we would have gone outside the organization only if we thought people on the inside were working double-shift. Maybe this was the situation down in New Orleans. If it was, then Mr. H. had a right to be worried. And he also was right about wanting it closed down clean and fast and with no publicity. This must have been what he was talking about a few months earlier when he said he didn't want any bodies floating to the surface.

I put the papers back in the briefcase and counted the money again. Twenty-five hundred tax-free ain't bad, I said to myself as I left the bathroom with the briefcase and the money. Nothing compared to what I was getting on the other side, of course, but the other side didn't come with hospital insurance. I was pretty cocky all right, as I thought about my first operation. But, as I remember it now, I was still in for a few surprises. I grabbed a cab back to the Lower East Side where I would have just enough time to pack a few things, lay my hands on some artillery, and get cleaned up before my flight. I would also have to square last night's disappearance with my mom, who was always worried, and tell her I was heading down to Havana for a little shore leave and some R &R. Maybe if I wrapped up this New Orleans job real quick, that's just what I would do.

Le Vieux Carré

The thing you always got to remember about New Orleans is that it's all below sea level. It gets flooded by the Mississippi River every spring and dead bodies bob outta their graves. Even legit graves. They got mosquitos as big as handballs that breed in the bayou swamps, bite you right through your clothes, and leave bleeding lumps the size of boils. They got roaches as big as pigeons and rats that are bigger than schnauzer dogs. You go into one of those restaurants in the old French Quarter and you see all kinds of animals crawling up the walls. You bend over to eat your gumbo and something with a long tongue looks up at you from your plate and winks an eye. They got whores walking up and down the streets and giving you the come-on out of every doorway. And the whole damn place is afraid of a curse some voodoo witch mama put on them a hundred and fifty years ago. In spring and summer the air's so hot and wet down there, you can't breathe. No wonder the locals go crazy every year at the end of winter.

Family business in New Orleans isn't like Family business anywhere else. A lot of the gambling and booze operations are run by Frenchies or Creoles instead of Sicilians, even though the head of the Family takes his orders out of Chicago. The hitters down there like to use knives instead of guns. That way they can hold you nice and close and look you right in the eye as they push the blade between your ribs. It's a wide open city with a pad that ran all the way up to the Mayor. I guess that's why the Old Man expected me to set up my own operation with locals who knew the lingo instead of bringing in heat from up North.

You see, Mr. H. knew that somewhere along the line people were going to have to be hit, especially if some of the intelligence guys were running a double operation. And hitting a guy in New Orleans has special problems because you just can't dump the stiff in the drink and expect it to disappear. Bodies in New Orleans have a nasty habit of washing into the middle of a city street because the place always floods. We'd hear about a hit that went sour because the goons who pulled it wrapped a chain around the body, tossed it into the Gulf and went to get soused. Two days later, a rain storm floods the shit out of the joint and the stiff turns up on Bourbon Street looking like last night's corned beef hash. And even if they were to take it out into deeper water, a more expensive job because of all the traffic in the channels down there, you still get no guarantees because of the floods. So, the Old Man meant for me to bring in the local talent to make sure that whoever we hit stayed hit.

Now I'd never seen Mardi Gras before, but the way the people down there talk about it, you'd think it was the most important thing in the world. Everybody dresses up like clowns, gets drunk, gets into fights on the street, and fucks whoever they wake up with in the morning. By the time I'd landed in New Orleans, Mardi Gras had just ended and everybody was walking around like a bunch of hung-over zombies from a Bela Lugosi movie. I figured this might make my job a little easier. I was wrong.

Whatever skim these intelligence boys were running, they were running it smart. I spent my first two days getting the feel of the landscape and nosing around the military bases in the area as far west as Galveston. I didn't find a thing. Even swabbies who were falling dead drunk off their bar stools in river-front dives didn't seem to know about anybody spreading around money for military documents or information. I was drawing a blank.

I had gone back to my room at the Fairmont after spending my second night covering the bars along the river on the east side of town. It was especially warm for March. The smells of stale beer and sharp spices were hanging heavy in the air, mixing with the lonesome sounds of muted trumpets and reaching through the wrought iron and tumbledown streets of the French Quarter. I guess I was still a little wobbly because I didn't see the two flatfoots waiting for me in the hotel lobby. They waited until I had gone up to my room, followed me up in the elevator, and pounded on my door like they were going to bust it in if I didn't open it.

I have to admit that at first I was rattled by the pounding and my natural instinct would have been to reach for my gun and plug whoever came through the doorway. But I was a reasonable young man. I figured that nobody was going to hit me in my own hotel room and that unless King Kong was on the other side of the door, I could take care of him myself.

"Keep your shirt on," I yelled at the door.

"Police. Open up," someone called out.

I opened the door, and two big, sweating slobs pushed me out of the way and forced their way into the middle of the room. They looked me up and down, satisfied themselves that I wasn't packing a gun, took their hands away from their shoulder holsters, and gave the room a quick once over.

"You Mike Milan?" one of them asked.

I nodded.

"Answer yes or no," the other said.

"I'm Milan," I said.

One of them took out a badge with a crescent moon on it.

"I'm Sergeant LaFaye," the first cop said. "Investigator out of the parish prosecutor's office. This is my partner Detective Livoni."

"Sergeant," I said nodding in his direction. "Detective Livoni. Can I help you gentlemen?"

"You got any i-dee, Milan?" the sergeant asked.

I showed him my New York driver's license without answering.

"You got any military i-dee?" the sergeant asked again.

"No, sir," I said. "Been out of the service since the end of the war."

"You've been talking to a lot of sailors along the river front," Livoni said. "You down here to make new friends or do you have any special interests?"

I clammed.

"We can do this at the station," LaFaye said. "Or we can be nice and polite over a couple of drinks. Up to you."

I picked up the phone and asked room service to send up a bottle of bourbon and lots of ice.

"Make yourself at home, gentlemen," I said. "But I don't know if anything I have to say is going to interest you."

The two cops sat down, said nothing, and stared at me until room service knocked at the door. It took about five minutes. Then, after I poured a round of drinks, LaFaye continued.

"I'll get to the point," he said. "You're rustling up too many feathers and giving the wrong people the jitters. I don't want to be explaining to our mutual friends in Washington that we didn't give you any Southern hospitality down here." He took a slip of paper out of a small black leather notepad and handed it over to me.

"Let's us all save some time and get you out of here on your feet instead of in a box," he said. "Go ahead and read it."

The paper said Nitano Funeral Home, St. Charles Place.

"We had our eyes on this place for the past year," LaFaye continued. "And it was us that told some of them FBI boys about the traffic goin' in'n'out at the damndest hours. Lots of stiffs goin' in. Even more stiffs comin' out. If you was to keep count, there'd be more stiffs in there than the en-tire population of Baton Rouge, but the FBI don't seem to want to know. So we keep on goin' back for a looksee every now and then. No change."

Livoni picked up the conversation. "Then we hear proprietors of some of our local wagerin' establishments in the Quarter tells us that ree-pairman was coming down from up North to patch a few leaks that hadn't been turned off since the war. Then you shows up. We figure we're gonna be in for some fireworks so the sooner we get'em over with, the sooner we get back to business."

I nodded without giving away anything.

Now it was LaFaye's turn. He stuck out his glass and I poured in three fingers of bourbon. He held the glass up and turned it around in the light as if he was thinking about how to say what he really wanted to say. Then he downed the glass of booze in one gulp. He leaned forward in his chair.

"I don't give a shit what's goin' on over at Nitano's, you hear. Just you finish what you got to do and get the hell out of town before somebody up and decides you been around too long already."

I got his meaning.

"Can you boys cover my ass for a coupla days while I get some men to wrap this up?" I asked.

"You don't leave no blood out in'a open, hear?" Livoni said.

"Agreed," I assured him.

"Y'all got what's left of this week. Then we gotta close it down. If it's gonna take any longer, then we gotta make it official," he continued. "And I know you don' want that."

LaFaye and Livoni helped themselves to another round "for sociability's sake" and headed for the door. As they left, LaFaye took a small key out of his pocket and dropped it on the night table. "Make sure you leave this in the lock," he said as he left.

The key was to a luggage locker—which I now understood was the preferred method of passing information back and forth—at the small local airport in Metarie over in the next parish. There was no sense waiting around the hotel any longer since the visit from the cops told me that this thing was quickly coming to a head. The sooner I wrapped it up and got out, the healthier I'd be. I threw on a jacket, jammed my .38 in an inside belt holster I liked to wear against the small of my back, and left the hotel. There's a lot of nightlife in New Orleans, and with plenty of cabs cruising on the street even at that late hour, I caught one to the airport within minutes.

The luggage area of the airport in Metarie was deserted—not even the sounds of footsteps. The cops had timed it perfect. They knew I'd hightail it over there as soon as they gave me the key and they knew the place would be clear. But I knew to expect a double-cross since the whole operation was based on federal agents playing both sides. When I looked back over toward the parking lot, I saw a New Orleans police car sitting idle under a lamppost as if it was on permanent station there. That was La Faye's message to me that the detectives had posted another set of eyes to cover my trail.

I found the luggage lockers on the very far wall of the baggage area and quickly matched the key to the locker. I opened it and found a handwritten list of the names and addresses of Army intelligence agents who the New Orleans cops considered suspicious. Why were they suspicious? I didn't know then, but I guessed that cops like La Faye liked to know where every loose end was flapping around in their jurisdiction. There were a lot of New York cops like that. They didn't care who was good or who was bad as long as they didn't get any surprises. In fact, most cops I knew would rather be dealing with bad guys instead of good guys because, as one of them once told me before they wheeled him away on a stretcher, good guys will almost always become bad guys at least once. Bad guys never change. If you play percentage, stick with the bad guys because that way you can always come out ahead. I guess that's how La Faye and his partner also played the game.

After reading over the list, I knew where to start. From the airport, I would pay a visit to Nitano's to see what made the cops suspect the goings on down there. Next, I'd have to recruit some local button pushers first thing in the morning. I'd stay away from the FBI field office since they'd already done enough damage, but I would sure as hell call the Washington telephone number when I had something to report.

I flagged down another cab back to the hotel. He was just waiting at the terminal for one of the red-eye flights to land and was more than happy to see me spinning out of the arrivals building. As we left the cab stand, I checked in the rearview mirror to see if the police car followed us. It did, although the cop was smart enough to lay off by a few car lengths until we got into town so he wouldn't be spotted on the back roads.

I ditched the list of agents in the hotel, made sure it nothing incriminating was sitting in plain sight in case the room was tossed, and wrapped up my set of burglar tools and a glass cutter. These would get me through any office door or into a low-security building, provided there was no automatic burglar alarm. I hid these tools inside my jacket and checked again that my gun was in place. I don't care how long you've been in the business—checking for your gun will always be an automatic reaction. Then I hoofed it over to St. Charles Place.

Once outside again, I was surprised at the number of people still on the street in the dead of the night. New Orleans being what it was, I knew there would already be a few people cruising for action, but I never figured there would be this many. Some of them may have been residue from Mardi Gras, but I had the impression that most were regulars, out every night to get whatever they could drag home. Most of them seemed like loners rather than party-goers, real losers who wouldn't last a minute if they wandered out onto New York streets as drunk as they were down there in the murky heat.

St. Charles Place was in a residential neighborhood along the trolley line, but outside the French Quarter district. As I left the Quarter, the number of people milling around the streets grew smaller until by the time I reached the funeral home, the entire town seemed deserted. Nitano's itself was almost desolate—completely dark except for a single outside light all the way in back by a ramp entrance where the meat wagons unloaded the stiffs. The building was just an oversized house, like the kind you'd see in movies, with big double doors in front and a porch as big as a baseball diamond. There were also porches on both sides of the house and each of them had smaller entry doors. I did the obvious thing first and tried all the doors just to make sure they were locked. They were.

Next, I worked my way around to the rear of the house where there were two empty hearses and a coroner's wagon backed up against a garage. So this guy Nitano worked for the city coroner as well as doing his own business. Very handy, I figured, for the body-bagger to sit in bed with the doc who signs the death certificates for the city. We did it like that in New York, and it was an easy way to cut off homicide investigations before they even became investigations. Nothing sends a homicide dick off to his wet lunch faster than the words "natural causes" on a death certificate.

There was a sudden, loud barking from somewhere in the darkness. I reached for my gun. The last thing I wanted to do was plug some crazy mutt and wake up the entire neighborhood, but I wasn't about to watch my arm get carried off in a pair of jaws while I was trying to make a run back for the street. Luckily, the dog's bark was picked up by a howl and then a chorus of yelps from the other pooches on the block. They soon quieted down, almost as if by some prearranged signal, and I was left in silence once again.

I got down on my hands and knees and crawled around the foundation of the building until I could peer into the basement windows. They were dark. I felt around the windowsill for burglar alarm wires. Yep, they were there. I knew from my months during the war working as an undercover OSS agent out of naval ordinance on the Ranger that if anyone tried to open the window or cut the wires, the whole place would sound like an air raid. So I struck a match for light to see if the wires themselves crisscrossed the actual window pane. They didn't. It was an antique burglar alarm system more to satisfy an insurance company, probably, than for real protection. The window pane was just large enough for me to get through without slicing up my face if I cut the glass as close to the wooden frame as possible and didn't nick the alarm wires.

Using the suction cup with my glass cutter, I held the glass pane in place with my left hand while I made a light score around the edge of the frame. I worked deliberately rather than quickly, going over my score again and again until I heard the soft but distinct crack that told me the glass was broken. I worked the rest of the score until I felt the entire pane loosen from the frame. Then I tapped the lead ball at the other of the cutter gently against the glass to break it away from the frame, raised and tilted the suction cup so that the bottom of the pane was angled toward me, and slowly lifted the pane out of the frame. So far so good; the alarm hadn't gone off.

Now with the glass pane out of the window, I pulled the tiny pieces of glass out of the bottom of the frame so I wouldn't tear my ass off as I slid into the basement. I only had to hope that I could jump in without busting my ankle and that I could get out as easily as I got in. First I leaned head first inside the window and felt around the wall toward the floor with my hands and figured that it was only about a four-foot drop to a ledge against the wall. I backed out, slowly turned around, slid my legs through the window opening, and, without pulling on the wires, lowered myself to the ledge in the darkness. Then I felt for the floor with my toe and brought my other leg down.

Now I was inside the room and groping along the wall until I could see clearer in the grey darkness. At first I could make out the shapes of long boxes on what looked to be lab tables. Then I could see the shelves that held bottles of chemicals which reflected the light from the dimly burning light on the garage outside. I was very careful to stay against the wall so I didn't knock over any tables and cause a ruckus that might bring the cops. After all, I was technically breaking and entering, even though the district attorney's own investigator had given me the lead. He would have to deny it anyway if the cops picked me up, and that's assuming that whoever was behind this skim would let me walk away from the place without a bullet between my ears.

As I made my way along the wall, I listened carefully for the sound of any people upstairs. It was safe to figure that the place might have a guard or two because people sometimes wanted their relatives to be buried with their valuables. That sounds like a load of bullshit if you ask me, but the *goyim* have strange customs when it comes to planting one of their own. Maybe I'd lift a few diamond rings on my way out of this joint just to make it look like it was a break-in and robbery. No sense making them any more suspicious than necessary if a window was kicked in but nothing was heisted.

I needed light, but I was afraid to strike a match because of my fear that the heavy alcohol fumes that were already making me dizzy would set this place off like a torch. Finally, I bumped into and almost knocked over what I thought at first was a floor lamp. However, it wasn't really a lamp, it was more like one of those standing studio floor spots that photographers like to use when they shoot the cheesecake for magazines. Benny Siegel took me to a studio once when one of his girlfriends was getting her picture taken for a theater marquee. This was the same kind of light.

I drew the shades over the bulb to shield as much of the glare as possible, turned on the bulb, and threw a narrow beam of light into the center of the joint. I quickly became aware of the interior of the whole room. It was like a giant high-ceilinged cave, cast in deep shadows by the indirect light from the shielded floor spot. As my eyes again adjusted to the dim light, I could see among the shadows that row upon row of coffins were lined up like artillery shells in a depot. There were plain pine coffins, black and shiny mahogany coffins, coffins with gold and silver filigree, and the metallic-looking boxes that were used during the war to ship the soldiers' remains home for burial. This room looked more like a processing plant than a family funeral home.

How could this guy have so much business? I said to myself. There couldn't be this many stiffs in all New Orleans. Then I realized that Nitano was probably the contractor for most of the body disposal business in the area, if not the entire state. You could imagine how big that might be. Guys get hit by the Families, the police put guys away either by accident or on purpose, maybe even the government has to make people disappear. And you can't just plant all these stiffs in a swamp.

You also have to make sure that nobody's going to be digging up your grave site to lay a foundation for a high school or a hospital. That's why you need a good funeral home. These guys can stack two or sometimes three people in the same grave. They can run bodies into the cremation oven one after the other on a conveyor belt. They can cut up the remains of an adult and bag them in the same coffin with a child between the time the family leaves from the funeral and the box is loaded up on the hearse. A good contract mortician has a hundred tricks up his sleeve and is usually worth his weight. I know, because the families do a lot of late-night business with the neighborhood contract morticians in New York.

The rest of the basement room was like an army medical field station filled with rolling work tables, IV stands, surgical trays and equipment, portable overhead lights, and stacks of wadding, paraffin, and theatrical makeup for cleaning up the basket cases. I also noticed that most of the coffins were tagged with those five-copy carbon-paper bills of lading that professional movers always use. It was like the boxes were ready to be loaded up and shipped off somewhere. Something didn't figure. Even if this guy was contracting for half the Families along the Gulf, he still wouldn't be shipping bodies out of town unless he was doing his regular business on the up-and-up. And this guy was not on the up-and-up. Had to be something else.

Then I found it! More than half of the names on the shipping tags were identical. Worse, all of the identical name tags were being shipped overseas. The rest of the shipment tags were for cemetaries up and down the East Coast. I told myself that I would make my phone calls the next morning just to check some facts, but right then and there I was willing to lay odds that Nitano was processing military remains coming into the country from overseas and sending bodies back overseas that were either misidentified or had not been claimed by their Families. That seemed straightforward enough, especially if he was doing business with the Families. They could easily throw military contracts his way without anybody in Washington even bothering to verify the signatures on the reimbursement checks. But the identical name tags told me something more. The cocksucker was smuggling something out of the country by covering his tracks with the paperwork for the real shipment and not filing any paperwork for the fake shipment. It was an almost perfect skim. And it would have kept on working forever except that both the FBI and the Families that were keeping this Nitano in business figured something was wrong.

The FBI knew that information was being smuggled out of New Orleans. It didn't know how or where, but stuff just kept on turning up missing. At the same time, the Families were getting nervous because there was just too much traffic at Nitano's to be kosher. There's nothing the Families put a stop to faster than when somebody's making private phone calls on their dime. So the Old Man sends me down to New Orleans to sniff around—so far so good. Then the families, hearing through friends of friends that a New York contractor is coming down for oysters in the French Quarter, has its cops send him to a trouble spot that they're worried about. And whaddya know—it's the same spot.

That's enough snooping for one night, I told myself, and made my plans to exit. I looked around for any valuables that a kid might take to make it look like the obvious break-in. I found a lot of loose folding money and some change, a couple of gold wristwatches, a box of rings. I'd lay these off on the two cops as I left town. I also opened up a couple bottles of booze and poured the liquor on the floor. This way whoever called the police would think some kids had a party in the embalming room and robbed the place. Then I took some lipstick from the theatrical makeup table and wrote "Fuck You Nitano" on one of the walls. Now they would think the kids were assholes as well as punks. This would get Nitano so good and mad he might never figure that someone was onto his skim. At least not yet. Besides, Nitano might be protected and I didn't want to step on any big toes. I wanted at least two days' worth of complete surprise because when I closed the door on whoever was running Mr. Nitano's operation, I wanted him to be looking the other way.

The Skinner

I got myself out of the embalming room through the same window I came in. Climbing out was trickier because I kept catching my balls on the window frame every time I hiked up to street level. One slip backwards, as I tried to pull myself up on arm strength alone and roll head first through the broken window pane, and my career would have been over right then and there. So I was very careful about that particular get-away. Even during the war when I was willing to give up a lot for my country, I wasn't willing to sacrifice those. I sure as hell wasn't going to hang'em up on Charlie Nitano's windowsill now. I finally made it through the opening in one continuous movement by holding my breath and pushing myself straight up with the strength of my shoulders and back.

Once outside, I didn't waste any time getting back to town. I had a lot of ground to cover and I knew that when the place was opened later in the morning, Nitano would either be calling the police because his place was hit or screaming at whoever he was working for that somebody was onto him. I was betting he would call the police first and I wanted to be ready with an alibi I could sell when LaFaye and his partner pounded down my door.

I still had a few hours before sunrise, so I figured I'd pay a visit to Johnny Santos, the biggest of the Family businessmen in town. He was one of the local people the Old Man expected me to check on. I figured that Mr. Santos'd be able to tell me which of the names on my list of suspicious feds rang a bell and then maybe I'd be able to place my phone call to Washington and close up shop. At least that's what I hoped. So I caught the milk-run streetcar back to the Bourbon Street stop and hoofed it over to Johnny Santos' River Front Lounge. It was late, I knew, but even if no one was home at Johnny's, I'd still be able to get me some of that Frenchie coffee and sugar doughnuts the town is famous for.

As I walked toward the river, I kept my eyes open for any late-night gamblers roaming the streets with loot in their pockets. In case there was no action at the Lounge, I'd only have to follow one of them to find another joint where my credentials were good. But it turned out to be no problem at all. The two or three stragglers I picked up were already heading over to Johnny's. Soused to where they could hardly keep their eyes open and pitching like they were on the deck of a ship, they staggered down the narrow streets towards the river like they couldn't wait to empty their wallets on Johnny's tables. His was the only joint still running this late.

The Lounge was real close to the river and the smell of rotten fish heads, dead rats, swamp weed, and tanker oil made you want to chuck up your gumbo before you even got around the corner. There was no sign or anything to tell you where it was. You just had to know that the small wooden door smack in the middle of a crumbling brick wall, no bigger than a mouse hole, opened into the heaviest gambling joint in town. The brick wall was all covered with river moss and the door opening was so small you had to stoop all the way over to get in so you wouldn't smash your head on the overhanging beam. If you knew to duck under the beam, the rumor went, Johnny figured you were connected and extended you the courtesy of the house. If you cracked your head, you were a mark and your wallet was as good as gone.

Even in New York the bookies and shylocks looked at Johnny Santos' operation with green faces. Johnny had his pickings of the local gamblers, bargemen from the cities upriver, longshoremen from the Gulf, oil riggers out of Texas, and even the foreign merchantmen who seemed to save their money just to spend it in New Orleans. When bigtime gamblers came to town, they paid visits to Johnny out of respect, like they were payin' a toll just to stay in town as guests. Drop a coupla grand at Johnny's and the boys'll show you a good time. Don't pay Johnny your respects, and you'll get pinched before morning and spend the next week in the can while the judge tries to figure out what you were pinched for in the first place.

The Mott Street boys had told me about the beam before I went into the service, just in case I was stationed down on the Gulf, so I already knew all about Johnny and it was strictly on the level. I put my ear against the door and heard the sweet sounds of dice clattering against one another. I could pick that sound out even in the middle of an artillery barrage. I also heard the shuffling cards and the sound of a ball bouncing in the slots of a roulette wheel. All of this made me crazy for action, so I pounded on the door like a drunken sailor until it opened. My fist was still in the air and suddenly I was looking straight into the cloudy, blood-shot eyes of a hundred-year-old negro. He just stood there like a ghost, saying nothing but staring at me like he was the *capo di tutti capi* himself. He was wearing jockey's silks and had a horseshoe shaped bald spot in the center of his head, with white slicked back hair along the sides. His eyes were big, red, sad; all cloudy from age and watery from the thick grey cigar smoke that curled around the green velvet tables. Booze was heavy on his breath and he was moving very slow.

"You fixin' to knock down the door? 'Cause it opens by itself. Y' know," he said, real deliberate.

"I'm Mike Milan outta New York here to see Mr. S. on a private matter," I spit out like an NCO to a dogface just out of boot. And before the doorkeeper could open his mouth again, I ordered: "Make it fast, I got business."

He didn't answer, but very slowly turned around to look at someone inside where I couldn't see.

"Mistuh S?" he finally said, raising his eyes just a little and rocking back on his heels. "You out uh; *New* York you say?"

"That's right, Mike Milan outta New York for Mr. S."

"Ain't no Mistuh S. heah," he said with a straight face. "We gots a Mistuh Sala*zar*, we gots a Mistuh San*tu*cci, and we gots a Mistuh *Sil*verman, but we ain't gots a Mistuh *'ess.*"

This wasn't gonna be easy because I had to be real nice at the local establishments. Extra special nice. Wherever you go, you take your Family' honor with you. Dishonor yourself and you dishonor your boss. More than one punk has gotten his face slapped in public when he got home because he forgot that rule.

"Do you have a Mr. Santos?" I asked in a honey-sweet voice that said I could wait all night for this guy's song and dance to go into encores.

"Oh," he said with gravel in his voice. "You means Mistuh Johnny."

"Johnny Santos?" I asked.

"Yes *suh*," he said. "You means Mistuh. Mistuh Johnny. That'd be." He paused while he rolled his red eyes all around in their sockets in big, slow circles. "Mistuh J." He paused again, looking up to the ceiling as if he were thinking about it with all his might, and laid a finger alongside his nose just like in the Christmas poem. "Now if you axe for Mistuh J., I says we gots a Mistuh J." Another pause while he looked directly at me. "You wanna see Mistuh Johnny? And who shall I say is calling on Mistuh Johnny?"

"Please tell Johnny Santos that Mike Milan outta New York is down here to see him," I said.

"All the way from *New* York, mah-oh-mah. That'd be *New* York City, wud it?" he asked as he slowly turned toward the inside of the room again. "Gots to be sho' bout dese things. 'Cause y'all don' wants Mistuh J. to gits eny *mis*info'mayshun." He emphasized the "mis" with his pinky finger jabbed right at my eyes. " 'Speshully when the *mis*info'mayshun com'n fr'm *New* York boys wit' no mannuhs and no rispet fo'age. Y'all git *mah* meanin'?"

I was burned. My face must've been looking red as a coal. He dressed me down like a punk and if I even thought about slappin' him around, I'd be sent back to New York with no hands. Mr. C. would finish off the rest. There was no need for me to say anything to the old man. I put my head down and nodded like a yo-yo after a schoolyard fight.

"Hey *boss!*" the old man yelled into the room with a voice that seemed to come right out of his nose. It pierced through the air like a musical note and echoed off the far bank of the river.

"Send him in," I heard a heavy Siciliano voice call out from the back of the room.

The old man pointed a twisted black finger toward a far door and nodded in that direction.

"Mind yo' mannuhs, son," he said in a gentler voice. "Mistuh Johnny *give* all 'e yo'duhs in heah. He don't take'em."

Johnny Santos was short, even shorter than me, with hair so black and shiny it looked like he'd slicked it down with the packing slime that pit monkeys use to keep ball bearings from seizing up. They called him "The Skinner" because once during Prohibition he caught a driver who'd heisted a case of red-eye hootch. It wasn't the kind of booze you'd kill a man over, but Johnny figured to make an example. He skinned the man alive, starting at his ears and working down the sides of his body, and he left the carcass to rot in the dank gutters of the French Quarter as a message. The name stuck, and over the years even the craziest mulattoes out of Storyville, those who'd put the evil eye on you just 'cause you'd crossed their path on the narrow streets, came to fear The Skinner's sudden thunderstorm temper and savage fury.

Mr. Santos was wearing a tan-on-white linen Gene Autry shirt with round pearl buttons, long pointy collars, and a Jack Frost lace pattern around the pockets. His armpits were dark yellow from sweat and there was a dirty brown stain around the collar where I would have given 11-to-7 that oil had been seeping in for a week. His skin was a deep yellow, which told me that his kidneys were giving out, and his hands were the hands of a leather tanner, wrinkled and dry like the skin on mama's roasted chicken when I'm late for Friday night dinner and she keeps it warming in the oven too long. He was smoking a long fat Havana that looked like a black piece of horse shit and smelled even worse. He was motioning me toward a door at the back of the room past the card tables and crap shooters and behind the silver-tipped roulette wheel sunk into its mahogany base. I wanted to look around at all the action, but it would have been a sign of great disrespect to take my eyes off Johnny Santos.

"Ya got business fuh me?" Mr. Santos asked, his cigar smoke filling up the small room he pointed me into. There was something Spanish about his accent, or maybe it was a type of Sicilian I hadn't heard on the streets of New York. Instead of answering him directly, I moved my head around the room, motioning to the corners of the ceiling, and waved my hand back and forth the way I'd seen Mr. C. do it when he was unsure about who was listening. Johnny Santos knew what I meant immediately.

"Room's good," he said. "Ain' no ears here but ours." Then he leaned close to me and said in very hushed tones, almost as if he were *davening baruchot* in temple. Send the *padrino mi rispetto*. What service does he ask? There is none so great that I would not gladly perform for him."

"The *padrino* asks that you help me in whatever I ask. He will consider it a great service and a token of . . ." I paused for the word.

"*Rispetto* for one of his friends," I said, using the same old-fashioned tones that Johnny Santos had lapsed into.

"Of course the *padrino's* friend is a friend of mine and of all my friends." He used a formal Sicilian phrase that I hadn't heard in ten or so years, but it was a sign of honor that meant I wouldn't be touched by anybody in New Orleans who wanted to stay alive.

"Please help me," I asked. "I need some information about a man I believe to be one of your regular guests." I reeled off the three names from memory that were on the list that LaFaye had left for me. "Jack Sable?" I asked. "Is that a name you know? Or Leo Nuñez or Lawrence Keener?"

"Nuñez," Johnny Santos said to himself. "Leo Nuñez! Used to be a Shore Patrol cop down here during the war. He still works for the feds now. Plays the horses a lot. Into me for about five-and-a-half g's. But lately he pays on time."

"Did he ever stall on his payments?" I asked.

"Used to. I slapped him around a coupla times. Rapped him across the knee. Had someone bust up his car windshield once. Gave his girlfriend a message for him that sent her packing for Chicago. He understood. Now he's on time."

"Never told you how he makes his payments?"

"Never asked." He belched up a foul cloud of smoke and gumbo sauce. "What these people have to do to make payment is not my business. If they steal from my friends, I take off their hands. 'Sides, it's the business of others. Does this man Nuñez steal from my *padrino?*" Mr. Santos asked, biting off the cigar-end of the word. "I swear to Frank Costello he will make restitution before he dies."

"No," I said. "He does not steal from the *padrino.* Do you recognize any of the other names?"

"Maybe this Nuñez brings them here. Maybe I've seen them, but I don't know."

"Can I ask you one more kindness?" I said, pressing my luck.

"Name it," Mr. Santos answered, puffing out his little chest, proud that Mr. C. regarded him so highly he asked this service of him.

"I will need to visit Leo Nuñez and ask him where he makes his extra money," I said. "I will need to know the names of other people he works with. Then he will disappear. This is a confidence that I must keep and take care of this man myself, and I would not do you the disrespect by disclosing it. I will make good on his debt to you and I mean you no dishonor by guaranteeing it. This is your domain, and I ask for your blessing and your permission to fulfill this contract."

Johnny "the Skinner" Santos said nothing as he extended his hand towards my face. I knew the ritual and kissed the cracked and wrinkled skin on the back of his hand. I smelled the old-man smell of death, and I knew that Mr. C. would soon have to sit down with the commission to name a new *capo di familia* to fill Johnny Santos' chair. *"Grazi, seignor,"* I said, and tried to figure out how I could break the news to Mr. C. without violating the Old Man's sanction.

The Coffins

It felt like I had just dozed off when I heard such a crashing on the hotel room door I thought the whole thing was going to give way. I looked at my watch. Four hours of sleep. Enough to hold me, because I'd been in the Navy and I'd learned how to sleep in four-hour snatches. In the Navy your whole damn life is lived from watch to watch so when the door started banging, I had had my four hours and was ready to go ten rounds.

"Room service," a voice called out from the hall.

I hadn't ordered any room service. I pulled the .38 police special from under the pillow and put on a pair of pants. I crept over to the door and flipped off the safety on the revolver.

"Just bring it in and leave it," I called out, pulling back the hammer on the gun.

"No key," the voice said again.

I reached out and slowly turned the bolt in the lock, went into the bathroom, closed the door, and peered out through the keyhole.

"Door's unlocked," I called out. "I'm in the can."

I heard the door open and saw the room service car roll into the room. Then I saw two sets of legs behind the cart.

"Hey, Milan," a familiar voice called out. "We ordered us some breakfast. Figure you're hungry after a big night's work and y'ain't mind treatin' ya buddies to some eats."

I released the hammer real slow so it wouldn't make any noise.

"You start eatin', Sarge," I said through the door. "I'll be out in a minute."

Then I wrapped the gun in a towel, groaned a couple of three times to make it sound like I was having a tough shit, laid him a big fart, and flushed the toilet.

"It all comin' out OK in'ere?" Livoni sang out between slurps.

"You-all shoulda eat'em up ya gumbo, Milan. Makes ya livin' easy," LaFaye joined in. "Hope ya got room for some grits."

I ran the bathroom faucet nice and loud, splashed water on my face to wake up, stuck the towel-wrapped gun under my arm and walked out of the head.

"You boys are up with the sun," I said as innocently as possible while I shoved the towel in the creases of the bedcovers.

"We got to git movin' 'fore it gits too hot," LaFaye said. "This here's the South. You boys from up North you'all like to work at night. We party at night, 'cept I hear from friends that you partied last night, too."

"I saw the police car at the airport," I said. "Thanks."

"That's the local service we provide for VIP boys who treats us with *ree-spet*," LaFaye said, emphasizing the word "respect" so it wouldn't slip my mind. "Now we'd like to be privy to what's on yawh agenda for today."

He scooped a large helping of bone-colored grits from the serving bowl onto his plate, hollowed out the mound in the center of them, and dumped on a huge pat of orange-yellow margarine. The margarine began to melt even before it hit the grits and ran down the sides like the lava flows out of volcanos in geography textbooks. "Y'all should try some of this," he said, holding up the plate like he was a billboard ad. "Put *hayre* on ya chest. Ain't no maht-soh bread but just as good." Then he forked over a slice of ham and spooned some red-colored gravy over it. *Chozzeray*, I said to myself. My mamma would have a heart attack, and I'd be on the toilet for real for the next week.

"I'm gonna visit your list of suspicious people and ask them their spending habits. I wanna know who they pay and who pays them."

"Whaddya think y'all 'll find?" LaFaye asked.

"Guys workin' overtime 'cause they're in over their heads," I answered. "I have to pay a few visits first, but I think I know what's there."

"Y'all 'll be kind *ee*-nuff to let us in before you say good-bye?" Livoni hinted, leaning towards me with a very hungry look in his eye.

"No names, no places, no dates," I said. "And on the q.t."

They put their plates down, satisfied that I would tie up some of their loose ends.

"Then we'll close our books and forget about it," Livoni slurped, gulping down the last of his coffee and burping as he got to his feet. LaFaye also stood up, adjusted a white-handled .38 that he wore crossdraw style in a hip holster, hiked up his pants, and headed for the door.

"Mistuh Santos asks us to leave this heah address for ya," he said. "I 'spect y'all knows what to do 'bout it?" Don't fuh-git now, heah?"

I nodded as they left and went back to the bathroom to shave before getting my own cup of coffee and figuring out where I was going to cross the path of Mr. Nuñez and what I was going to do to him once I found him. I didn't spend much time over the coffee. They put some kind of spice in it that burned the back of my tongue and killed the taste. So I just said the hell with it and drank the cream instead. Then I got out of my towel and dressed real quick so I could get an early start, shining up the fronts of my shoes with the polish cloth compliments of the house, and throwing on a khaki military tie and my Navy fatigue jacket. I tucked my roll of lock-picking tools into the belt of my pants because I wanted to case out Nuñez's place first before I did anything else.

This was my M.O. I always liked to check out where a guy hangs up his coat and cooks his breakfast before extracting what I needed out of him. Tommy Lucchese taught me this on the Lower East Side while I was still a kid. I didn't understand why, at first, but eventually it made sense. As it turns out, knowing how your mark lives gives you the edge every time. You get familiar with his habits, you see whether he closes the toilet when he's finished, whether he leaves dishes in the sink, and how much cash he hides in his drawer under his socks. You know something about him but he doesn't know anything about you. This way the more you know, the easier it makes it for you to whack him when the time comes. And the time always comes. Besides, I wanted to pull information out of this guy before the hit. The odds were if he'd been dealing both sides he'd have a stash of information he'd want to exchange for his life. It was the information more than his life that I really wanted. Nuñez would have to bite it because Mr. Hoover said so—as a warning to anybody thinking about selling out our military secrets. Rat out your Uncle and you'll disappear without a trace.

There was something else I wanted to know, more for myself than for the Old Man: what made Nuñez tick the way he did? Sure, I liked to throw the dice, make my point the hard way, and bet the long-shot nags running at Belmont. Bet on the Clipper, too; whether he'd put a 3-and-2 pitch into the left-field deck or whiff it. Who didn't? But to get so deep in the hole you'd sell out your own side just to keep on playing, that was different. I had to know why.

My father never bet a dime on anything. He always said betting was a sucker's game. You had a wife, a family, a business; that was a big enough gamble for anybody. To take money out of what you knew and risk it on whether a horse didn't take a good enough shit after his morning feed, you might as well just throw it down a manhole. I didn't think that way, but my father was from the old country and he had his point. It wasn't that I couldn't understand it—I could. But it was more that I never had to run away from Cossacks so I never had to worry about somebody taking away something that was mine without me being able to get in my licks first. Maybe I just had it easy in this country, but I never thought of myself as anything other than an American, a born-in-New-York-City American.

Leo Nuñez was a paper-pusher who worked out of the Army's local war records' office in the federal building over in the business district—at least that's what his yellow sheet said he did. I had a funny feeling it wasn't the truth because the only war records' office I ever heard of was in Washington and everybody said it was run by fat-assed brass and a bunch of dried-up broads. This local office had to be a cover, but a cover for what? I couldn't squash the hunch that Nuñez was either a federal cop on the take or a field intelligence agent for some government department somewhere because he seemed to be able to move around a lot and didn't have to answer to nobody. I just had the feeling that there was something bigger going on around here than Mr. H. had told me about.

Nuñez lived in a rooming house just north of the French Quarter in what they called the Hotel District. It was really a part of town where the old whorehouses had been rousted by the cops and cleaned up for GIs coming home from the war. Since it was still early in the morning, I figured I had enough time before staking out this guy's place before he left for work to look around for a while before breaking into his apartment and going over his betting slips. So I walked over to the rooming houses and found where Nuñez was staying. Then I waited while groups of guys all wearing the same kinds of light-colored seersucker suits and porkpie rain hats that were the uniform of most office workers in New Orleans caught the streetcar for the downtown business district. I walked around the neighborhood a little, seeing how many kids got taken to school, looking at the pregnant women pushing baby carriages around, and trying to guess at how many people stayed at home during the day. I always like to get a feeling for the number of potential witnesses to whatever I have to do.

I walked around the narrow streets and the wood-frame, iron-trellised buildings until well after eight when the knots of people at the trolley stops looked like they were thinning out. But I still waited down the street from the hotel because I didn't want Nuñez to see me standing around the front. Just in case he was the suspicious type, which I expected he was because of the situation he was in, I didn't want to give him any reason to get his guard up. He might just as likely have thought I was one of Santos' boys getting nosey and plugged me before I had a chance to plug him. So I gave it another fifteen minutes and then I headed back to Nuñez' rooming house to case out the lobby.

I walked up the wide wooden steps at the front of the building, checked the handwritten list of room numbers on the front for the name Leo Nuñez, stuck my head inside the wood-framed, frosted glass doors, stared at the room like an idiot, and blinked my eyes to see if it would disappear. I couldn't believe it. Walking into the lobby of the rooming house was like walking into the middle of a saloon in a Hopalong Cassidy movie, only without the honky-tonk piano player banging on the keys in the corner of the hall. If it was possible to go back in time, I had just jumped back by a hundred years.

The inside of the lobby was decorated all in red and black wallpaper and shiny satin. There were ruffles around the windows and lace over the frames like it was a whorehouse or something. The walls had wood panels along the bottom that were painted a deep green, like the color of a forest, and there was a round rooming house desk directly across from the door with a bank of mailboxes behind it. The old guy at the desk sorting letters and rifling through pink message slips was wearing a striped shirt with a round, frayed, starched-stiff collar and rubber bands around his shirt sleeves to hold up his cuffs. He was so thin it looked like a skeleton was inside the shirt instead of a live person. I stood in a corner and watched him for a few minutes to see if I could slip by him and get up the narrow staircase to my left. The desk clerk didn't seem to be noticing anything besides the envelopes and pieces of paper on the desk which he was putting into stacks and stuffing into the mailboxes behind him.

I waited until he had picked up one of his envelope piles and turned his back to the front of the lobby. Then I walked by the desk as if I lived in the place and continued up the stairs to the third floor where Nuñez was renting his private rooms. There was nobody in the hall on the third floor, but I didn't want to take the chance of being discovered, so the first thing I did was to check for empty broom closets or janitor's sinks. I found an unlocked cleaning closet that was right across the hall from Nuñez' room. I hid there for a minute, waiting for the voices of anyone coming down the hall. Except for the sounds of talking and some radio music from nearby rooms, everything else was quiet. I held my breath, slipped out of the closet, and quickly cut across the hall. Then I put my ear against the door for a minute to listen for sounds from inside the room. I didn't hear any noise so I inserted my pick and long-handled pliers into the lock and began working the tumblers the way any kid from the Lower East Side streets was able to do. The old-fashioned lock was so simple that picking it was quick business. I could have sneezed the door open and Nuñez would never have known the difference. It was clear that the tenants didn't expect any break-ins because they relied on the old man at the front desk for security. What a mistake. Anybody could slip this guy a half a C-note or crunch his skinny bones and have his run of the place for a couple of hours. If I was a crook, I could have made a nice day's haul out of this place and still have gotten my main job done.

I felt, more than heard, the tumblers click into place, retrieved my pick and pliers, and turned the doorknob. I pushed my weight against the door and let it open a crack. I waited, holding my breath to hear if there was any movement inside or the sound of running water. Nothing. I edged the door open further, slid into the room, and knelt behind the door while I drew my .38 and quickly scanned the room. No one was there. I closed the door behind me, throwing the door lock back into position, and holstered my revolver. Now I was satisfied that I was alone in the tiny three-room apartment.

The inside of the room was in heavy shadow with an indirect light leaking in from around the edges of the shades like a halo. Probably because he was afraid, Nuñez had kept his window shades drawn and his curtains all the way down even in the sunlight of the early New Orleans morning. It looked like he wasn't taking any chances about being seen from the street. And it also told me that he knew he was in danger.

After I crept through the door, I knelt down immediately and stayed there in a crouch position while I waited the second or so for my eyes to adjust to the darkness. If I'd had to shoot at something in that light, I probably would have missed. That must have been just how Nuñez had intended it to be in case somebody broke in on him in the early morning. The room itself was stuffy, unventilated, and smelled of bed sweat and the stale insides of shoes just like the joint of an old man who was hanging onto life by his fingernails and trying hard to make ends meet every month. And some months he didn't. Nuñez was in the same sort of trouble.

The look of the room also told me that he was in a position to make a quick getaway with as few of his possessions as possible if he had to. There was a pile of stuff on top of the chest of drawers and on his night table—loose change, a few bills, a checkbook, cufflinks, collar studs, slips of paper, cigarettes, and some .45 rounds from a military issue automatic—that looked like they were moved around a lot. The rest of the stuff in the room looked dusty, like no one ever touched it. Nothing else seemed to be permanently arranged. Undershorts and ties were thrown over the one chair; there were a few sport jackets and a suit at the end of the bed, and three or four ties were hanging over the footboard. There was more clothing in the closet, including a set of Army fatigues from the war and one of those yellow golfing jackets I'd been seeing in magazine ads, and the closet was just deep enough for me me to hide in if I had to disappear in a hurry. But I still had the feeling that Leo Nuñez could have wrapped up the whole wardrobe into one valise and been out of there in a matter of minutes. He was probably a guy used to taking it on the lam fast.

I looked through his betting slips on the night table as best I could without moving them around. No sense sending him a signal that somebody had searched his room. The slips, some of them from his bookmaker and some made over to Johnny Santos, showed that he was a heavy better. But they were current and showed that he was paying his losses even though he was a loser who didn't know when to call it a night at the crap table. I left his bedroom and went into the bathroom to see if I could find any drugs he might have been taking for a heart condition or nerves or something. Nothing doing except some aspirin and cough syrup. I looked in the garbage for empty liquor bottles. Found a couple of fifths of Four Roses so I knew he liked his booze, but nothing that said he was a walking 'still. Then I nosed around his kitchen, checked what he was keeping in his hotel-sized icebox, and looked through the drawers.

It really wasn't a kitchen like the kitchens I knew; it was more like a narrow closet with an overhead bare bulb, two electric burners on a small tabletop counter with an icebox alongside, and a tiny sink with a couple of shallow drawers beneath. You couldn't cook up a *Pesachdich seder* here or anything, but you could boil water for a pot of coffee and maybe heat a can of meatballs without setting the tinderbox on fire. I opened the icebox door and almost fell over from the smell. The guy was keeping a small bottle of buttermilk in there, which was already starting to sour, or maybe it could have been the very soft stick of bright yellow oleo that looked like it had begun to run that was turning rancid. I couldn't tell without sniffing, but I wasn't getting close enough to care. The foul odor coming out of the icebox was so intense that it was not only keeping me from looking through it as closely as I wanted, it was also smelling up the room—a dead giveaway that somebody had been poking inside the kitchen. Then I remembered. This was an old OSS trick that Bill Sullivan had used behind the lines during the war. The underground would hide messages in drawers with food that was rotting, and it would keep the Gestapo away. If the Germans opened the drawers to search, the smell in the confined space would let the underground know that the hiding place had been compromised.

OK, I thought, Nuñez is using an old wartime intelligence trick. It may mean everything; it may only mean that he has friends who've been around. I'd know soon enough. Meanwhile, I still wanted to find out if he was hiding anything in the icebox. So I opened all of the windows in the rooms to air them out while the icebox was opened, making sure I noted whatever pieces of paper or string were on the sills and ledges, and then returned to my search. I held my breath at first and squinted when I opened the door and felt around the bottom of the icebox and soon found an unsealed envelope. This guy must have been either stupid, careless, or lazy. If these were still the days of the old Rainbow Division, Wild Bill Donovan would have taken care of this guy himself. I closed the icebox door and brought the envelope back into the bedroom light where I opened it to see what the Ruskies were paying for.

I have to admit, I'm not an expert in military secrets, but even with no training at all I could tell that what this guy was giving over wasn't worth the paper it was photographed on—let alone the money he was getting. There were lists, just lists, of the divisional strengths of the American mechanized brigades facing the Soviets in Germany. It was dated 1946, so it wasn't even the latest list. It just didn't make sense. Why would the Russians pay for something that wasn't today's news? Why would they have to go to this guy to get it, when they could probably get the same thing from some library somewhere? And how could a guy who was in the OSS be such an easy mark? This whole situation was smelling worse than what was inside the icebox, but I wasn't down there to figure out who was right. I was only assigned to use my ability to enlist the local boys to close down Nuñez and his friends. And that's what I was going to to.

If I was as smart as Mr. H. or the people who worked for him on the up-and-up were, I would have started figuring out right then and there what I would stumble across by accident fifteen years later in 1963 when it socked me like a left hook to the gut when I figured out that all these guys ate from the same plate. But I was still a kid in 1948 who used his hands too much and his brains too little. I just did what Mr. H. and Mr. C. told me to do, plugged who they told me to plug, and kept my ears open and my mouth shut. If the list in my hand didn't make any sense in 1948, I figured it was the Old Man's problem and not mine. But, standing there in that rooming house apartment with a list of American tank divisions in my hand, I wasn't going to take the time to think about the big picture, especially when I heard footsteps on the wood floor outside the door, the rattling of a keychain, and the sound of a key fumbling against the outside of the lock.

I stuffed the list back in the envelope and flipped the envelope back into the icebox. Then I took off for the closet to hide in. I left the door open just a crack to be able to see who came in and took out my gun just in case Nuñez had come back, smelled trouble, and wanted to play for keeps. I heard the tumblers turn in the lock and the door opened, but it wasn't Leo Nuñez at all. It was a tiny dame, maybe four-and-a-half feet tall, and she had red hair. She came through the door like she owned the place, took her key out of the lock, and put it back in her purse. She looked like she was surprised to see the light in the room, shook her head as if she thought Nuñez had been stupid enough to leave it that way, and closed the windows I had opened. So much for my surreptious break-in and entry, which is what Mr. H. liked to call these kind of assignments. Mr. C. called it hitting a mark's joint before he hit yours.

The woman took a white envelope out of her purse and peeled out a wad of bills, counted them carefully like she was making sure the right amount was critically important, then walked out of my line of sight into the kitchen. I heard the icebox door open and close, and she came out carrying the envelope that I had just put back. At least I was doing one thing right, I thought to myself. The woman rifled through the envelope as if assuring herself that what she expected to be there was there. Then she took one final look around the place, went back into the kitchen, opened and closed the icebox door again, and walked out of the small apartment. I heard the key turn in the lock and her footsteps echo on the wood floors as she went back down the hall. Then all was quiet again except for the sounds of kids playing in the courtyard below.

That was easy, I said to myself as I slipped out of the closet. She put the whole thing right in my lap. I went back into the kitchen and took the money envelope out of the icebox and noted that she had replaced the original envelope. That seemed strange, but at least now I had all the makings of a trap that would knock Nuñez off guard, bounce him off Johnny Santos, and send him flying right into my net. And I could do it all in one night. I checked Nuñez' slips again to see whether the money in the envelope that the redhead had left was enough to cover the Santos markers. More than enough. Nuñez probably had a night of spending all lined up. So whether he was double-crossing the Ruskies or somebody was double-crossing him or whether everybody was just too stupid to know they were all running around in circles double-crossing each other was not my worry. I could still wrap it up by tomorrow morning if things broke right.

Since the woman had locked the door again, I still had a shot of making Nuñez think he was being double-crossed by the Russians. I put the money envelope in my pocket, made sure the windows were all closed and his paper booby traps were back in place so that Nuñez wouldn't know the windows had been opened, and left by the door. I used my long-handled, needle-nosed pliers to trip the lock tumblers back into place so Nuñez wouldn't know somebody had ever broken in.

I worried about getting by the guy at the desk again, but I figured going out was easier than coming in. I was right—even before I got to the second floor landing, a group of women were coming out of their rooms and I just followed them down. The old man barely looked at me. He must have decided that I was the guy who had just had a good time with the girls, smiled to himself about the good old days, and went back to his mail. My next stop was Johnny's.

I called him from a drug-store phone booth, first to extend my respects and then to ask his permission so I could pay a friendly visit.

"Of course, Michael," he said over the phone. "*Prego,* come for a cup of espresso and perhaps a little breakfast."

I didn't waste any time. I took a cab over to the river front area and found Mr. Santos sitting out in back of his place, swishing away flies in the sun, and slurping espresso in long, loud gulps out of those little half-cups all of the *Unione* boys go nuts over. He extended his hand and waved me to a chair like the polite old don that he was and put his hand to his mouth when I started to speak.

"First some espresso. Then you will ask your service," he said. "Your impetuousness makes me forget my manners."

"Then I ask your pardon, Don Santos," I said, nodding in his direction like I was bowing. If the boys on Mulberry Street ever saw me going this far, they would fall on their faces laughing. I took the cup he offered and drank it in one gulp. Then I smiled as I tried to keep from throwing the stuff back up all over his white linen jacket.

"Now you have had your coffee and you may ask your service," he said, refilling my cup without asking if I wanted any more.

"First, and please forgive me, *padrone*," I said in order to clear the air and give the old man what I knew he wanted, "if this is seen as a sign of disrespect, I am sorry, but I want to make sure that all of Leo Nuñez' financial responsibilities to you are paid. Therefore, before paying Mr. Nuñez the visit that I spoke of and obtained your permission to pay, I give to you all of what Mr. Nuñez owes so that you will suffer no loss on account of what I will have to do."

Mr. Santos took the envelope politely out of my hand, but I could see that he wanted to rip it open and count every single bill that the little redhead had put there. I wondered if he would refund me whatever was extra.

You gotta know right up front here that I hadn't taken any money out of the envelope. You also gotta know why. It was because of the sanctions by Mr. C. and the Old Man never to cross the line between their two worlds. To have helped myself to the extra money in the envelope and to have told no one would have been to have to cross that line. That was something I was not going to do. And if there's anything you should know about me it's that once I give my word, I keep my word. As old fashioned as that sounds now, back then it was the only contract you needed—and a contract that people enforced.

So I found myself sitting across from Johnny Santos in a typical test of the ways the Families worked. Mr. Santos knew that I knew exactly how much money Nuñez owed him. He also knew that I couldn't reveal it: it would have shown him disrespect to pay him to the penny. If he felt like taking all the money for himself, that was his right as the old *capo* of his family—his judgment—and there was nothing I could or was supposed to do about it. In those days, there were very rigid rules which told people how to behave.

It was not like today when any *giambon* can jump out of a BMW, shoot up a neighborhood with an Uzi, and write his own ticket.

"I'm sure it's all here," Mr. Santos said, flapping the envelope back and forth alongside his ear. "But it would not be a dishonor to make sure."

Mr. Santos began laying the bills out on the table before him, snapping the newer bills once or twice and holding them up to the light to make sure they weren't counterfeit.

"I expect," he said, hissing uncontrollably through the tightly clenched false teeth of an old man, "that you obtained this by taking from whoever was paying Nuñez." I nodded. "For if this was your own I would be doing you a disrespect."

"Not at all, Don Santos, this is your home and your business and I understand that," I said.

"Business is business," he whispered. "Your own *caporegime* must have taught you that if not the Don himself."

I nodded again, still wondering what he would do with the extra grand or so I had already counted out.

"There is a discrepancy," Mr. Santos said as he laid out all the bills in front of him. I held my breath. "In your favor," he said, breaking into a laugh that must have thrown terror into hundreds of people during the days of gin running along the Gulf coast when he and his boys mopped up the toughest Cuban syndicates with brass knuckles, Tommy guns, stilettos, and the blade of a hunting knife. "In your favor," he repeated as if surprised by it all. Then he counted out fifteen hundred dollars and pushed it across the table to me. "This is for you, my son," he said as gently as a *capo* ever could. "I want you to go out and buy yourself some silks. Spend it!" he urged. "I'll know if you take it back to New York and put it in the bank."

I breathed a long, but silent, sigh of relief as I took the money and folded it into my pocket without counting it. Mr. Santos knew that he was giving me a commission of five hundred on the money I collected for him.

"Thank you, *padrone*," I said. But before I could continue, he spoke.

"I thank you, young man, for collecting this for me. I expect that Mr. Nuñez is not aware of what has passed between us, and for my part, he will never know. But he will soon be calling me with apologies just as I'm sure there is some additional service you ask me. You ask and I will grant it."

I adopted my best formal tone in a voice that I had heard many times before when the *soldari* on the East Side addressed their *caporegimes*. "How can I thank you enough for the honor you have shown me, *padrone?*" I asked. "And it is true that I would ask you for an additional service. It is this: when Leo Nuñez calls to beg your favor in granting him an extension of time on his marker, will you require him to ask it of you in person? And when he stands here in person, will you grant him only one night? I will be here, in the shadows, of course, and will follow him wherever he goes. All debts are cleared, and Nuñez has to go."

I saw Johnny Santos' eyes narrow and his old man's death stare suddenly hardened, almost as if what I said had suddenly breathed youth into his lungs. For a moment, there was a cold chill in the springtime air that surrounded us. Then his eyes softened, he put up his hands in front of him, and sighed a sigh of fatality. "Business is business." Then the corners of his mouth turned up in a very pale imitation of a smile. "I would not want to be on the receiving end of your business," he said. "You have my blessing, of course. One of my men will be at your service this evening, if you should require it."

"Molto grazi, padrone, y buongiorno," I said, rising, bowing from the head with a sweep of my hand, drinking what was left of my espresso and choking on the bitter grounds in the bottom of the cup. I smiled at the old don through the tears of pain in my eyes and took a glass of water to ambush the coughing.

"Buongiorno, buongiorno," he said laughing at the show. "Take yourself some more water so you don't drop dead before seeing Mr. Nuñez." Then he laughed harder. "If he saw you now, he'd laugh so hard he'd bust a gut and save you the job of pluggin'im." He was wheezing so furiously by the time he finished the sentence that two of his men had to rush up and pound on his back to get him to stop. As I left, he was still waving to me, coughing up his espresso all over his white linen pants, and falling back into his chair with fits of laughter like he had never heard a joke before.

I'd be happy when I left this place, I told myself, and headed back to the Fairmont to place a call to LaFaye.

"Ya shuh y'all c'n close this up tomorruh?" LaFaye asked, a little peeved that he wasn't going to be let in on any front-page collars that would get him his lewie's bars. I had called him from the pay phone in the lobby to make sure no nosey operator was listening in on a party line.

"By tomorrow I'll be on the plane back to the Apple and you'll be slurpin' up yuh gumbo knowin' that everything's back to normal," I assured him. "I'm stashing the Nitano loot under my bed, if you'd care to clean up my room when I'm gone," I told him. "No follow-up, no bodies popping up in embarrassing places, and no feds!"

"Say, it's that 'no feds' that I'm most partial to," he said, ignoring any reference to the jewelry. "Y'all keep ya word, heah." And he hung up.

I put down the phone and looked at the clock hanging over the front desk in the lobby. It was almost noon. I figured I'd stand down from watch, catch up on some winks for a couple of hours, grab me one of them poorboy sandwiches, and head over to Johnny Santos' joint before sundown.

But I must have caught more winks than I figured because it was just sundown when I rolled over in the bed and realized where I was. I just kept on rolling myself into the bathroom where I stuck my face into a sinkful of ice cold water to wake up. As I was gritting my teeth in pain, I remembered that I had spent most of last night creeping around a bunch of coffins and paying respects to Johnny Santos so, I told myself, it was OK to take an extra hour without feeling like a Sad Sack about it. If I dressed in a hurry, I would be able to get some eats over at Johnny's before Nuñez showed up. So I threw on what I wore that day, packed my revolver and two pocketfuls of extra rounds, took the stairs out of the hotel, and took a short cab ride over to the River Front where my friend at the door let me in with a smile and a nod and even offered to show me to the employees' all-you-can-eat table.

"Mistuh Johnny say y'all be doin' a night's work what needs a full belly," he said.

This time I only grunted because I hadn't eaten anything all day except for some shit coffee and a little cup of espresso grounds that made me cough like I was choking to death. But I remembered my manners and thanked him for showing me to the food table.

"Go slow," he cautioned. "Sick man don't shoot straight. Man y'all's lookin' for shoot straighter'n you. Eat slow and keep yo' edge. I'm 'a make sure they's plenty left when y'all gets back."

This guy mighta been old but he knew what he was talking about so I slowed down. No sense getting sloppy over a few meatballs and some bread. And I didn't drink anything either. No matter what they show in the movies, when you're on your Uncle's or your *capo's* clock, you don't drink. If you're ever seen acting drunk in public or if you make a fool of yourself because of booze, they call it an *infamia* and it's worth a slap in the face if not a full-fledged beating. I didn't want no *infamias*, especially now, so I just drank Coke with lemons and those little shiny cherries until I heard Mr. Santos yelling at someone on the other side of the door outside in the dusty open lot behind the small woodframe building, which is why I figured he made sure I was sitting where I could take it all in. Then I heard the sound of a sharp slap.

"You playin' me for a sucker?" Mr. Santos screamed. "You think I'm some guinea pushover, some fuckin' dumb-ass dago you can jerk around the corner like a goddamm duck on wheels?"

"Mr. Santos, it's only one fuckin' night," the voice pleaded. "I'm tellin' ya, the bitch double-crossed me. She was supposed to leave off an envelope fulla dough, you woulda been a hundred percent covered. But she pulled a double-cross."

"You mean that redheaded pinprick of a cunt?" Santos said, his voice breaking into the crazy squeal-like sound of fury that only Italians can make. "Listen Nuñez," the old man's voice had broken completely now, and he could only wheeze at Nuñez in a threatening whisper. "I don't care what the bitch did. She doesn't owe me. You do. And you insult my honor by using a woman as an excuse." There was the sharp sound of another slap and a whimper of pain. "Nobody holds out on me and walks away on his own legs to tell about it. I'm gonna start on this leg . . ." There was the sound of a billy club—a sound I knew all too well from my neighborhood days—thudding against someone's skin. Then another cry of pain.

". . . then I'm gonna break this leg. But I'm gonna break 'em slow so the bone'll pull apart instead of split clean. That way you'll always have a pair of crutches to remember me by."

"Mr. Santos, please," the voice that was Nuñez pleaded again. "If you break my legs and I can't work I'll never pay you. You might as well kill me now and get it over with."

"That's still a possibility, Nuñez," Mr. Santos said. "I ain't ruled that out yet. If I break your legs first or not has nothing to do with if I kill you afterwards."

"But you'll lose the money that I can still get. And what was stolen from me is nothing compared to what's still coming," Nuñez said with a tone in his voice that made me believe him.

"From that bitch?" Mr. Santos screamed again. "How do I know she won't double-cross you again? Now you insult my intelligence as well as my honor."

There was another thud of the billy club and the sound of a man falling in the loose dirt. Then a final thud and the sound of wretching.

"Get up, Nuñez," Mr. Santos said. "I'm going to offer you one night to save your life. But now the money is doubled. Double or nothing, *capice?*" I only heard scraping on the ground and the sound of a man breathing very heavy and painfully.

"I'm sending a man along with you, Nuñez," Johnny Santos hissed. "He's gonna sit next to you in your car, go with you to collect from the bitch, sit by your bed, and stand there while you shit. If you even look at him cross-eyed, he'll blow your balls right off and bring you back here. I'll finish the rest." Mr. Santos pounded on the door so hard I could see the door rattle in the frame and the rust fly off the inside hinges.

"They's callin' ya numbuh, son," the old doorkeeper said as he smiled at me. "Mind y'all keep ya edge. Is all ya got."

He threw the bolt back on the door and pulled it open. It was fully dark outside, but I could see a man with a bloody gash in his head, bloody saliva coming out over his lower lip, a torn suit jacket, and dirt all over his face. He was being supported by two bulls. He raised his head just enough to look up at me and then let it drop against his chest. Mr. Santos drew a long hunting knife with a menacing blade and pressed it hard against Nuñez' cheekbone, right below his eye. This was his infamous skinner's knife, I figured, and probably so did Nuñez.

"You go with him," Santos said to me. "Take this with you." One of his button men held out a .45 automatic, popped the clip, shoved it in Nuñez' face to show him it was loaded, slammed it back into the handle, flipped off the safety, and handed it over to Mr. Santos. The Skinner took the gun in his left hand and pointed it directly at Nuñez. "Use this; it's cold. Not your own," he said to me. "And if he gives you any trouble," he put the nozzle directly into Nuñez' eye, "ba-da-boom!" He sang it out like a war cry. Then he pressed the point of the blade into the soft skin right below Nuñez' eye. "Or even better, bring him back to me." He drew back his lips, grinning at what he was about to do. "I'll take his eyes one at a time like this . . ." He screamed as he twisted and jerked the knife away, prying off a piece of Nuñez' face with the point of the blade. Nuñez screamed too, farted a loud, liquid fart, and squirted pale shit right through the legs of his pants.

"Ayyyyie," Santos screamed and held his nose as the stench of a coward's shit hung heavy in the air. One of the bulls brought his own gun butt down flat on Nuñez' shoulder and the mark fell face forward into the dirt again. The bull kicked him in the stomach, flipping him over on his back, and we could hear the sound of soft shit as it squirted up his back. "Get this bum cleaned up," he screamed at the old doorkeeper who was standing inside the room. You, go with 'em," Johnny Santos said, turning to me and handing me the automatic. "I don't want to see his face again unless it's double what he owes."

"Thank . . . thank you, Mr. Santos," Nuñez said as he tried to get up. "I'll get your money and I won't give nobody no trouble." He started to get to one knee. "You know I can help you, Mr. Santos. I got this job in the government, see? The people I work for, some of them are connected in high places. They know things. They tell me things. Things that are worth money. Things like who gets to be the federal prosecutor, who gets to be a federal judge, what comes in the port of New Orleans and what goes out." Nuñez was giving it up right then and there and Santos knew he would hear too much. So he wisely cut him off at once with a kick directly into his kidneys. Nuñez fell over forwards again and rolled on the ground.

"I already know who's gonna be what," he said as Nuñez whimpered and shook his head " 'Cause I hand pick'em in advance and pay'em what they're worth, you cocksucking rat. This whole fuckin' town works for Johnny Santos." The blow had taken all of Johnny's strength and he had to be supported by one of his bulls until he got his breath back. "And you'll fuckin' get my money, you heah?" Santos said through heaving breathing. "Because you only got one day left." Then he wiped the toe of his shoe on the ground. "It's like I stepped in a pile of dogshit," he said as he walked back inside his club.

The bulls yanked Nuñez to his feet as if they were hauling a piece of slime out of a river. Nobody wanted to touch him. He could barely stand up on his own because of the beating he'd gotten and the fear which had weakened his knees to the point where they were as wobbly as a fighter's who was just hanging on until the knockout punch put him away for the night. Nuñez heeled over to his left and his right and both bulls pulled away, afraid he'd get shit on them, too. It if had been left up to either of them, they would have plugged him right there and thrown a mound of dirt right over the spot where he lay. I almost felt bad for the sonovabitch. This wasn't his fault, really. He had done his job and gotten his money. Too bad he had double-crossed the wrong people in the bargain. Now he was a shitass who had almost given Johnny Santos the information he would later give me. He was about to die a rat's death.

"Y'all c'n wait back heah," the doorkeeper said to me as he circled one of his long arms around Nuñez' neck, grabbed his collar, and pushed him forward against the outside wall of the building. He was strong for an old geezer. "We gots some clothes in the slop basket for this chump," he assured me. "After I run the hose on him. Then y'all does what you wants wiv'em."

The bulls guarded Nuñez while the doorkeeper hosed him down, clothes and all. I kept a watch on him from inside, but said nothing. The less I spoke, the more threatening I would be when the time came and I had to get him to spill his guts before he died.

"Now y'all dry off and wipe ya ass clean," the doorkeeper said to Nuñez after he finished hosing him. "Gots to git rid of that shit smell 'fore y'all goes out court'n." He shut off the hose, disappeared inside the house, and came back out with a pile of khakis. He threw them at Nuñez. Nuñez dried himself off, dressed, and then stood in front of me, waiting for me to tell him what to do.

"Where's your car?" I asked him.

He limply pointed toward the front of the building.

"Then let's go," I said, and I followed him around the building to a black Buick that was parked in front.

He got in the driver's side and I opened the passenger door and got in beside him. He just stared at me, not knowing what to do.

"Get the money," I told him, assuming that he would lead me right through the pipeline to whoever was buying the information from him.

"We gotta make a stop first," he said.

I reached for the automatic in my pocket in a way that made it obvious to Nuñez what I was doing.

"Don't worry," Nuñez said. "I won't pull any tricks."

"I ain't worryin'," I said. "You already got your death sentence."

"Just one stop," he said again. "It'll get me all the money I need, and there'll be some left over for you, too."

This was even better than I'd planned. "Go ahead," I told him. "But you can't run far enough or fast enough to get away from what's gonna happen to you if pull anything funny."

"I said don't worry," he repeated, this time with an edge to his voice. "Mr. Santos'll get his money and I'll get outta this alive as soon as I get my hands on Tatia."

"Tatia," I said out loud to myself as the car pulled into the street. "Foreign dame?" I directed it at Nuñez.

"Calls herself Ginger when she's in town. Wears a red wig," he said, not answering my question at all, but telling me what I needed to know. "She stiffed me on the dough I owe to Johnny S. I do some business with her." He paused and made an "uh . . . uh" sound as if he was thinking about what to say next. "Uh, like I said to Mr. Santos, where I work I can get my hands on lots of useful information. I can be very useful to Mr. Santos, maybe you can tell him that."

"Maybe you should just tell me," I said. "Might be a start."

"We gotta make one stop," Nuñez repeated. "I gotta collect some papers first and then you can see for yourself."

As I expected, Nuñez drove right through the French Quarter and turned north onto St. Charles Place where he kept going until we came to Nitano's. This was all beginning to seem as familiar as a movie I had seen again for a third time. Nuñez drove by Nitano's to see whether any lights were on—they weren't—and made a U-turn across the empty thoroughfare and parked across the street from the funeral home.

"It's in here," Nuñez said while I pretended to stare at him dumbfounded. He turned to face me while his hand fumbled for the door handle.

"Whaddya gonna do, get it outta a stiff?" I asked like I was as stupid as I looked.

"Just follow me," he whined. "You got the gun. All I got is an ass full of shit and a bullet with my name on it in your clip."

He left the keys in the ignition and I followed him to the ambulance entrance in the rear of Nitano's where he turned on the outside light switch, inserted an Allen wrench kind of key in the garage-door lock, and pulled down the big door handle. The doors swung open in tandem from either side just far enough for the two of us to squeeze through. He turned on the inside lights, pushed the doors closed, and I found myself in the main receiving room of the funeral parlor right above the basement room where I searched around last night. Nuñez didn't say a word, but pulled a leather briefcase out from under a doctor's examination table and went right to work unloading papers and spreading them out on the tabletop. I walked up behind him, but stayed far enough away so he couldn't take a swipe at me by surprise. He was getting edgy, though, I could tell by the way he hunched over as I walked up.

"This ain't your business," he spat out at me. "All you got to care about is your boss's dough. Just stand back and let me earn it for him."

"You spouted off pretty good when you was layin' in the dirt with your pants full of shit," I said as I kept moving in. I didn't like the way he was acting. "Told Mr. Santos you could put your hands on valuable information. You said there was plenty more dough you could get. Offered to cut him in." I waited to see what he would say, but he just kept on sorting his papers and rummaging in the briefcase. "Isn't that what I heard?"

"Yeah, but I done some thinkin' in the car," Nuñez said bitterly. "All's I gotta do is pay you and then Santos is taken care of." I should have heard the tone of his voice changing. "Just a lousy twenty-five Cs and it's over with." You should always listen not only to what a man says, but how he says it. "No law says I gotta keep bettin' those crap tables and payin' good dough to Santos." You should also always watch his hands. If you're lucky, like I was in those days, you get on-the-job training. You get the chance to learn from your mistakes. If you're not lucky, you can only get one turn at bat. That night, I was lucky.

"Say, you're right, pal," I said as flat as I could. I was getting edgy. I wanted to finish up and put him in the drink, but I needed to know how he ran his operation. I fingered the automatic in my pocket. Maybe I would just beat it out of him. I knew he scared easy.

"Sure," he continued, his voice boiling over like a guy on a bad drunk. "You and Santos beat the shit outta me for a lousy few hundred and I just hand it over. But there's a lot more in this job, and you ain't seein' none of it."

He turned quickly, too quickly for me to get the automatic out of my jacket or to spin for cover, and flipped the briefcase at my head. When I had blocked the flying case, I looked up and found myself staring into the nozzle of a .45 with the hammer cocked. I didn't even have the time to chamber a round in the automatic, much less draw and aim.

"Drop the gun, punk," Nuñez said. He was almost swaggering, proud that he had gotten the jump on me. But he didn't know about the .38 in the holster inside my waistband. Now it was my turn to play for time.

"Nuñez, you can't be that stupid," I spit back at him. "Don't you realize what Johnny Santos is gonna do? If I don't turn up tonight, you won't just die, you'll beg for death. Think you shit tonight?" I said, laughing into the nozzle of his revolver. "They'll be pumpin' your shit out of the river by morning."

"You think I don't know your orders?" he asked. "I hand over the dough to you and you take care of the rest, right? This way, you're my insurance policy for a while. Now drop the gun. If you're smart, you may live long enough for Santos to put you in my place. Then we'll see who shits."

I let the barrel of the automatic point down at the floor, slipping my index finger off the trigger and hooking it around the guard. Then I let the handle slip out of my hand. I put the pistol on the floor beside my foot.

"Now kick it over," he said. "Not only will you get your head blown off for botching this hit," Nuñez continued. "You'll also get your balls blown off for giving up the gun Santos told you to kill me with. You dishonored him. I'm gonna keep the gun as a trophy and let Santos know it. Guineas go crazy over that shit."

I still wasn't about to kick the gun over so fast.

"Now that you're the top of the world, Nuñez, why don't you tell me what we're doin' in this joint with a bunch of stiffs. This whole thing was just a lucky trap you got me into wasn't it?" I asked, trying to puncture a hole in his pride to get him talking. Talking too much had gotten me ahead of the game in the past. Maybe it would buy me the time I needed now.

"You dumb fuck. You'd like to think that, right?" he asked, forgetting about the gun at my foot for a moment. "Just a lucky trap, right, punk. Dumb luck, and you just got a bad deal. Not your fault. You may be too stupid to shoot 'cause you won't know when you're dead." He laughed because he'd turned the tables, enjoying the power he had over me. "Now push that gun away or I'll give it to you right now."

"So if this ain't dumb luck, what is it?" I asked, casually pushing the automatic away with my toe while acting like I was so interested in what he had to say I forgot that the sonovabitch was gonna kill me if he got the chance.

He kept the gun trained on me while he reached behind himself and picked up a sheaf of papers and held them over his head.

"If I show you these, then I got to kill you, understand?" he said.

"Either way you look at it, Nuñez, you're a dead man as of tonight," I answered. "You kill me, you die slower. You don't kill me, you die faster. One way or another, you're finished and you know it. I figure you're gonna kill me anyway so I might as well know what your racket is."

He slid the papers across the floor to me and I saw that they were only more lists.

"Go ahead, look 'em over," he said, and I knelt down to get closer. "Those are the names of our military personnel in high places in Germany," Nuñez continued. "How many of them do you think have family behind the Iron Curtain?"

I didn't know, but I bet the Ruskies did.

"There are people willing to pay a lot to get their hands on these names," Nuñez bragged. "And I can supply all the names they need. I just requisition the names from Washington and down they come in a government pouch. Just as easy as you please."

"And you turn around and sell them," I said. "But how do you get them out of the country? The dame?"

"Nah," he said. "We're onto her. She'd get picked up in a minute. Look around." And he gestured to the racks of coffins against the wall of the embalming room. "There's more boxes downstairs. Bodies come in here every week from overseas." He laughed again, proud to be giving up his private secret, but confident that I couldn't do a thing about. "Only nobody knows whose bodies they are. The French say they're American GIs. The Americans say they're British, and the British say they're German. Nobody knows. They send 'em over, we ID the remains and keep the ones that belong here and send the rest back. And the guy who runs this place has to rely on us to tell him who goes back in a box and who stays."

It was beginning to come clear. With bodies coming in and going out and with nobody knowing who was who, Nuñez had his own private delivery service by just putting the right labels on the wrong boxes.

"Pretty nifty, huh? I show Tatia the lists I'm supposed to send, she leaves me a cash payment, and I drop the lists in a coffin going back to the Germans or the Russians. Pretty soon, it's going to be more than lists of officers in tank battalions. When I get them to pay me what I want, they'll get our G2 officers. Then maybe the names of intelligence agents at our embassies." Nuñez was bragging now, certain that he was going to knock me off and maybe make a deal with Mr. Santos for protection. "It's a snap. When I show Santos that I can eliminate his own trigger men and cut him in for a percentage, I'll be in the driver's seat."

"But why kill me?" I said, figuring the angles as quickly as I could. "Like you said, you're dealing with Sicilians here. These guys don't take kindly to letting their people get hit one, two, three. For them it's you hit me, I hit you."

Nuñez seemed to be listening. Maybe I had shown him that his plan had some big holes in it.

"Play it smart. You been playin' it smart up to now, why get stupid?" I argued. "Just give me the dough to pay your marker and lay low for a few days. Santos'll be happy and he'll listen to gettin' more dough for protection, especially when he knows it's going up every time you jack up the price on the Ruskies."

"No hard feelings, no tricks?" Nuñez asked, hoping that he wouldn't have to go on the lam from Johnny Santos.

"You only got two choices," I said. "Either you whack me out and take off with the chump change you can get tonight or you cut your deal and stay around for the big payoff. But if you run, you won't get far. If you pay off your marker and ask for protection, you'll stay alive to spend the dough you've been workin' for." I paused to give him time to think about that. "But you don't have to take my word for that 'cause I got a vested interest in keepin' you and me healthy."

Nuñez slowly released the hammer on the .45 he was pointing at me. "I don't like it," he said. "You're makin' too much sense."

"I'm only tryin' to stay alive," I told him. "I don't give a fuck what you do for dough just as long as I don't wind up with a bullet in my head. Besides, all Mr. S. wants is your marker paid off. If he gets a cut of the action, that's OK by him."

"No tricks," Nuñez warned. "I still got this gun. You just turn around and walk out of here. Meet me outside of Johnny Santos' in a couple of hours. I'll have the money. If I see your face anywhere else before then, I'll blow it off."

I turned around, confident that the last thing Leo Nuñez wanted was to make an enemy out of Johnny Santos. That fear was going to keep me alive until I got the drop on him again. Nuñez followed me to the garage doors, kept the gun on me while I opened them, and pushed me outside. Then he watched while I walked around the building and closed the doors. I heard him throw the bolt lock from all the way down the driveway. I walked down to the end of the block just in case he might have been looking out a window to watch me go, but I kept his car in sight all the time. I didn't want him to get away. Then I worked my way back to the funeral home and crept to the basement window where I had broken in the night before.

As I figured, the window hadn't been replaced and I was able to slide through the frame without a sound. I didn't bother to turn on the lights downstairs because I was afraid of telegraphing the punch to Nuñez. Instead, I waited until I could see in the dim light coming from the outside and used it to find my way to the stairs. By the time I got to the main embalming room where I had left Nuñez, he was packing up to leave. Just as well, I told myself, to let him think that he's got time on his side. So I crouched near the darkened doorway behind a wall of pine coffins, breathed as quietly as I could while I sweated through the back of my jacket, and watched him put away each of his lists, dog-earing the pages like a street-corner bookie so they wouldn't come apart and stowing them in the briefcase. Then he put the .45 revolver he had pulled on me in his belt, snapped the briefcase shut, and turned it over and over in his hand like he was looking for a hole in it, and stuffed it back under the doctor's examination table. He took one last look around the place as if he'd heard something, pulled the automatic out of his belt and cocked the trigger, and slowly made his way toward the door.

He was a suspicious guy—I had to give him that—and he had a right to be. He was playing a dangerous game, funnelling information back out of the country in military shipments and going shy on the pot with one of the biggest gambling syndicates south of DC. He had crossed the line every which way.

Nuñez stood directly in the doorway, leaned forward, and reached over a stack of crates to turn off the lights. I mentally measured the space between my gun butt and his head. Then he released the trigger on the gun, put the automatic back in his belt, and flipped the switch, sending the room into absolute darkness. That's when I jumped up and brought the butt down as hard as I could.

He screamed out in pain and writhed away as the gun handle dug into the skin on the side of his head, caught on his ear, and kept on going into his shoulder. I'd hit him a glancing blow, but it did the job. He sighed and crumpled against me on his way to the floor. He was a heavy sonovabitch and almost knocked me over as he fell. But before I lost my balance, I dug the heel of my shoe into what felt like the middle of his chest. I heard a rib crack and then I fell into the coffins, scraping the side of my head on the rough pine wood.

I kept a good grip onto my own .38 as I fell so that when I got back to my feet, knocking over the wall of coffins in the process, I was standing over him in the darkness with my gun leveled at his chest. He groaned and started to come to. I heard him digging in his belt for the automatic.

"Freeze, Nuñez, FBI," I ordered, knowing that he'd be less likely to shoot if he thought he'd been collared by a fed. Feds aren't supposed to shoot you on the spot. I could just about see the outline of his body in the semidarkness. "Go for the gun and I'll shoot. Put your hands behind your head. You're under arrest."

I reached down and took the automatic out of his belt. I felt warm blood all over his chest and in his pants, and he was breathing heavily between groans and sighs.

"Roll over and put your hands behind your neck," I ordered.

"I . . . can't," he gasped. "Too . . . much . . . pain."

I dug my foot into the small of his back and pushed him over as hard as I could. He screamed as he flipped over on the floor like a dying fish on the deck of a boat.

"Hands behind your neck or I'll break both your arms," I barked.

He was in too much pain to recognize my voice, but I could see that he was doing what I told him. Then, when I was sure he was unable to move, I reached back, squinted to protect my eyes, and turned on the light.

My eyes adjusted quickly to the white, factory-type lights that flooded the embalming room, and I saw just how much damage my gun butt had done. The entire side of Nuñez' head was torn open and bleeding, and his ear was partially torn off. There was a stream of blood coming out of his mouth, and I figured that the rib I'd busted with my heel must have punctured his lung. He was in a lot of pain. I would get out of him what I needed and then put him away quickly with a round to the head. No sense in prolonging this.

"You," he gasped as he turned his head around to see who'd hit him. "You're not FBI, you're . . ." Then he caught himself. Maybe he thought he could still get out of this alive if he just did what he was told. "Wait," he said as if he'd just had an idea. "Shit, maybe you really are FBI. But you don't know about the operation. Lookit, I'm undercover. You gotta listen. You're makin' a mistake, this is CIA. You're steppin' into another operation here." He was talking so hard now that he coughed up a wad of blood and almost choked. The more he fought to catch his breath, the more blood he swallowed and that only made him wretch more. Then he threw up.

"I'm chokin' to death," he gasped, pushing his hands against the floor to pick his head up from the blood and puke. "This is killin' me."

"Get in a crouch," I ordered. "And put your hands back behind your head."

"You busted my ribs, you fuck, get me a doctor," he screamed.

I cocked my .38 and put it against his ear with one hand and dragged him up by the collar with the other.

"Get in a crouch and put your hands back behind your head," I repeated, my voice slowly rising like I was losing my marbles. "Or I'm gonna blow your fuckin' brains out the other side of your fuckin' head."

Nuñez got to one knee, and then seemed to sag in the chest. I yanked him by the collar again and he brought up his other knee.

"I'm on your side, you prick," he cursed. "I'm an undercover cop. I'm CIA!"

"You're a double!" I shot back. "You're sellin' to both sides just to cover your bets. The only way you're gonna stay alive is to spill it all. The boys in Washington'll decide. Not me. You give me trouble, and I just pull this trigger."

"I talk, then what do you do?" He asked, the faint beginnings of hope were crossing his face now.

"I tie you up. I make a phone call. They come and get you. I walk away," I said. "That's all there is to it. But you gotta give me everything so I can give it to them."

"This phone's no good," he said. "We've been listening to it since the end of the war."

"Phone's OK now," I said, not knowing what the fuck he was talking about.

"You sure?" he asked. "I mean the boys at the field office been running a tape recorder on it for weeks now."

"I been told the phone's OK now," I said. "Tell me about the boys in the office."

Now I was the one sweating bullets over this. Sure, I could pull the trigger on this bum and ring down his curtain, but that wouldn't solve any mysteries. It was that damned curiousity raising its head again. I had to know the whole story, what was making him do what he did. I wanted to get a full confession out of him, find out what the hell the CIA was and who *he* was and why I was down here packing up cops. If he really was a cop. And if he was, how come he was on the take? And who was he taking from?

"This whole deal's a setup," Nuñez continued. "Nothin's on the up-and-up here."

"What about those lists?" I asked. "And who's the broad, a Ruskie agent?"

"She's KGB," Nuñez said.

I knew who they were from the war. "And you're handin' over documents and stuffin' them in coffins to smuggle overseas?"

"All part of the plan," he said. "We're feedin' the KGB stuff we already know they have to make them believe they're gettin' live information. Shit they can verify by themselves in an hour over their own Teletypes from Washington," he explained like he was giving me a civics lesson. "The real stuff, get it?" he said, emphasizing "real" so I was supposed to understand what he was talking about.

"Then what?" I asked.

"Then they know it's real," he continued. "And they figure what we send 'em in the future is just as real, even when it's fake information we want them to believe. This is the way it's always done. Don't they train you guys in the FBI anymore?"

"Just keep talkin'," I ordered.

"That's it," he panted. "That's all of it. I give her intelligence she knows she can verify. Our side sets up the pipeline with me playin' the double. They think they can trust me and I work my way into their KGB ring in this area. Once I'm in, I'm the double for our side and send information about them back to Washington. I'm a counterspy, get it?" He paused. "Now what?"

"I gotta relay what you say to Washington," I told him. "Then they send the wagon for you and I'm done."

Nuñez seemed to relax for the first time.

"But I need names and details," I said, anxious to pry him open to know what he knew. "Who's in this with you?"

Nuñez rattled off a list of names that I never heard of so I made him stop. Then, while he was still in a crouch with his hands behind his neck, I got his briefcase from under the doctor's table, opened it, and dumped out what was inside. Sure enough, there was a list of his people as well.

"Now tell me how you got the information overseas," I ordered.

"That's the easy part," he grunted. His breathing was very shallow now because his lung was filling up with blood. Every once and awhile he would cough up another wad of blood and mucus. Then he would begin another fit of heaving and he would have to stop, wait, and catch his breath. I didn't know who Nitano was going to call to clean this mess up tomorrow morning, and I didn't care. By the time he would be sputtering into the phone, I would be on a plane back to the Apple.

Nuñez continued talking after he had gotten his wind back. "Half the coffins that come in here have bodies that don't belong in this country. The Army just checks the ones they can identify, notifies next of kin, and sends 'em out for burial. The one's they can't identify stay here to get checked against lists of GIs missing in action. Then there's the others, the ones that were sent by mistake. They have to go back to any one of four countries. That's where I come in. I have all the lists of names, bills of lading, shipping manifests, whatever I need. I just change the name tags on the coffins going back overseas to the names of GIs being buried so's I make double names, stuff the documents in the coffins I tagged, and, boom, they get sent. Nitano don't know nothin'. He never checks the names until the day they go. Night before a shipment I come back and switch the name tags to the overseas destinations. Nitano ships 'em out and they're claimed by the KGB once they arrive. The double names are just for my benefit in case anybody pulls a search down here. I erase 'em once the bodies are dispersed. The only name that stays on the list is the name of the body that's buried in the States. Sounds complicated, but it ain't."

"And you say it's all legit," I replied.

"Hundred percent!" Nuñez said, snapping his elbows for emphasis. "We're setting up the other side."

"How do I know you're tellin' the truth?" I asked. "Who do I call?"

"You don't," he said. "This is a classified op so you got to take my word for it."

"Time for my phone call," I told him.

"Can't do that either," he said, and I knew he was playing out a hand he thought was golden. "You blow my cover in this operation and they're gonna shoot you down from upstairs. Be the end of your career in the service."

I didn't answer him at first. Instead, I stood back from him and watched him go through another bout of retching up the slop filling up his lungs. He turned to look back at me, blood all over his lip, but confident that he'd explained everything away and now might even have something on me.

"Now get me a doctor before I bleed to death," he said as if he was a gunny sarge giving me a order. "And then we better figure out what we're gonna do about Santos 'cause we gotta make sure you keep your cover." He started to his feet, taking his hands from behind his neck to help him get up. And he was getting talkative, too, just like we were partners on a job. "Give me a hand, here," he said as he staggered forward a little bit. "You drive. I know a doc that'll tape me up. Then we'll pay a visit to Ginger and get Santos' dough."

I was enjoying this performance more than I should have. It was time to bring the curtain down on the job and get the hell out of New Orleans.

"Last thing," I said. He paused midway up, teetering on the fronts of his shoes and staring at me with wide glassy eyes because he realized that I hadn't put away the gun yet. "You pocketed the dough."

"Huh?" He dropped his jaw so that his mouth was hanging wide open.

"You pocketed the dough," I repeated. "Even if you been tellin' the truth, it don't mean you get to pocket the dough they give you."

"No . . . you don't . . . understand," he stuttered. "I'm freelance. I'm not on Uncle Sam's payroll. I get to keep my commission."

"You're a fuckin' double," I said, sighting down the barrel of my .38. "Takin' grease from both sides and cuttin' your own deals on the side."

"No," he said with a catch of fear in his throat. He knew that it wasn't over yet, that he was in worse trouble than he thought. "No, you still don't get it. This is how it's supposed to happen. The KGB runs checks on all company people. They know who we are, we know who they are. That's the way the company has to run with independents once in awhile. I have to make it look good or else the whole thing fails."

"Company?" I repeated.

"Company, COMPANY," he said, his voice rising as it dawned on him that he and I might just be the same. "You ain't regular FBI," he said finally. "You'd know about the Company, the *C-I-A,* the *en-ter-prise.*" He stared very hard at me. He rolled his eyes and fought to stay upright.

"March over to that box," I ordered, motioning with the gun in my hand.

"You can't kill me if you're FBI. How you gonna explain what you did?" His head must have been spinning because he couldn't come up with anything that made sense. Either I was FBI or I wasn't. Either I was working for Mr. S. or I wasn't. I couldn't be doing both. So who was I? "Unless," he continued. A real edge of fear crept into his voice. "Unless you're one of them. KGB."

But I wasn't getting paid to give him any answers, just to get answers from him. And I had my answers.

"Look, I don't know what the fuck you're doin'," he pleaded. "But I can make it worth your while to work for me. Whoever you work for, together we can knock off Johnny Santos, if he's your boss. We can take over his action. You're tough, the boys'll listen to you. I can work this game. I'm in tight with the Company men in DC."

"Stand over there," I said. I was much calmer now. It was all going to be over soon. "Just stand there. Nothin's gonna happen if you just do what I say."

"Sure, sure," he said. "Don't do anything stupid. Nothin' you can't undo, know what I mean?"

"I just gotta think for a second," I said. "And you're rattlin' my brains."

"OK, I'll just stand here," he promised.

He shut up, stopped moving, and leaned against the pine coffin that he'd already double-tagged. It was sitting on its own table, ready for the next stiff and stash of documents he was supposed to send. Nuñez was breathing with greater difficulty now, and I almost thought that if I just stomped out some more ribs, he'd die on his own. But that was not the way I was supposed to work. Finally the tension seemed to be breaking him down. I cocked the hammer on my .38

"What the fuck are you doin'?" he screamed.

"It's a contract, Leo," I said. "Plain and simple. A hit. You're a rat, a *goniff*. You been judged, sentenced, I've got your warrant, and you're gettin' what rats get."

"No," he screamed again. "You're only a fuckin' hitter. You don't know what you're doing. It's a bigger picture than you can see. I'm CIA and you're a . . . a . . . *HITTER!* I'm on the right side and you're workin' for the bad guys. You're the enemy!"

A .38 police special is a loud gun. The cops like it that way 'cause it scares the shit out of anybody who's never heard a gun go off. But I'd used it many times before and know how much it's a real conversation stopper. So I didn't have to get in position or flinch when I squeezed the trigger. I just let the sound of the shot echo off the walls while Leo Nuñez reeled over backwards into the coffin and tried to hang on for his life.

My round had hit him square in the chest. It also must have bounced off two or three other ribs and entered the lung again 'cause he was spitting up volumes of blood from both his mouth and nose. But he didn't fall. Instead he tried to stagger towards me, his hand reaching out like a monster in a Boris Karloff movie when I squeezed the trigger two more times in slow succession. This time he spun backwards on the first shot and took the second round in his kidney. I heard him pissing like a tinkle of water through a busted pipe and then saw it just come pouring down his right leg. Then he let go his shit and slid off the table to the floor. He lay there; his eyes half open, his left foot twitching like it wasn't attached any more, and his breathing as shallow as the tray of water on an old lady's steam radiator.

The rat would have laid like that for another hour and I would have missed the last plane out of town. So I stood over him, stepped back so his brains wouldn't splash all over my pants, and aimed the gun straight up his nose. That way the round would ricochet away from me and keep on going into the wall. The force of the blast took off most of his nose and drilled his brains through the top of his head. His head jerked all the way back and arched him up, then he collapsed and stopped moving once and for all. I heard air gurgling out of the back of his head.

I shoved the gun back in my holster and looked around the embalming room for one of those rubber bags that they wrap around stiffs after a bloody car accident. I found a bunch of them by the stack of coffins, dragged one across the floor, and dropped it over Leo Nuñez. With my foot under his back, I scooped him up and into the bag. Then I rolled him over on his stomach, brought the bag around, and zippered him up. The liquids were still pouring out of him so I lifted him up quickly and dropped him into the open coffin before the bag got too slippery to handle. The floor was still a mess, but that was Nitano's problem. Once I closed and sealed the coffin, I knew Nitano would stash it and send it off. He didn't want any trouble from the cops or the family. He would simply have one of his boys wash down the floor, hand him a C-note to shut him up, and make believe none of this happened.

Before I left, I took the briefcase, stashed the automatic, shut off the lights, and got behind the wheel of Nuñez' Buick. I could hear sirens in the distance. The neighbors had called the cops, I figured, and I wanted to get out of there real fast. I started up the car and drove back down St. Charles, past the three squad cars that had just turned onto the boulevard, and went into the French Quarter where I would leave Johnny Santos his automatic and Nuñez' car. That was my last loose end, and Mr. Santos would know what to do with them.

I didn't forget to place the phone call from the airport either. I reported in, telling the voice at the other end of the line that the package of strawberries had been delivered to its destination and that I was returning that night and had the bill of lading with me. The voice simply asked me to leave the bill in a luggage locker at LaGuardia. Someone would get it later.

"Nobody saw you go, right, Mike?" the voice asked.

"Nobody," I said. "But two local cops asked me to tie down their loose ends."

"Not to worry," the voice said. "They belong to us. We'll take care of them. Any questions?"

I started to ask about the Company, but the voice cut me off as soon as I began.

"That's not your problem either," it said. "You did your job. Now forget about it and take a vacation."

"But Nuñez said he worked for our side. What did the CIA have to do with this?" I pushed.

"You're not followin' orders," the voice said. I could hear the irritation at the other end. I was going too far.

"I wanna know if I did right," I continued. I didn't care what the voice said. I had to know.

"You did right. Don't ask any more questions!"

I didn't answer. I backed off.

"Come home, Mike," it said in an almost soothing tone. "It's over for now."

The Hilo Hotel

I first learned about Hawaii from travel posters in bars and from the radio news broadcasts on the morning of the attack on Pearl Harbor. Blue water, white sand, ukeleles, brown-skinned girls in grass skirts, leis floating on the water, natives paddling outrigger canoes through the surf, the smoking USS Arizona: flames licking out from beneath her superstructure, listing hard by her bows, and heeling well over near the dock; the riddled bodies of sailors in their khaki Mae Wests floating face down through oil slicks and rising over the crests of the breaking whitecaps. I'd never been to Hawaii, but I'd seen a lot of movie newsreels since the war.

Hawaii was a whole world away from me. The only beach I'd ever sunned on was Rockaway. And when I was a kid the closest thing to an outrigger canoe I'd ever paddled was the lifeguard boat we used to steal early in the morning until the police launch would come after us and tow us back to shore where the lifeguards would slap us around after we hauled it up on the sand. Then we'd slip into the Turkish bath houses like Curly's on the boardwalk and lift billfolds and loose change out of the old men's lockers while they spent their ninety-five-degree days sitting in the *schvitz* and *kvetching* about the heat, their jobs, and their Coppertoned wives who were playing mahjong and canasta on folding tables near the water's edge. Maybe that wasn't the South Seas but it was the only beach I knew until I received my marching orders from the Old Man a few days after New Year's in 1950.

At first I was a little sour that Mr. H. had pulled me away while I was still enjoying the little black RCA table-model television I had just bought my momma for Chanukka. That was the first time she'd ever seen the Times Square ball drop from real close up. And the next morning, after she woke me up by banging the frying pan in the kitchen sink, she couldn't stop bending my ear at what she'd seen the night before on television. *"Mendela,"* she said, clucking her lips the way she always did whenever she was impressed by something. *"Ischt ein goldineh medineh.* A whole new *voild!"* The television was the first real present I'd gotten her that seemed to make any difference in the world she still lived in, that told her I was succeeding in my world in my own way. She would complain to me about the *goyische momsers* the neighbors told her I palled around with, but when she watched Molly Goldberg leaning out her window and yoo-hooing across the courtyard and laughed when Menasha Skullnick said, "Not a Cadillac but a *Cadillac!"* she didn't care what the neighbors said. The television meant that I was a success, the toast of the town, and I wanted to enjoy it for as long as I could. But when Mr. H. said it was time for another job, there was no calling for a time-out.

So I left the cold New York January and flew west on one of the new TWA Constellations to Los Angeles where I caught the Pan Am Clipper for the trip to Hawaii. Wings over the world, I was thinking to myself on the final leg of my trip to Hilo as I sat bumping around in the cramped, makeshift passenger seat of a Piper island-hopper: the small World War II-vintage artillery-spotter plane that had had its camouflage painted over and the insignia of the South Pacific Airways decaled on its wings. I never liked flying in the first place; it always made me nervous, and a flight where you could touch all sides of the cabin at the same time and count the hairs coming out of the pilot's nostrils only made more logical the fear of airplanes I had since my days on the Ranger. It was a fear I never even admitted to myself.

I had already been hit by the solid wall of wet Hawaiian midday heat when I got off the Pan Am Clipper in Oahu. It fell on me as I stepped onto the tarmac, and I had my jacket and tie off by the time I reached the luggage counter. It smelled like a million flowers all coming into bloom at the same minute and it made my shirt cling to my back like it was glued there. My white starched collar was wringing wet like the red and white checked napkins that the Sicilian dock workers drew tight around their necks even on the hottest days. I had opened my shirt all the way down to my belly button, letting my undershirt show through. Disapproving ladies in their pastel dresses, wide-brimmed hats, and lace garden gloves looked down their noses at me in the Oahu terminal, but I didn't give a shit. I just wanted to get me one of the loose Hawaiian tropical shirts with the green and orange flowers on it and a pair of chinos and leave whatever I was wearing right there at the baggage counter. I even blended into the local population because all the Honolulu gumshoes wore their shirttails out, leaving lots of room for a holster inside the belt. I'd wear mine the same way.

The Piper Cub dipped low over the breaking waves along the beaches, the pilot figuring to show me the local color while demonstrating the hedge-hogging techniques that kept him alive over the beaches of Normandy when he was spotting where the AEF's shells were landing. The pilot skirted a jagged outcropping of mean-looking cliffs by about six inches, it seemed from inside the cabin, and suddenly banked inland toward a bright patch of green with a lot of construction equipment parked around a giant crater.

"What you're looking for is down here," he said, yelling over the buzz-saw of the prop motor and pointing down like a wing leader motioning to the rest of his flight.

I nodded and tried to crane out over the window to see exactly what green patch he was pointing at, but the angle of his turn was too steep for me to see anything at all. Then he went into a sudden dive and buzzed the treetops until he circled over a small grassy landing field just to the north of the construction site with an orange windsock flying above it. Then he turned back to look at me directly and shouted, "You're staying at the club, right?" He pointed vehemently down at the ground and pumped his hand out the window as if he wanted me to jump. I nodded again. "The Hilo Hotel," he shouted. "The pride of the islands." And then he threw his head back as if he expected me to start laughing.

We were so close to the trees by this time that I was beginning to feel sick. But he pulled the nose up at the last minute, banked into a turn, flattened us out directly over the landing field, and dipped the plane toward the ground. In what seemed like a minute, the wheels bounced off the turf, the tail dropped, and the Piper skidded to a shortfield landing.

"Couldn't ask for better service," he said. "Door to door."

The pilot was opening the hatch even before the plane came to a dead stop. He slid out between the wing struts and vaulted to the ground like a kid in gym class. Then he reached out his hand to help me down. I was no old man, but when I almost fell face first into the grass because the drop was longer than I expected, I let him help me out.

"It's a service we provide for all our passengers," he said just a little too smugly for my money. Then he crawled through the door back into an area behind the cockpit, handed me my suitcases under the wing struts, and swung down like a trapeze flyer again. "Hilo Hotel," he said gesturing toward the construction site with an open hand like a ringmaster. "They don't build'em any classier."

The structure itself looked like the hotels that were going up in Vegas and Miami, especially the Flamingo Casino that Benny and Meyer were putting up along the Vegas strip. I'd already been to a few of'em, mostly on business for Mr. C. Unlike most of the old hotels in the Apple and down in Philly and Atlantic City, this one was entirely glass and stucco. It looked more like a big ranch or a hacienda than a hotel.

The sight of the bright green trees and tall grass all around and the thick bushes with leaves as big as car doors was something out of a fairy tale. Everywhere was green, like I'd just been dropped by the tornado into Oz and suddenly the world was in RKO technicolor. Once your senses adjusted to the green around you, you were able to pick out other colors coming through the background. There were the bright pinks of flower blossoms, a bright, bone-colored sand, lots of reds and lots of blues. But all of them were intense colors, not like in the city where the only colors you could see were like little holes in a black and white movie. This place was looking like a cartoon land where no matter how many times you got dropped on your head, you'd just flatten out and spring right back into shape.

Only it wasn't going to be as simple as that. As I hoisted my luggage over my back, I had to remember that my orders from the Old Man were as dangerous as any of my jobs during the war, and they gave me no fire escape in case they blew up in my face. I was settling an eight-year-old score, a shiv that had been dug deep into the ribs of most anyone who knew the real story of the Bataan Death March when the Japanese forced our garrison in the Philippines to march through the jungle to their prison camp. It wasn't just that people died on that march. It was that nurses, chaplains, and GIs who were so wounded they could barely stand were shoved forward at bayonet point to march until they dropped. And when they dropped, they were shot, right there on the spot, and left to rot in the jungle like meat for the monkeys. There were no medicines, no rules of war, no Geneva Convention. Those were rules that only the good guys had to obey. For the Japanese, the more people who died or who were killed meant fewer faces to feed and more rice for the guards to eat. What did a pile of dead GIs mean to them anyway? The Americans had already disgraced themselves to the Japanese by surrendering. The world would never know what happened and would never care. That's what the Japanese thought. And they forgot about it as the years passed and they grew rich on American money.

But old scores are there for the settling. They burn in your blood. In my world you do business as long as you have to; you kiss your enemies on the lips and save your revenge 'till the very end. The longer you wait, knowing what you will do, the sweeter it becomes. That was the reason the Old Man chose me for this assignment: a simple straightforward execution like it was done in the old days. The body disappears, the message is sent, the other side knows that you've avenged the wrong. And now it would be Colonel Kyoshi Moro's turn to feed the monkeys.

Putting out a hit on Kyoshi Moro was important enough to the Old Man that it was one of the few times up to then that he ever gave me an assignment in person. I had gotten the call slip for the face-to-face from a homicide dick at the Number Six Precinct. Two uniforms picked me up as I was walking along Houston Street and threw me in the back of a car for an hour before this cop walks up, leans over like he's gonna pass me some advice that's good for my health, and slips me a piece of paper through the open slot at the top of the window that says Carlyle, 842. Then he tells the uniforms, "Let'em go! Wrong punk." But I got the message OK, went home, threw on a good-looking suit so I could mingle uptown, and headed in a cab to see Mr. H.

"This one's a tricky sonovabitch," the Old Man said to me, sitting by the little writing desk in his suite, staring out the window and watching a dry, early January snow powder against the streetlights along Madison Avenue. It was hot and stuffy in the hotel room and you could hear the steam whistling out of the radiators and the banging of the water in the return pipes. Mr. Hoover was feeling the heat even though he was only in shirtsleeves and wearing a dark brown tie. "You know who you're gonna visit? Kyoshi Moro, the bastard that G2's been after since the march out of Bataan. When MacArthur gave up on the war trials, the Army turned his file over to me. Now I hear Moro's supposed to've been working for our side since '49. CIA has him as one of their informants pointing fingers at the KGB boys working in China. He sure must have made his deal fast."

As was usual in these meetings, the Old Man started out by doing all the talking. All I was supposed to do was nod in the right places, ask him dates, names, and locations, and say, "Yes, Mr. Hoover" when it was over. But I noticed something different this time. Maybe it was because I'd opened up a hornets' nest in New Orleans by turning over a double agent in an intelligence operation and whacking him instead of letting him get back to the Agency for cover, but Mr. Hoover seemed to want to tell me everything in advance about the jobs the Squad was doing, even the little details. I guessed he didn't want me to have any doubts the next time I pointed a cocked revolver at my target and the guy screamed "CIA. Don't shoot!"

"These CIA boys are getting in my way," the Old Man said, still looking out the window like he was looking for answers in the snow. "And soon it's gonna be war. They're just a bunch of pipe-smoking Harvard pencil-dicks. They sit in their offices, read their books, and look over a pile of numbers. Only know what they read. Then they meet over a teatable in the White House and tell Truman how the world is run. None of 'em ever even looked a real spy in the face—they would pee in their pants. Yet they talk from behind their books like they have have all the answers. Burns me up."

I nodded, mumbled "uh-huh," and didn't say anything else. You just agreed with Mr. Hoover when he was like this. He'd been around long enough—since the Great War, in fact—to see people in Washington come and go. He'd made a long list of friends and enemies on both sides of the line and knew how to hedge his bets.

"This isn't like the good old days, Mike," he said. "That was when you could wait for a punk like Kelly or Nelson in an alley and hit'em with fifty rounds out of a tommy gun until his guts splashed all over the bricks. Now you gotta negotiate with Professor Fancy Pants over in the White House who tells Truman he's the best thing to happen to this country since sliced bread." He coughed a deep phelgmy cough into a handkerchief, wadded it up, and then put it back into his pants pocket. "Guy couldn't even run a hat factory right; how's he supposed to run the country?"

"Yes sir," I said. But I had to wait for him to continue at his own speed. You couldn't rush J. Edgar Hoover into anything.

"You finger a guy on the other side and Dulles pipes up and says, 'He's ours; national security,' and he smokes up a storm with his pipe. You don't know the dust you kicked up because of that double agent down in New Orleans. They knew he was greasing his wheels but they were willing to look the other way and we blew the lid right off. That's why I'm using you again. Let Dulles know I ain't backing down from a fight. I don't want to send you down there. I'd rather play this one right by the book. Wait 'til Moro comes to Los Angeles, slap him with a federal warrant, and bring him to Washington in cuffs. Put the bastard on trial right in front of the television cameras. Let that sonovabitch Nixon take a whack at him like he did Hiss. Then we strap him in the chair and throw the switch." He rapped his fingers on the desk and then stood up to face me. "But that's not the way it's gonna happen. You're gonna hit him, Mike. You're gonna plant'em somewhere and leave a message where the CIA can find it. After that, I don't give a shit."

"Do I set up the hit myself, Mr. Hoover?" I asked.

"Any way you want," he answered. "You're gonna make contact with him through a nightclub owner named Li Chin, a Chinaman with no backbone and no loyalties to anybody. Bastard worked for both sides before the start of the war. But as soon as we busted up the Jap fleet at Midway, Li saw which way the wind was blowing and claimed he was really working for us all the time." The Old Man pummeled his fist against the top of the desk and clenched his teeth hard. "At least if you're working for a government, work for the government. You can't ever trust the guys who turn double on their own people because the tide of war changes. When it changes back, they'll turn double on you." He leaned over to me. "Li's the real problem here, Mike. He's like an eel—catch'em here," he said, grabbing at thin air with both his hands as if was strangling someone, "and he slips out here. If it was up to me, I'd have you shoot Li Chin's eyes out right where he's sitting. But I can't sanction that kind of hit. The CIA says he works for us. My boys say he runs errands for the KGB. He tells the local hoods down there he works for Benny Siegel out of Vegas."

Mr. Hoover saw my face go white. I didn't even nod. I clammed.

"Don't say nothing. That was just so you'd be in the know when the time comes," he said, trying to put things back on keel. "I'm not telling you about any other business Li Chin has. He's not connected in this country so you can do what you have to if you have to protect yourself. You have my word on that. My guess is that he's worked for the Chinese heroin rings for years, bringing the stuff in through Hawaii, shipping by couriers to his distribution network in Los Angeles and San Francisco, and sending the cash back to the Chicoms. You and I both know that he's the type who'll work for the guy that pays him the most. We can't shut him down unless he makes the first move, but you are to leave him a message he'll never forget. You understand?"

I nodded. Li Chin was to know but not to know—right up to the line. And if he figured it out, he was supposed to be too scared to do anything about it because then no one, *NO ONE*, could protect him.

"I'll send you all the details you'll need through the boys at the Number Six in a day or so," Mr. Hoover concluded. "Pack your bags and dress light. I want you looking like one of the locals. There are plenty of Americans setting up shop down there, and that's exactly what you'll be." He threw up his hands as he said this. "But I'm not telling you how to do the job. Work your own way. When you're finished you can take a couple of days R &R in Honolulu. I'll pick up the tab. Be careful." And with that he grabbed my hand, shook it with both of his hands, and walked me out of the room all at the same time. He always made it clear when your time with him was up.

Li Chin

The long hike from the landing strip to Li Chin's Hilo Hotel resort was all up an incline and tougher going than I thought. And by the time I got to the glass doors, I was panting like a hound on a dog day. Even for a twenty-six-year-old guy like me who was still in pretty good fighting shape, the heavy air took took a lot of starch out. That was something worth remembering if I had to go hand-to-hand with Colonel Moro. Standing there with my bags under my arms like a greenie just off the boat, I could hardly wait to strip down into the native costume and mingle with the tourists milling around the front of the hotel wearing winged sunglasses, funny flower hats, Manila cotton shirts, and carrying green-and-blue-colored drinks with bamboo umbrellas coming out the top.

The printed sign on the green-tinted heavy glass doors read "It's Koooool Inside!" with little icicles and a penguin hanging off the "Kool." I put down my bags and took a long gander through the door at the folks sitting in wicker lounge chairs arranged around glass tables like little islands in the plushly carpeted lobby. I took in the scene as completely as I could before pushing open the doors, more to confirm my first impressions of the place than for any logical reason. Even though it was still seriously under construction, the place looked rich, like it was being floated by a lot of money that had to be laundered so it wouldn't turn up looking too conspicuous in any one place for too long. This was the new way of doing things when money was changing hands faster than anyone could bury it in untraceable bank accounts.

When I opened the door I noticed the change in temperature right away. It was like an icebox on the other side of the glass to anyone just walking in from the outside tropical heat. People must be getting a lot of colds going back and forth from the hotel to the outside, I thought to myself, as the damp shirt clinging to my skin started to make chills run up and down my backbone. A short Oriental guy with very yellow skin and shiny black hair slicked way back along his head with vaseline waddled up to me.

"You Missah Moran?" he asked, his mouth wide open and his eyes blinking like he was sending semaphore messages to the rest of the fleet.

"Milan," I said. "Mike Milan." In my line of work, I was glad to be looking down at someone instead of straight up into the red of cop's nose.

"Das whaddai say, Mike Moran," the guy said. "Boss say you come have drink say hi. Hokay?"

"Who's your boss? Li Chin?" I asked.

"Missuh Ri, Missuh Ri. You come now have drink wiv Missuh Ri, hokay?" And he bowed and waved me through the lobby and down a hallway past the front desk. He started to take the suitcases out of my hands but I pulled them back. He pulled them the other way. "No, no, boss say I take bags to room. You no carry, I take, you boss guest."

"I'll hold onto this," I said, keeping my overnight bag with my revolver under my arm. "You can take the rest."

"You keep, you keep," Li Chin's errand boy said. "I take rest." And I watched him heave my luggage onto his back like he'd been carrying it for his whole life. "Boss door straight," he said nodding with his head to a wooden door at the end of the hall.

I followed his nose to the door and knocked twice to make sure my host was ready for me. The door opened before I finished my second knock and revealed a large wood-paneled room that looked like it had been flown in from a Wall Street banker's office building the night before. I had never seen such furniture in any other place, not even Wall Street: oversized leather couches, shiny forest-green leather winged-back chairs, standing ashtrays everywhere, and a huge, wooden lawyer's desk with a globe as big as a beach ball beside it. A long, green-shaded banker's lamp was on the edge of the desk, and plenty of smaller lamps were on the three coffee tables arranged in the office.

The tall and broad-beamed Polynesian-looking guy wearing thick, black-rimmed eyeglasses and sitting behind the desk must have known that I was a little surprised at his posh setup because he laughed as he watched me give his place the once-over. "What'd you expect? Grass huts, torches, and a uke-ukelele?" he asked in perfect English as he got up to walk around the edge of his desk to face me. "This is the U.S., Mike. New York, big business." And he laughed as he took my hand and rung it like a slot machine. "I expect that you want to get a shower, maybe have a swim, change into the local uniform, and get a drink before we talk. I've taken the liberty of checking you into our VIP suite, sending some shirts and bathing suits up to your room, turning on your whirlpool, and stocking your private bar. When you're comfortable, call me on the house phone, and we'll have some dinner. We have a lot to talk about. Now get out of here and relax. You New York boys always want to get things done in a hurry. Well, out here you play by the house rules and they are: rest first, then work. Chop, chop," he said grinning a grin that only a mother could love.

"Mr. Li," I began.

"Chin, Chin," he interrupted. "My friends, and we're gonna be good friends, Mike, call me Chin."

"Chin," I said. "Your reputation as a host and a gentleman is no exaggeration. I expect our business to be friendly and profitable."

"That's just the way I want it, Mike," he said. "Friendly and profitable, for your people *and* mine."

And with that I left his office and walked back towards the front desk where the clerk, when he looked up from his register and saw me, began rapping the bell like he was playing the drums and motioned to the bellcap himself to show me my room.

It all felt like it was too easy, too friendly, like separate welcome mats at the threshold of every doorway, all of them tempting little scraps of bait leading me into the middle of a giant spider's web. I'd been down this road before, walking both sides of the invisible line between the Families and the Squad, and each time it was the same. Does the guy who's oogling you from behind his Fu Manchu mask suspect anything? Does he see through your cover? Because you know what you know, you always think sometimes that you're just like a sandwich man walking down the street with a big FBI sign hanging over your shoulders. But what does the mark know? Sometimes they make it too easy for you, and that's when you start to doubt. When your marks lay back and expose their bellies like dumb mutts sunning themselves in Tompkins Square you ask yourself, do I just put the knife in or are they going to take my hand off when I make my move? Thing is, you never know until you make the move. And that's exactly what I was coming up to now.

The sight of my room almost knocked my eyes out. They had a fuckin' waterfall right by the windows. A waterfall! Bubbling away like Old Faithful was coming right through the floor and sounding like a toilet sounds when someone doesn't pull the chain all the way so it keeps on flushing. At the base of the waterfall was a fountain with floating leaves and posies on it that twirled around in the current of the circulating water. The room had a TV set as big as a table against another wall with black leather couches and easy chairs arranged in front of it. The rest of room was laid out with wicker furniture and big leafy plants, like Tarzan was gonna come swinging through any minute on the next vine. And from the entry foyer, I could see the sliding glass doors at the far end of the room that opened onto a terrace where there was a glass and wicker table-and-chairs set. The entire scene was washed in so much late afternoon sunlight coming from so many different reflections that the place looked like it was sitting on top of a glowing volcano. It looked as if Li Chin was catering to a well-heeled crowd all right, and he was spending a lot of money to let them know he knew they were well-heeled. And I hadn't even seen the bedroom yet.

"Anything else, boss?" a Hawaiian-looking bellcap asked as he came out of the bedroom. "I put bags on top of bed, want me to unpack 'em?" And he stood there waiting.

I dug in my back pocket for the loose bills I had especially folded in there, knowing that the way I tipped the bellcap would also tip my hand to Li Chin. Too little, and it would mean a sign of disrespect for him in the eyes of the Families who had supposedly sent me down here. A careful tip would mean that the Families had sent down someone who was low on the totem pole and that they really didn't know who they were dealing with. I had to make Li Chin feel that he was held in wide esteem by the Families and they were confident in whatever I chose to do. I had to make Li Chin feel confident as well, so confident he would have no doubts about trusting what I could do for him. I pulled out two half-C notes and obviously laid them across the bellcap's open palm.

"What's your name?" I asked the kid who stared down in astonishment at the money he had just gotten.

"Call me Frankie," he said.

"When I want anything I'll call you Frankie," I said. "And you'll take care of me personally?"

"Any time. Boss," he said. "Don't call no one but me. You tell downstairs it's Mr. Moran on phone and I knock on door before you put receiver down."

"I've got my eye on you, Frankie," I winked at him. "Do good for me."

"Yes. Boss. You call, I come." And he bowed like a Kamikaze pilot, spun around, and headed out the door.

I was alone, trying to put together what I had to do in the next few days while keeping my cover intact. Was Li Chin already placing calls to the West Coast to check on my story in advance? Would any of the boys from back East be showing up here unannounced? I only had a few days to make this work, set up a connection with Kyoshi Moro, and get out with my head still attached to the rest of me. Only the steady grinding of the air conditioner pumping icebox cold air through the place answered my questions. I would have to play through the game like I was on the level and hope that Li Chin was falling for my line.

I closed the door and flopped backwards on the couch. The cold air flowed around me and took me back to the icy New York January I'd left behind. With my eyes closed and the chill breeze blowing around my ears, I felt like I was still on the plane—like my stomach was going up and down every time we hit a bump in the clouds. I was walking down Mott Street into Little Italy for a bowl of pastina and butter with a little soup splashed on top. Then I was rolling a pair of bones against the brick wall of the graveyard on Chrystie Street when one of Lucky's *gumbas* grabs me by the back of the neck and shakes me 'till my brains rattle against my ear drums.

"Ya palmin' the iv'ries, ya little hebe," he says over garlic and onions and spinach in my face and then the phone rings.

"Are you freshened up yet, Mike?" the articulate and well-educated voice says at the other end.

My mouth was all full of spit and I was still staring at the *gumba* waiting for my slap in the face.

"Do you need a few more minutes?" I must have grunted something because the voice said, "Why don't you take some more time and call Frankie when you're ready. I'll wait for you."

"Yeah, yeah," I heard myself saying. "Just be a minute.,"

"Don't rush. Relax. Spend some time in the whirlpool in your bathroom suite. We'll have all night to talk over dinner and play some cards. Don't bring your money. This should be your vacation and you're my guest, Mike. The games are on the house. You're only here to have fun and to let your people back East know that we run a clean show down here. We want to be your friends, too." Then it hung up.

I stumbled into the bathroom, still not sure whether Chrystie Street was real and Hawaii was the dream or vice versa. But I wanted to know what a whirlpool in a bathroom felt like. If the Hilo Hotel was the dream, then I'd have a hell of a story to tell when I woke up. If this was the real thing, then I wouldn't be able to tell anybody because nobody was supposed to know where I was, except the Old Man and he didn't bullshit with nobody. I was voting for the dream because this bathroom was larger than most of the living rooms I'd been in. It reminded me of the woodcuts of the Roman *schvitzes* that were in my high school history book, except here there was no little kid in a skirt whipping some fat guy with a switch stick.

The bathroom was walled with mirrors, and the light seemed to be coming from somewhere inside the ceiling. The floor was a pink marble tile, not the linoleum I'd grown up with on the Lower East Side. And in the center of it all was a large, round bathtub sunken part of the way into a raised platform. Steam rose off the surface of water in the tub and I heard the sound of bubbling water. I climbed the three steps and looked in. Water was sluicing into the tub from who knows how many nozzles in the side. But instead of water, the tub looked like it was filling with seltzer and foaming up with a thick head like the top of a chocolate egg cream only without the chocolate. And it was hot and steamy and making sweat even though there was cold air coming into the room. I peeled off my clothes and slid into the water, letting it bubble up around me and tickle my nose and ears.

This was no dream. The water was so hot that my muscles turned to jelly and I slid all the way to the bottom. I could have fallen asleep right there in the water, but I was having too much fun. I put my back against the nozzles and then my scalp and finally my balls. Too bad I couldn't tell the boys about this gizmo, I thought. This was really living. I climbed out before I turned into a raisin, shaved while I was still steamed up like a soggy *kreplach*, and dried off. Then I threw on one of those bright Hawaiian shirts that were hanging in the closet and a pair of white pants. I slicked back my hair like I was a piranha fish moving in for the kill, phoned Frankie to let Li Chin know I was ready, and headed downstairs in the glass elevator for some eats and the sitdown.

"It's just gonna be you and me, Mike," Li Chin said when he saw me standing in his doorway, all shiny like a boiled lobster from my whirlpool. Frankie led me through Li's private office into a dining room with long table with lots of tropical plants on it. Only they weren't plants at all. They were dinner.

"That's quite a gadget you got up there, Mr. Li," I said, careful to show him the respect of a local boss, even though the Old Man really wanted me to put two rounds through his eyeballs.

"Let's get this on a friendly basis, right now," he said. "You call me Chin, like the rest of my buddies."

I was more interested in the food that was piled in the center of the table on copper plates than I was in being anybody's friend. Chin had pineapples as big as bowling balls and coconuts split in half so you could see the milky meat piled thick in the inside. And he had a big roasted pig over at one corner of the table. It looked fat and juicy, but my mamma would have reached out from New York and slapped my hand off if I'd touched it. I hoped there was a nice piece of chicken hidden there somewhere. Chin saw me oogling the pig.

"You ever eat Hawaiian roast pork?" he asked.

"Never tried it," I answered. "And I don't think I ever will. No disrespect, of course," I said in a hurry, "but I'm not allowed to touch it. Looks great, though."

"Forgive me," Chin said as if he'd just insulted my family. "I should have known. You're one of Mr. Lansky's people." He rang a bell that was hidden somewhere under the table and a busboy in white coat appeared at the door. Chin spoke to him in machine-gun Chinese and the busboy bowed three times like he was on a rope, picked up the pig like it was a piece of shit, bowed to me twice, and tiptoed out of the room.

"Then you must try the sweet and sour duck, or maybe some of our local fish," Chin offered. And as I nodded, he ladled chunks of duck, peppers, and pineapple in a thick, dark-red sauce onto a copper plate and passed it over to me. "You like rice?" he asked.

"Love it," I said, and Chin piled a bowl high with white rice and passed it across as well.

"Dip your duck in the rice, Mike, and try the chopsticks," he said. "Eat up. We have a lot of talking to do so that you can spend the rest of your time here on vacation. You're gonna be our ambassador of good will. When you tell the boys back East about what you've seen here, they'll never want to see Havana again. No disrespect to Mr. Lansky intended at all by that, you understand."

I didn't even grace Li's remark with an answer. I just smiled at him with my usual idiot smile and dug into the sweet-and sour-sauce.

"Tell me about Las Vegas, Mike?" Chin asked as he watched me fumble with a pair of chopsticks and send a piece of duck spinning across the thick hemp carpeting on the floor of his dining room. Maybe it looked stupid to see me play with them, but I figured it wouldn't hurt to let Li Chin believe that I couldn't use my hands. If I had to use them against him later, I could be at a real advantage. What do the Chinese always say about surprise? What did the Japanese do to us at Pearl Harbor? I'd be chopping his sticks soon enough, I told myself as a chunk of pineapple went flying off the table as well.

"Las Vegas?" I repeated. "Ain't got the weather you got down here," I said. "Desert. Some sagebrush. Mostly a lot of sand and very little water. It's good for people with asthma or tuberculosis, I hear. Years ago, even right before the war when most of the New York apartment buildings didn't have any central heat, the old people would get sick and their doctors would send them to Nevada to get their lungs back. I don't think people go there that much for health reasons anymore so the land's cheap and there's plenty of it."

"That why the New York Families are buying up every acre they can get their hands on?" Li asked. "Poor little Chinee merchant can't even buy a hill of sand."

I saw an opening and jumped in like I was born to sell real estate. "Depends who you're buying from," I said. "And it depends on what you want."

"Maybe a nice Jewish boy can get me in on the ground floor?" Li asked.

He didn't know that Old Man Hoover wanted to get him in under the ground floor. But, I promised myself as he mouthed the word "Jewish" as if he were spitting in a toilet, there would be time enough for that, even if it took the next twenty years. "Actually, Mr. Li," I said emphasizing respectfulness over familiarity the way Mr. Lansky always taught me to do when you're doing business with someone you're gonna plug later on, "you may be able to acquire some interest in the properties that are going up out there. That's part of what I was sent here to talk about."

"Am I being offered a deal?" he asked, putting down his chopsticks and letting his eyeglasses slip to the end of his nose.

"I was told to say that the possibility of a trade exists," I began.

"With a little cash consideration thrown in, of course," Li said cynically.

"They can send a lot of business your way," I said. "Especially since you want an interest in the Las Vegas action."

"How much money are your people willing to put up?" Li asked, getting to the point immediately.

"As much as necessary to acquire a substantial interest in the new development on these islands. They would want you to represent their interests down here, of course," I tried to assure him.

"Their interests?"

"They would become your silent partners," I said. "Just as you would become theirs in Las Vegas."

"And would I have to deal with the *gumba* bag men every month?" he asked, showing a surprising amount of disrespect for me and the Families. "Taking their cut right off the top until they decided that they wanted more than just a piece of the action?"

"Not at all," I said, letting him assume that I hadn't really understood what he said. "This would all be strictly on the up-and-up. You deal with their lawyers. Their lawyers deal with your lawyers. You take care of your people, we take care of ours. Strictly business, Mr. Li."

"Chin, Chin," he said leaning across the table and letting a piece of shellfish slide out of his mouth and into his bowl of rice. It didn't matter, I supposed; he was mixing it in his bowl before he put in his mouth. He might as well have mixed it after it was in his mouth. Looked the same anyhow. "How much control are we talking about here?" He asked after he wiped his face with a damp cloth.

"For their part, they would expect you to make money," I said. "That's not unreasonable since you're obviously making money now."

"Then," he asked, getting concerned about the directions the conversation could take if he wasn't careful, "Why do I need them?"

"You want a piece of the Las Vegas action, a way to invest some of the money you're taking in down here," I repeated, happy that he had thrown me the unexpected bone at the beginning of the conversation. I wasn't going to bury it now. "You figure there'll be a profit in it for you, a return on your investment. Cuts both ways. They want a return on their investment. You take care of your business, they'll take care of theirs. But both sides can share the wealth."

"And if I don't need them, they'll make sure I do?"

"Chin, I'm here to offer you a proposition," I said. "Your new construction is stalled because you need cash to finish it. Any kid just out of school can see that. You've had some union problems, delays in getting materials to the site, maybe your work permits have been a little slow in coming. The people in Las Vegas can take care of all that for you. They can make your construction move along faster."

"My new partners," he said sarcastically.

"Partners can make all the difference," I said. "Besides, look at what you can do for them in Las Vegas. You can get them the acts they need from down here. And you can send them business just like they can send you business."

"Sounds handy."

"It's the way we've been doing business back East since before the war," I said, remembering the way I'd heard Mr. Lansky say it a hundred times before. "If you act like businessmen, you make money like businessmen."

"What's the next step?" he asked.

"You send one of your people back East to work out the details. Someone you trust. That way you keep a safe distance and never have to handle any money," I explained.

"And how to we move the money?" he asked again, now very interested in the details.

"Special bank accounts over in Europe," I said as mysteriously as I could. "That's all I can say about it now. You move money into an account we give you. You pick up money from that account when we tell you. Nobody uses names, only numbers."

"Where do I get the numbers?" he continued, acting like an inscrutable Oriental who trusted only what he knew firsthand.

Now I planted the bait for Kyoshi Moro. "I've brought some cash with me as a . . . a . . ." I paused, letting Li Chin wet his lips over the thought that I had a bag of money for him, that I was really a *gumba* bag man after all. ". . . a kind of deposit. A gesture of friendship between partners. I will give this deposit to the person you designate to make the trip back to New York to work out the details of our partnership."

Li Chin nodded; calculating, I imagined, how much money might be in my bag; calculating how much money he'd need to send back to New York. And I knew that his operation was gobbling up as much cash as he could toss into it. He didn't know a thing about construction. And from the condition of his work site, I could tell that his local contractors were taking him for as much cash as they could sponge up. In New York, we knew how to deal with people like that. They'd become part of the construction site, usually somewhere in the foundation.

"I will introduce you to that person tonight," Li said, pausing again as if he were flipping the pages of a roster through his mind. I was hoping to get a score on the first go 'round. "A Japanese gentleman, older than yourself, who I've known for many years. He has my full confidence and trust."

Bingo! I thought to myself. It could only be Kyoshi Moro. Damn, but the Old Man was right again. Moro was the only person Li trusted, I'd lay odds on it. The telephone rang and Li Chin suddenly got up from the table. I started to get up also.

"Sit and finish up, Mike," he said. "Let me take this phone call while you enjoy the rest of the meal."

He left the room briefly while I tried some of the other dishes on the table. He was back in a few minutes, poured out two cups of Chinese tea, and toasted the future.

"Now indulge your sportsmanship at my tables as my guest. I have some arrangements to make."

And with that he ushered me out of the dining room, closing the door behind me with a hollow thud, before I could even ask him where the crap tables were.

"He there now, boss," Frankie whispered to me just outside of Li Chin's private office. I had waited to follow Li after I left the dining room, but he never came out. Then Frankie caught my eye and motioned me into one of the bathrooms off the casino floor. "We pass in hall. He wait till clear, but I hide. Saw him use key in your door."

"And he hasn't come down yet?" I asked.

"No, boss. No come down. I wait."

"How come you told me and not Li?" I asked again.

"You bigger boss. Li Chin afraid. Not know you. Not saw Li Chin afraid ever. You bigger. I tell you."

"You did the *right* thing, Frankie," I said. "You were smart and you'll get a big reward."

"Mebbe go Vegas. Deal Blackjack?" Frankie said.

"I'll see to that," I told him. "Now come up to the room with me and keep watch while I get rid of him."

Frankie followed me to the elevator, his eyes straight forward as if nothing was wrong. He carefully avoided looking at the desk clerk.

"You plug'em?" Frankie finally asked as we got into the only working elevator and took it up to my floor.

"We'll see," I whispered and waited for the doors to open, revealing an empty hall. There was no one by my room. "You wait here by the elevator," I whispered again. "And watch for my signal. Then you come in a hurry."

"Hokay," he said, bowing emphatically as I left him standing by the elevator while I walked as quietly as possible toward my door.

At first, when I put my ear to the keyhole, the gurgling of the waterfall muffled any other sounds of movement from inside the room. But as I got used to the rhythm of the water, I was able to pick out the thudding of closet doors opening and closing and then the banging of someone working on the lock of my brief case. Somebody was tossing the room, all right, and someone on the inside had given him the key. I assumed that Li Chin had sent him to search my room while I was supposed to be betting at the tables. I also assumed that the person inside wasn't Kyoshi Moro. After all, why would Li Chin play his best card and leave himself no graceful back door in case someone popped his stooge? Which is exactly what I was about to do at that moment.

I waited until, from what I could hear of his footsteps, it sounded as if he'd gone into the bedroom. Then I slid the key into the lock, dropped to my knees, and slipped into the room. I closed the door behind me and crawled behind the couch while the stooge was still trying to open the suitcase on my bed. He had left the bedroom door partially open. From my hiding place, I could just see the side of the man's head reflecting in the wide strip of mirror on the bedroom wall. He was Oriental, bald and shiny as if he'd been oiling his head, and well-tanned. I couldn't see much of his face because he kept his head down as he searched through my clothing. Then he turned his back to me and began going through the chest of drawers by the bed. I stayed low to avoid being seen in the mirror and cakewalked to the edge of the bedroom door. The sound of the water fountain muffled my movements as it had muffled his earlier.

I looked around for a weapon. I wasn't going to stand there and throw punches at this guy because I'd seen too many of those "how to fight a Jap hand to hand" training films in the war. I knew this guy could probably kick my balls in while I was setting up for a left jab. No sir. When he went back into the walk-in bedroom closet to rummage around in my clothes some more, I quickly ran over to the bar, grabbed the heaviest bottle of champagne I could find in a hurry, and crouched back behind the bedroom door.

"Ahh," I heard him say from inside the closet. And then he made a bunch of sounds like he was throwing up his dinner the hard way. I raised the bottle with both hands, stepped through the doorway into bopping range, and as he threw back his head laughing at the cache of money he found in my overnight bag, I kept my eyes open and brought the Dom Perignon down on the top of his head like it was a bright bullseye.

BAM! The bottle exploded like a grenade sending glass in a hundred directions. It bounced off the top of his thick skull like it was made of tank armor, but opened up a small cut in the skin, sending a thin stream of blood down the side of his face. The sonovabitch didn't go down. He spun around, his eyes wide and glassy, waddled from side to side like a walrus as he tried to get into his fighting stance. I uncorked a right uppercut with the full force of my body as he sagged forward, and the Jap sailed back into the closet, still kicking and aiming to get to his feet. It was gonna take another A-bomb to knock this guy out.

I yanked him out of the closet by his feet while he tried to shake himself out of it, sat on his chest, and began unloading rights and lefts to the side of his chin with all my might until his eyes rolled back into their sockets and closed. I slapped his head to the side so he wouldn't choke on his tongue and noticed that blood was filling up the inside of his mouth. Tough shit! He was lucky the bottle hadn't killed him. Then I dragged him by his feet through the living room and out into the hall.

"Hey, Frankie," I whispered. "Help me with this thing."

"Shit, boss," Frankie said as he ran up. "Itsa Hong, Missuh Li's man. You hit'em good, boss. Hong nevuh down. He karate kiruh."

By this time, Hong was starting to kick back at me and he looked like he was gonna be trouble. I looked around for something to hit him with again when Frankie stood over him and made his left hand into a flat-edged shape, almost like a spade with his knuckles pointed at Hong's throat.

"Watch, boss," he said. And as Hong tried to get up, Frankie took a deep breath, screamed, and at the same time shot his left hand straight forward, catching Hong square under the chin, just above the Adam's apple. This time Hong spit up a small volume of blood fell backward and stayed there. "Little lower and I kill," Frankie said, obviously proud of his punch. "I karate man too," he preened. Then he pointed to his head. "All in here, boss," he said. "Not here." And he pointed to the hand that had done the damage. "Speed! Not strength. Pffft!" And he snapped his hand back and forth like it was on a spring. I'd never seen anything like it before.

"Frankie," I said. "You come to New York and I'll make you the next lightweight champ in six months." I figured if I bet the odds just right, I'd also make a killing on the side for his first few fights at least. Then the East Side book would catch on and you wouldn't be able to lay a bet on this guy even for the combination to Fort Knox.

"I join mob?" Frankie asked.

"Yeah," I told him, laughing at the stupid situation I was in, with Li Chin's bodyguard flat on the floor and me promising to get some Hawaiian fighter made. "You can be in the mob. You can live in Vegas and screw Hollywood movie stars." I laughed, even as I tried to figure out what we were going to do with this guy's body before he came around and started to swing like King Kong. "Where can we stash him?" I asked.

"Feight erevatuh," Frankie said. "Take up woof. You know nofing, say nofing." And he took out a thick key from his belt chain and turned it in the lock on one of the elevator doors. Then he pointed at the body bleeding all over the hall carpet. "Hong wake up, he not know own name. You, me in creuh."

When the freight elevator came up and the doors slid open, we dragged Hong inside and Frankie motioned me back into the hall.

"I work for you now, hokay, boss?" He asked.

I dug a C-note out of my pocket and slipped it into his hand.

"You're on the payroll, Frankïe. All the way." I figured I'd be buying Cadillacs by the dozen if I could get him a license to box in New York. I'd even figure out a way to explain him to Mr. C. and the boys on Cherry Street. "I dunno what you got, but when we get back East, you go into training." Frankie flexed his muscles to show me what he had and puffed out his chest. "I take'em outta here, boss," he said, and the elevator doors closed.

I hurried back to my room to check on the dough in my overnight bag, cover up any blood that spilled out of Hong, and put my clothes back in the closet. By the time Li realized that Hong was missing and came puffing up to my room, I had to make it seem as if Hong had just disappeared and I was simply waiting for Li Chin to set up the meeting with Kysohi Moro. Even if Li had his suspicions about what happened, he would never accuse me of flattening his prize goon. Whatever he might think, he couldn't admit to my face that he had ordered the heist. It would be a sign of disrespect to the New York Families.

I repacked the dough in my overnight bag, straightened out the living room, and waited for my host. Within a half hour, I knew my guess was right on the money. Li Chin came knocking at my door, sweaty, the tail of his flashy shirt hanging out over his belt, less confident than he was at dinner, but still as polite as he had to be so I wouldn't get edgy that something was wrong.

"The meeting's all set, Mike," he said, panting as he spoke. I wondered if he was worrying about Hong.

"Yeah?" I said, leading him into the room. "When?"

"Few minutes. We're going to meet outside away from any eyes that might be watching."

"When I talk to your associate, I have to be alone," I told him, making sure that he knew I was not gonna hand over any money in front of him.

"I understand," he said nodding. "I'll leave it all up to you. I want your friends to understand that I have complete trust in the way they do business." And then he added, "I appreciate their offer of good faith. I hope you'll convey to them my appreciation and thanks."

"You can count on it," I assured him, letting him think I didn't notice the difference in the way he was acting.

"You have what you need?" he asked while he motioned me out the door.

"Right here," I said and lifted up my overnight bag without opening it. I could hear him licking the inside of his dry mouth, mentally counting the money he believed was inside. He was so desperate for the cash, he would have had Hong kill me just to make sure he could get his hands on it without giving anything away. I'd get him back for that someday, I promised myself, even though it was hands off for now. Old Man's orders. I stuck the overnight bag under my arm and gripped firmly so that Li would know that I wasn't about to open it in front of him. He either trusted my word or he didn't. "I will arrange with your associate how and where to give him the cash."

Li raised his eyes as if to ask why I wasn't going to hand it over right then and there. I answered his question before he had time to speak. "You have to allow that we have our ways. One of the rules is that I don't hand over any money personally to anybody I don't know. You can understand that. Just leave it to me. Now where can I find Mr. . . .?" I paused, giving him ample time to answer. "Your associate?"

"If you follow me to the front entrance, I will point you in the right direction," he said, not taking the bait. "That is, unless you want me to show you the meeting place myself."

"How will I recognize him?" I asked.

"He'll find you, Mike. I already told him how to recognize you."

I threw on a jacket and followed Li Chin out of the suite and down the elevator to the front entrance. Most of the guests were outside or on their terraces, leaving the lobby strangely empty for a resort. We stood in the doorway looking into the darkness.

"As you can see," Li said, once more acting like a tour guide, "we haven't completed the outside lighting yet except for a few areas."

The moon was bright and I could see well into the trees surrounding the resort even though there were only a few lights. Li was pointing toward a dense section of trees near where the pool was being completed.

"Walk in that direction," he said. "He will introduce himself." And I followed his hand into the darkness. Once through the glass doors, I was hit in the face again with the real temperature of the outside world. Only by now it had gotten much cooler, almost chilly, because it was so damp. I was glad I was wearing my jacket. I was also glad that my jacket had my .38 snubbed-nose Police Special and twelve extra rounds in an inside zippered pocket. I headed toward the dense section of trees at the edge of the resort clearing that Li had pointed out from inside the lobby. As usual, I was improvising this operation until I knew for sure that I was dealing with Moro. Then I would know what to do.

"Pssssst!" The hiss, cutting through the sound of breaking ocean waves, was clearly human, not the insect hissing that is a constant background sound in Hawaii. At first I didn't know where it was coming from.

"Pssssst!" It started up again, only this time from a different direction. I looked around and slid my hand into my jacket to unzip the inside pocket. I figured if Hong was hiding behind one of those trees, I'd plug him first and answer Li's questions later.

"Milan!"

I was no expert, but I had ears. And the English sounded too educated to be Hong's, even though I had only heard him grunt a few times while Frankie beat the shit out of him. I flipped the safety off on the .38 just in case, but left the hammer down. I didn't care who I was facing—I could get off three shots and put one of the rounds in between the guy's balls even if I had to blow holes in my best golf jacket to do it.

"Just keep your hands where I can see them!" The voice commanded. I froze and took my hand out of my jacket. I would wait for my chance once I saw what he was pointing at me.

"Now, without turning around, drop that bag to the ground and kick it in front of you."

I kept the bag exactly where it was. I barely breathed.

"You hear me?" The voice said.

"You want the bag, you drop me here," I said, playing out a bluff. "But you'd better know that what's gonna come down here after you won't be worth twice what's in this bag."

I heard the loud cock of a hammer on a large-bore heater. Its click drowned out the ocean like the sound of a deadly animal.

"You can cock that thing a hundred times," I called out. "But I ain't lettin' go of this bag. And after I'm planted, you and whoever you're workin' for better find a hole and crawl into it. Because sure as shit, the guys who come down here after me ain't gonna let you get away with just a bullet through your eye."

The hammer released. I could hear the springs groan as the tension was relaxed.

"You got balls, son," the voice said. "Big ones, too."

I exhaled, finally.

"Just had to make sure what they were sending down. I ain't getting into a deal with a Family that sends down a pussy to do a man's job."

"I'm gonna turn around now," I said. "And I hope for your sake I don't see no gun."

I turned in the direction of the voice and saw an outline of a short, thin, bald man. He looked old and sinewy, but he carried authority on him like a cape.

"Am I supposed to know who you are?" I asked.

"I'm Kyoshi Moro," he said in a voice heavy with sarcasm. "Your evening appointment. You were told to expect me."

I could see that Moro had put his gun away. Whatever chance I had taken, it had worked, and he seemed convinced that I was on the level.

I looked at him as closely as the light would allow. He was a slight man standing in the moonlight like the fading image on a yellow tintype. He was as bald as the Man in the Moon and his head shone in the dim glow that was filtering through the trees. He was smiling at me through a set of white teeth that I knew were false because they were too even, too perfect. It looked like he could use them as weapons when he had to.

"See, Milan, I put my gun away like you wanted," he said. "We can be colleagues. Work for same boss."

I didn't answer him right away, nor did I move any closer.

"Li Chin tells me to pack some dough and get ready for a trip to Vegas," Moro continued. "He tells me that we have to work out the details."

I looked at Moro's face as closely as I dared without setting him off, taking a snapshot of it for my own mind. He didn't look like a flat-faced Japanese soldier at all. His eyes were too round and his nose was too straight and long. He looked almost European. I guess I stared too long and hard because he suddenly became aware that I was up to something.

"What you lookin' at, boy?" he said with an instant tone of command that almost had me apologizing like he was brass or something. "See something you don't like?"

It took me a minute to get myself out of the Navy and back to the present.

"Just that you don't look Japanese at all," I said before I caught myself. I tried not to make a face, or at least not one he could see in the moonlight.

"Who told you I was Japanese?" he shot back.

Too late! This guy was not stupid. Now I had to come up with an answer or blow his brains out right there and then.

"You have an accent," I said. "Your name is Japanese. You don't spend time in the Pacific like I did without knowing what a Jap sounds like." I hoped I'd sounded nasty and stupid enough to make him mad. That would keep him from thinking—which is what he'd started to do—and allow me to play out my hand.

"Fought the Japs in the war?" He asked with an edge of bitterness in his voice.

"*Killed* Japs in the war," I added, hoping that it would make him mad enough to forget worrying about why I'd assumed he was a Jap without anybody's telling me.

Kyoshi Moro sucked in his breath. He was holding his temper. Maybe he was measuring me for a bullet. But what I'd said was making his brain smoke for the time being, and that was good. Then he smiled his tiger's smile. "War's over," he said with a forced assurance of authority. "Now we do business."

Not for you, Moro, I told myself. "Down to business," I said.

"Mr. Li says you have specific instructions for me?" Moro began again in a businesslike tone of voice.

"That's right." I assumed the same tone. "Tomorrow night, you will find an address and the name of a contact who will be expecting a message from you in the next few days. You're to arrange a meeting with him in New York. He'll give you an introduction to one of his associates in Las Vegas. You will fly to Las Vegas to meet him. If your meetings are successful, the people you work for and the people I work for will be partners."

"It's as simple as that?" he asked.

"Simple as that!"

"You have nothing else for me?"

"No," I said, and let my answer hang in the night air. "You will find everything you need, including what Mr. Li and I talked about, when you make your pickup. Make plans to leave for New York immediately and bring along a suitable show of good faith for your new partners. That will be up to Mr. Li."

"You and I will meet again?" Moro asked.

"No," I repeated. "I'm just the messenger. You will deal with whoever you deal with. Tomorrow you will find a message telling you where the pickup will be. Everything will be explained in the information you will find. There will be no further conversations. If you follow your instructions, the deal will be made. If the instructions are not followed, then it will be up to Mr. Li to do whatever he does."

I could see Moro smiling. "You are as inscrutable as an Asian in the way you do business, Mr. Milan," he said. "I mean that as a compliment. Your people have done well to choose you to carry their messages."

I looked over at the edge of the clearing to plan my route back to the hotel. I wanted to get out of this meeting without Moro taking any shots at my back.

"Thank you," I said. "I compliment Mr. Li on his choice of trusted associates." Moro bowed his head ever so slightly, acknowledging my sign of respect. "You will understand," I continued. "That you will have to leave this meeting place first, and I will follow."

"Just as you say," he whispered, fading into the darkness.

I stood back out of the light so that Moro wouldn't have a target if he decided to try his luck from behind the trees. I took out my own .38, and waited until I could no longer hear the sounds of his footsteps. Then I dropped into a crouch so I would be hidden beneath the shadows of the tall bushes and slithered my way back to the hotel clearing. I didn't like being this exposed to a target, especially when that target was a POW commandant who'd caused the deaths of thousands of GIs and nurses. The guy had a streak of cruelty that ran through him deeper and wider than any old Sicilian Moustache Pete who'd cut the throat of his own cousin during the Castellemare Wars. I always told myself that I never really enjoyed hitting a guy—it was always business only—but now I was going to double enjoy hitting Moro.

When I got back to the lobby, I asked around the bellstand for Frankie. I didn't want to make anybody suspicious enough to go running for Li Chin, but I wanted to keep Frankie handy. I also needed to know where he had stashed Hong because having Hong sneak up behind me was one surprise I didn't need during the next day. I figured I'd see how much I was worrying about it. If I was worrying to much, I'd hit him before I hit Moro. Then I'd be leaving two presents for Li Chin and the Old Man wouldn't mind that at all.

I caught up with Frankie pumping slots in the casino where I couldn't help but see right away he was losing everything he'd made the day before. I slipped an eagle into his pocket and leaned over next to his ear.

"Play through what I put in your pocket and pay me a visit in my room," I whispered. "We got to make some plans."

"You bet, boss," he said as his face split into a toothy grin. "What if I keep on winning?"

"Don't worry," I told him. "Chances are these slots are as weighted as the dice Li Chin's dealers are givin' to the shooters. But you be at my room in a half an hour."

I took the elevator up to my room where I began preparing the bag of money for my trap. When you set traps like this, where you want your mark to spend his time counting money instead of worrying about the gun that's about to go off next to his head, the trick is not to go light on the dough. Stuff the goddamn bag full of money so that it pours out like butter out of a roasted chicken the minute you punch it open. I can't tell you how many people who baited traps with newspaper shavings or betting slips instead of the real thing wound up getting plugged by their own marks in the end. By the time they tried to get the drop on their marks, the marks were so mad they didn't care if there was a bazooka between their eyes. They chewed the nozzles off the guns and stuffed the barrels up the asses of the people who were holding them. Never stiff your mark. Give 'em more dough than he expects, then shoot 'em through the eyes. You get the dough back anyway in the end.

I changed bags so the stash of loot was nice and full by the time Frankie rapped on the door. And after saying ten times, "You right, boss," about how much money he had just lost, he was able to tell me about some of the most isolated spots around the hotel. So for the next couple of hours, he drew me a bunch of maps of different locations and approximate distances, places where I could set up a drop and be sure of getting under cover there well before Kyoshi Moro showed up to get the dough. I finally settled on an old swamp that Frankie was hot about. "I swear it, boss, Mr. Li don't even know the place is there. Me and only one other guy sneak out there and smoke up Mary Jane." If I thought Frankie seemed a little strange, now I guessed why.

"You can show me how to get there so I won't get lost?" I asked.

"I take you there," he said. "I'm in a gang, right?"

"You in a gang, wrong," I said. "You take me there and hightail it out before there's any trouble. I don't want you gettin' hurt before you climb in the ring." I very much didn't want Frankie finding out who I was when I extracted Moro's final confession 'cause then I'd have to hit Frankie as well. And I had big plans for him in New York.

"But, boss, look at how I take care of Hong."

"Yeah, you did a good job," I conceded. "But this is different. If things get outta hand, there may be some shooting. Don't worry, I'll take care of myself."

"What you say, boss," Frankie said, nodding his head and wearing his smiling mask. "What time I meet?"

"You be here after midnight," I told him. "You'll lead me to the swamp and wait for me to get back after sunrise. Then we'll both be on the morning flight to Honolulu. And remember—you don't talk to nobody about this. As far as anybody's concerned, you're workin' here the rest of your life. Send'em a postcard from Vegas when you're the lightweight champ."

I just about had to push Frankie out the door so I could get to bed. I figured if Li Chin was as smart as he was supposed to be, he'd be keeping an eye on Frankie and assume that wherever he went, I'd be there as well. So I planned to be as visible as I could be tomorrow until it was time to set the trap. Then I'd give Moro very little warning before the meeting. The less time they had to think about staging an ambush to steal the money, the better my chances were of pulling it off.

You can never count on the honesty of the other side when you're this close to the edge. And this was Hawaii, the wild frontier of organized gambling where all kinds of crazy-looking Island people, Japanese, and Chinese were scrambling for the bucks that were falling out of the American tourists' pockets. There would be no formal agreements among the syndicates down here. The rule would be take: take first, and take as much as you can before the other guy took from you. And I was there for a hit, walking into a shootout with a war criminal that our own CIA had set up to run his private operation. Anything was possible.

Sayonara Colonel Moro

I wanted to be as conspicuous as possible the following day. I showed myself around the casino after breakfast, talking to the dealers and watching them set up for the lunchtime gamblers. Then I hung around the pool all morning looking like one of the tourists and acting like the old men at the cabana clubs on Atlantic Beach who fried themselves in the sun all day and then complained that it was too hot to breathe. I had to let Li Chin see that for me it was business as usual, nothing that would set anyone on edge— just another day as far as I was concerned. I could feel the heat of his eyeballs on the back of my neck, magnified a hundred times by the lenses in his thick glasses like he was a Boy Scout starting a fire by focusing the rays of the sun. But I played it like I was on vacation and not afraid of anything 'cause I wasn't doing anything wrong.

I could see Frankie from time to time watching me, making sure that none of Li's gorillas were following too close behind. That was my only worry—that Li would be stupid enough to send a tough message to the boys in New York by knocking me off and letting them know it. But Sometimes you got to take that risk because you know if somebody knocks you off, the next guy from your side will take extra special care to pay him back in spades. Besides, I figured that the quiet beating we gave to Hong would convince Li that we were on the level and wanted this deal to happen.

I didn't see Moro at all during the day even though I knew in my gut that he was keeping an eye on me as well. If I had been in his shoes, I would've been peeking out from behind every tree trunk in order to keep my nighttime appointment in my sights. And the first time the guy crossed his eyes funny, I would put the bag on him and sweat out his story. But since I knew what Moro would be worrying about, I acted like a kid on the first day of summer vacation.

I enjoyed myself at lunch. I knew that because I'd be making all my moves right after dinner, I wouldn't be able to load up on the free eats. Too much food makes you slow—that's why fat guys make lousy contractors—so you eat light before a hit. Also, if you're nice and hungry, you have an edge and a bad temper that can keep you from making a fat man's mistakes. So I ate Li Chin's chicken and pineapples, which I was developing a taste for, and pressed duck with little fruit slices and anything else that didn't remind me of dead porkers. And then I lounged around the pool in the early afternoon sun.

I could tell that people were beginning to get nervous around me because of the number of times Frankie passed by and paused in front of me just long enough to block the sun. Like he thought I was lying down on the job or something or that I was really a lazy slob underneath it all, and it was gonna take a punk like Frankie to kick my *tuchas* out of the foxhole. He was like a fucking baby, standing there in the light and throwing his shadow in exactly the right spot so that even with my eyes closed I could see the changing colors on the inside of my eyelids. But he wouldn't say nothing. He only stood there, looked at me like he wanted his week's allowance, and then he moved on. And if he was making me nervous, think of how nervous he must have been making Li Chin.

Finally it got to be too much, and the next time he went to the bar, I got up and followed him. As he passed by one of the potted palms on the way back to the pool deck, I grabbed him by the elbow and motioned him out of sight.

"Are you crazy?" I hissed. "Don't you know that half the world is watching me right now? And they've seen you pose in front of me like you were a broad waiting to get discovered for the movies?"

"But boss, I got to tell you," Frankie said. "I hear Mr. Li tell Hong follow you all day. What I do?"

The kid had good ears.

"Where's Hong now?"

"He watch you from casino. Now, I figure, he come this way look for you in pool."

"Is he gonna try anything?" I asked again, now getting worried that I'd have to plug Hong before I plugged Moro and give away the whole game.

"Naw, he just a lookout. Mebbe he follow you to Moro. Keep it even-Steven," Frankie answered.

More than likely, I thought to myself, Li was doubling down on his bet by protecting Moro and whacking me for good measure. Either way, Hong would have to go.

"You keep your eye on Hong," I told Frankie. "And if he looks like he's gonna make a move on me or my room again, get to me before he goes anywhere."

"Hokay, boss," Frankie said, darting away towards the bartender who was looking around frantically for him.

"But whatever you do, don't get in his way," I warned him. Frankie shot me back a worried look. "Don't let on that you are in on this. Stay out of sight and tell me everything Hong does."

"When we hit'em?" Frankie asked, wide-eyed with excitement.

"I'll tell you when," I said. "Until then, don't even think about it."

Frankie disappeared into the guests around the pool and made his way back to the bar as if he had been doing his job all along. I could see the bartender shake his fist in the kid's face, yelling at him for oogling the girls or hustling tips from the guests. But Frankie kept his head and didn't even look back at me over his shoulder. I tried to pick Hong out of the hundreds of faces around me, but either he was well concealed or he just knew how to blend in. And to tell you the truth, I wouldn't have known what to do had I found Hong. In all likelihood, I would have begun to act differently and possibly tipped my hand that someone had slipped me the info. Then Frankie's neck would have been in the noose. I still had an excuse—Hong tossed my room and I flattened him. If Li Chin wanted a deal with the boys in Vegas, he would have had to eat the insult and do business as usual. Frankie would have simply disappeared. Maybe his ear would turn up in my luggage as I was packing to leave, a warning from Li Chin never to cross him again or it would be my ear in an envelope addressed to Mr. Lansky. So even though I knew that Hong was watching me, I didn't try to watch him back.

I decided to give Hong an easy afternoon, all the while making it easier on myself. I ordered a few drinks at the pool bar and tipped the boys extra heavy. That made them stumble over each other to get to me first each time I put down my drink.

"Refresh that for you, sir?

"Need some more ice, Mr. Milan?"

"Ready for another round?"

All this must have caused a ripple or two of noise as far back as Li Chin's office. When I was sure I'd stirred them up enough to let Li Chin know I wanted him to keep me in sight, I left the pool and played the slots for an hour or so. Again I stayed in full view, ordering drinks and leaving them at the gambling tables so the cocktail waitresses had to run after me with single drinks on their trays. During this whole performance, I made it a point to pay my respects to Li Chin, acting as if I were a tourist and going out of my way to treat Li like the most important man on the island. I wasn't afraid of Hong trying to hit me, and I had Frankie watching just in case Hong tried to toss my room again. I felt that my bets were faded for the time being.

I even made it obvious when I went to get the elevator back up to my room, announcing it to one of the bellcaps in an especially loud voice while Hong was sitting in the lobby. I double-bolted the door so that I'd hear it if anyone was fiddling with the lock, then waited for a couple of hours with my feet up on the couch to give Li and his boys time to think I was setting up an elaborate message.

It was still before dinner and very light out when I called the bellstand to ask for Frankie to come up and help me pack my suitcases. The bell captain was frantic at first. "Frankie not here," he kept on screaming into the phone.

"It's OK," I told him. "I can wait. Just send him up when he gets back. I'll postpone whatever I have to do to wait for him."

This made the bell captain even crazier. "Postpone? No, no. I find Frankie. Send him up right away."

It was almost as if the entire staff of the hotel was in on this, just waiting for me to make the drop for Moro so their boss could get them all jobs in Vegas. I realized I could use that to my advantage also. When Frankie finally showed up, I asked him to draw me a map of some of the best and most private spots for the drop, spots far enough away that nobody could hear the gunshot and where Hong could be safely planted for a lifetime without anyone ever finding his body again. I gave Frankie a piece of hotel letter stationery and he pulled a pencil out of his pocket and began scribbling like an accountant, marking trees, rocks, shrubs, and every landmark that he could think of.

"You sure I can find this place?" I asked Frankie when he'd finished the map.

"Sure, boss, it easy," he said, laughing. "It close by. Maybe I follow."

"That's what I want you to do," I told him. "I'll find the place all right, but Hong will also follow me so I want you to wait until Hong starts out first and follow him. In case he tries any funny business, I want you behind him. Make sure he sees where I went and then follow him back to Li Chin where he'll report the meeting place. I'll leave a different meeting place for Moro at the last minute. I want to make sure I'm alone with him."

"So you want another place?" Frankie asked, now confused.

"Do you know of one where if a guy screamed bloody murder no one would hear him?"

"Know of swamp near here—people got lost and never seen again," he answered. "Place I gotta take you to. You no find."

"I'll need a long head start tonight. Can you get one of the other bellboys to deliver an envelope with the map to Li Chin after we've left? And can you get back here fast so Moro doesn't see you?" I asked.

"What about Li Chin, boss?" he asked. "Moro don't turn up in the morning, he gonna wanna know."

"Li Chin and I will have an understanding before I leave," I told him. "He'll know what he has to know and he's not gonna ask any more questions."

"Ain't Hong gonna be mad?" Frankie asked, trying to puzzle through all of the players.

"Hong ain't gonna be around," I said. "That's why I want you to tell me where I can find him when I get back. Then you wait for me and we'll get right out to the swamp. Then you disappear. You don't know nothing. Just be on the plane with me tomorrow morning."

"When you wanna start, boss?" he asked, excited that it would all be over in a night.

"Now," I told him. "Before anyone notices you're gone. Can you get outta your monkey suit and disappear quick?"

"Where I find you?" he asked, not wanting to lose sight of me for a minute.

"You find Hong," I said. Then I looked at the map he'd just drawn, and told myself that by following his landmarks, the site should be a snap to find. The only trick was faking Hong into thinking I was scouting locations so I could set up the meeting for later. "Keep your eyes on Hong without anybody seeing you. Follow him after he follows me. Make sure he gets back to Li Chin and reports the location. Then tell me where I can find him. Then you get back up here and wait for me."

"Hokay, boss. I go."

Finally, I was alone. First I memorized the map the way I'd been taught in Navy survival school, mentally orienting myself in the right directions and walking off the path. Then, when I thought I was sure of where I was going, I collected my bag. I puffed up the money that was inside so the bag would look full to overflowing. I screwed the silencer on my .38 and stuffed it in my belt so that no one would know I was packing unless they patted me down. Finally, I strapped my bone-cutting knife to my ankle as a piece of extra protection in close quarters. Then I caught the elevator to the lobby.

I picked up the reflection of Hong's bald head in the mirror, even though I couldn't see his face. The man was not the inconspicuous stranger that most secret agents were supposed to be, but I supposed that Li Chin already knew that and had pressed Hong into service at the last minute. After all, I was sure he was thinking, what did the hebes and dagos out of Vegas know about secret operations? After tonight, Li Chin would realize a lot more about who he was dealing with.

I stood there in front of the elevator doors, pretending I was trying to figure out where I was going, just to give Hong a chance to pick me up. When I saw his head jerk up, I made a beeline for the rear doors of the lobby. I thought I could see a dumb smile cross his fat face, as if he was telling himself that he had me figured out and now he would have me for a midnight snack, but he ducked behind a group of guests as I passed. Then, once outside, I darted behind some bushes where I could see Hong follow me.

Frankie had laid out his landmarks with greater care than I had expected, and I found the crisscrossing paths he had sketched on the paper even before I came to the turnoffs. If I stopped real quick and held my breath, I was able to hear the sound of Hong's last footstep before he, too, stopped and listened. And I figured that because the bushes and trees were so thick, Hong was having trouble keeping me in sight. He probably planned to wait until I stopped and then come up slow. I was hoping that Frankie was having better luck and that he was in a knife's throw of Hong's fat back.

As the bushes got thicker, it became tougher going. I found myself having to slow down and examine the ground carefully before cutting off in a new direction. And then, before I even realized it, I pushed my way into a very small clearing. It was exactly as Frankie had described it: invisible until you were in it. And once you were in it, you could sense the movement all around you. That was how I figured out where Hong was before he could see me. I could also hear him swishing the underbrush. I got behind the nearest rock I could find and started digging, looking over my shoulder whenever I got the chance to see if Li Chin's *shtarke* was fixing to jump me. When I was convinced he was just angling for a better view—simply to tell Li that he'd seen me drop the bag—then I relaxed a little bit, knowing that he would try to get back to the hotel before me so that they could make their next moves. I was even figuring the angles they could play depending upon how much trouble they were preparing to get into. None of the options were pretty from my end of the barrel. But I planted the bag like I said I would and waited until I heard the sounds of movement recede into the underbrush. Then I heard Frankie's hiss.

"Boss, it's hokay, it's me."

I looked up to see Frankie peering out from a clump of tall grass. He was holding his finger to his lips as if urging me to whisper like him.

"You're supposed to be following Hong," I whispered back.

"No worry, boss," he said. "Hong like tank. I circle around him as he go by. Pick him up at hotel and stay out of sight. You go back now like nuthin' happened." Then he winked like a Chinese waiter in an old movie. "This gettin' good, boss." And he disappeared again into the dark green grass and the thorny underbrush.

I was suddenly aware of the roaring ocean. The crash of breaking waves was always in the background on Hilo, but now that I was alone, the noise became almost deafening. And the sun, which had been shining most of the day, was covered by rain clouds and the sky had become gray and misty. I checked the money bag one last time, making sure that it was only partially concealed by a big rock. Let whoever found it enjoy the paper. I scanned around the clearing one last time, making sure that I was really alone and catching my breath for the last run back to the hotel and my visit to Hong.

The light was slipping away fast now. As it was, there was hardly any dusk on Hilo—just bright daylight, fifteen minutes of evening, and then the darkest night anybody ever saw. And because the sun had already begun to dip, I gave myself ten minutes to get back to the hotel. I plunged into the bushes and bunches of kiawe trees, feeling more than seeing my way back to the hotel and trying to steer clear of the rough bark and the clumps of thorns on the ground at the same time. The more sure of the way I was, the faster I ran, racing the darkness that was now advancing in long shadows that made the terrain look like a scene out of a 1930s' grade-B black-and-white western.

I was trying to avoid the larger rocks near the path when suddenly I dodged into a rock that appeared out out of nowhere, caught my foot into a crevice, and pitched headfirst into a clump of sharp kiawe thorns that tore into my palms. I shook my head to clear it from the shock. My foot was stuck. At first I thought I had wedged it into a groove in the rock. But when I began to tug on it, it felt like there were sharp teeth biting into my ankle. And it was hurting more the harder I tried to pull it out. There was blood all over the ground, saturating into the lava topsoil and penetrating through my clothing. An animal? I kicked myself around to see how I was caught and, screaming out even before I knew what I was doing, found myself looking directly into Frankie's eyes. They were open, but without pain: the flat eyes of death staring directly into mine, accusing me with their gaze and at the same time making a kind of complaint: "I had the promise of a long life before I met you. Now I'm only one of the dead bodies you've left behind."

It was as if Frankie had joined the growing brotherhood of people who'd crossed my path. And now he was sitting on a jury waiting for me at the other side of the grave. I felt a chill go all the way through me like a knife blade of ice, and I shivered uncontrollably. But within seconds, another thought came pushing through the remorse that was welling up inside. And it tolled my immediate fate more than the death stare from Frankie's head. Hong. Hong knew. I had to get to Hong. I shook off the ice and slid my *tusch* through the blood up to the head where I gently tried to extract my ankle from Hong's little surprise. The trap of thorns and vines alongside Frankie's severed head had been set well because the more I tried to free it, the more impossible it was. It looked like Hong had hoped I would try to yank my foot out and tear most of the skin off in the process. Instead, I worked my fingers into the knotted vines and pried them apart. Then I pulled out my ankle, which I hadn't broken or sprained from the impact. That's when I heard the footfalls over the sound of the ocean and looked up into the two jagged rows of Hong's yellow ripsaw teeth.

He was leering down at me, half in hate, half in the grin of an animal tearing into its prey. His was the face of fear that stares you down. The face in your nightmares. The face you see in the half darkness by the window when you wake up in the middle of the night after rubbing out some poor, hopeless *schlemiel* for ratting a Seventh Avenue shylock out to the cops. It was my fear. And years later my friend and associate Cus D'Amato would tell me how to live with that fear. But in Hilo that night Cus was a lifetime away.

I didn't even have time to shit down my leg because, quick as the lash of a whip, Hong's hand snapped out in a flat blow to my face. Only my own prize-fighter's speed kept my head from coming off as I flicked my head to the side, rolled away, and picked off his chop with my left forearm. There was no pain from the blow, just the instant shock that left my entire arm without feeling. I kept spinning away from the advancing Hong, scraping my ass along the patches of the goddamn kiawe thorns that fall in thickets all over Hilo. My left arm was still hanging and I couldn't use it to keep him off me with jabs, so I snapped my right hand into the flat underside of his nose as he tried to butt me with his head. I felt the cartilage cave in as he screamed, and blood rushed over his mouth in torrents. He stepped back to recompose himself before his next attack, but by that time I'd grabbed a handful of thorny dirt off the ground and pushed it into his eyes. The sonovabitch didn't give up, though—he could barely see—but still he whipped out another chop that just about sheared off my ear as I ducked under the blow. He brought his knee up instantly and caught me a glancing shot off the side of my chest. I ooffed as I rolled off his thigh and kept on rolling before he could bring his other foot down.

No more games! I saw him reach for a weapon in his belt and knew that I was out of time. I feinted left and ducked right and dug into the back of my pants for my .38 as a spinning blade whirred just overhead, taking a piece of my scalp with it. My whole head was burning. I pulled on the handle of my gun and almost ripped off my pants as the silencer caught on the belt loops. I didn't give a fuck. Feeling was coming back to my left arm, and I cocked the hammer and aimed, firing off three rounds into Hong's midsection from a crouch while he tried to flip his next blade at my neck. The blade spun off his hand and into the air above his head as Hong was whirled backwards by the exploding soft lead dum-dum heads I had loaded. He hit the rough ground with a hard thud face down and kicking, trying to scramble out of the spreading pool of blood. He rolled over onto his ass and struggled on one arm to get up while his other hand cocked the kind of razor-blade sharp throwing disk I had seen the gook officers use in the Navy training films during the war. I fired automatically, putting my next two rounds right into his mouth and splattering his brains out the back of his head across the dried lava patches on the ground. Hong stopped moving. His eyes had burst out from the force of the bullets and the cavities were filling with blood. More blood bubbled out of his open mouth like water from a busted underground main and collected into pools around the base of his head.

I got out of my crouch and reloaded the gun, putting the spent rounds I took out of the barrel into my pants pocket. The burned powder coated my hands like an invisible paste that I automatically tried to wipe off even though I knew it would be clinging to my skin for the next week. The sound of the ocean waves breaking on the beach rose around me again and it helped me to bring me back to the immediate reality I was facing.

Frankie was dead. There was nothing I could do for him now. I didn't even know where the rest of his body was, but that was Li

Chin's problem, not mine. Fat Hong was also lying there in a lake of his own brains and blood. Li Chin would no doubt take care of him as well. I still had to hit Kyoshi Moro and fly the hell out of Hilo on the morning plane before Li Chin planted me. And it was as dark as pitch out here with not even a moon to show me the way back to the resort. I shoved my gun back into my pants and tried to orient myself on the map Frankie had drawn. I had a momentary thought that it might be better for me to hole up until first light and then make it back to the hotel, but the sight of Li Chin's gunsels waiting for me all along the dark paths in the woods make me think better of it. Then I realized that if I could follow the sound of waves toward the ocean, I might be able to pick my way back along the landmarks that I remembered from my plane flight two days before. It was a longshot, but the only shot I had. It would also give me a chance to think of what I was going to do about the story I was gonna have to come up with for Li Chin. If you want to know the truth, I was figuring on blaming the whole thing on Frankie. Dead men take the rap good, Tommy Lucchese once told me as the cops picked him up on a some bum homicide roust they were trying to hang him on.

"Out late, Mr. Milan?" a voice I knew all too well called out from behind me. "You don't think that only Mr. Hong was interested in your whereabouts today, do you?"

I didn't say a word. I let him talk into the dark, since it was clear he was enjoying the sound of his voice and the taste of victory.

"Or that Frankie was your loyal Number One Son, hey boss?" And he laughed at the joke of what he was saying.

I wanted to know more. I wanted to keep him talking because I figured that I'd find a way to get the drop on him again if only he was thinking more about what he was saying than about what he was supposed to be doing.

"You must be too stupid to understand," he continued.

I bit my tongue to keep from mouthing off.

"You thought that by handing Frankie a couple of bucks, you could buy whatever you wanted. You never figured he might be working for us. Jews only understand money," he said, almost to himself. "That's their biggest problem. But that's nothing you're gonna have to worry about after tonight. You're gonna tell me who you're really working for just so that you can die faster."

"You're getting to be a real nagging habit," I said reaching for my gun while a new wave of fear gripped at my throat.

"If I even think your hands are moving, I'll blow your head off," the voice said. "Just keep telling me who sent you down here."

Just because I got a pretty face doesn't mean I'm stupid. I figured for sure if it was so dark that I couldn't see my own hands, neither could Kyoshi Moro. But he thought I was just another slob kike working for an even dumber bunch of guinea heads.

"I don't hear any talking, Milan," Moro said again, only this time his voice sounded a little shaky, like maybe he thought I was too stupid even to fall for for what he was doing.

"Huh?" I said. Long pause while he moved around in the dark and I got into a low crouch and slowly took out my gun.

"Milan," he screamed, his voice getting louder and more frustrated while I pinpointed what I figured to be where he was standing. "You start talking *now* or you're a dead man!"

I fired a shot into the darkness and dived left and straight for the ground. Moro fired three shots, all of which hit the dirt behind me, and I fired back directly at the last flash. Even over the ocean I heard the unmistakable loud thud of a hollow headed round tearing through fabric and skin. And then I heard the crunching of a body hitting the ground.

"Fuck," Moro cried and fired another two shots at my flash, but I had already moved and froze in the new spot. Now there was only silence, the silence of the washing of the ocean and the nighttime fragrance of seaspray. I couldn't even hear his breathing.

I figured he was still laying down flat on the ground because of where his last shot came from. The muzzle flash was low and the angle of the shot was sharply up because the round hit the tree bark way above my head. So I waited. Waited until I could hear him move. Waited until he breathed too loud. Waited while I prayed that he was bleeding his life away into the lava-hardened ground. Waited to see who's courage would hold, who could stare into the blackness without flinching and without running away. Like two enemy subs running silent beneath the surface, circling for the best angle of attack, their sonarmen straining at their earphones for the single sound that will reveal the other's location in the blind darkness, Moro and I simply waited each other out.

When the roar from the waves subsided every now and then, I listened as closely as I could for the slightest rustle along the ground that would reveal that Moro was moving. And I was staking my life on my gut feeling that he was doing the same. So I moved nothing. But as the night wore on and the tiny sliver of a moon worked its way higher in the sky, I also realized that I had to finish Moro before Li Chin and his boys came looking for him. If Frankie was really working for the other side—and I intended to make sure of that before I put the final round into Moro's eye—then Li Chin had a surer hand than I realized. He probably had button men watching button men and trusted no one besides himself. People like that only thought they could stay alive longer. In the end, it was just the same no matter who you trusted or didn't trust. Some guy hunched over a push broom and emptying spit buckets who looked like he'd taken too many punches to the head in late rounds always wound up the hitter as you turned the key in the third lock early Sunday morning after counting Saturday's take. And you'd made the same stupid expression as you looked at the guy behind the flash of the gun and realized that he was the one person you never thought about, ever. And he'd look at you with the same stupid expression he used every day when you pushed him and his broom out of your way. And you'd think, right before your knees gave way into jelly and you fell head-first down the flight of stairs: who was stupider? What a fucking waste of a last thought.

My mind was drifting. The sound of waves, maybe because it was so rhythmic, was becoming like a lullaby and I was beginning to see things in the darkness. When I blinked my eyes and focused them again, the things went away and I was staring into an empty space. But somewhere out there Moro was also waiting, biding his time, hoping he could catch the first little bits of daylight before I did and plug me so he could crawl back to Li Chin before he bled to death. Or maybe he would become desperate, which is what I hoped, and take his his last chance on one roll at the crap table. But nothing happened and I waited and drifted, drifted and waited.

I was in New York, down near Greenwich Village with two Japanese sailors from the Quanset Point Naval Air Station. They got pissed off whenever anybody called them Japs. They were Americans. Just like the Rhode Island dagos, they said, who loaded the scrap fish heads off the boats at the wharf for Friday night's stew. But Roscoe McFall had sent me up there because he was worried about a leak. The Japs had been squawking over their boxes for months about the plans for the new Hellcat torpedo sight. Now McFall was tracking'em down. I'd liquored these Japs up good at one of the downtown jazz clubs run by Good People and promised them a night with a pair of Lucky's broads. They told me how I could make some easy dough. I worked in the ordinance filing section, didn't I? they had asked. The warrant officers let me come and go as I pleased. No special passes for me 'cause I was a PC. Had I ever seen one of them little Jap cameras? Fit one in your palm and nobody'd ever know you were carrying it. Just a few clicks over some plans and I'd make myself a quick couple of grand. Everybody knew the Japs would lose the war anyway, so who cared? Dough was dough right? Hey, I say, that's Jake with me.

Look, Mac, they say. Have some dough right now. We pay cash. And they fold me a wad of bills right into my hand under the table. Don't count it, Mac. Plenty more where that's from. Plenty! Hey this ain't rotgut we're drinkin'. It's the good stuff. You know how to show some guys a good time, Mac. Where're the broads? You got broads? Sure—I got plenty broads. You want'em blonde, red-heads, dagos, coon pussy. I got what you want, clean broads. Used to work for Mr. Lucky Luciano, but now he's in the joint. I got an in with the guy what runs'em now. Thinks I'm aces. You boys wait here. I'll set us up with the broads. Take you outside. Wait. So we're in the alley and they say, hey, Mac, where's the broads? Why we out here? Cops, I say. The heat. You want Shore Patrol pickin' us up? Gotta do this my way or we're all in the brig. Sure, Jake, you're aces. Whatever you say. Want some dough? We got plenty. You boys head down the alley. Broads are waitin' for you. This way, Jake? Yeah, right past those garbage cans. See over there. Say, what the fuck, Jake, put it away. Jake, this a heist? You can have it, Jake. Take it all, just ease off the hammer. Jake, you dago hood, put away the rod, we're all aces. Say good-bye to the Emperor, boys. Two rounds and they're rolling in the garbage. Then two more rounds apiece. Right in the temples. Can't hear a thing. Just the music and pop, pop! And there's blood all over my shoes. Can't even stand up straight 'cause of all the blood. Why don't they close their eyes?

"Ayieee!" I only heard the sound echo over the waves, coming right at me in the first dim gray mist of the Hawaiian dawn, and I froze right where I was, holding my breath, praying that he couldn't see me just as I couldn't see him. "Ayieee," it sounded like the fury at the end of the world, and I almost puked my insides up. It was almost on top of me, but I held my fire and didn't move. I heard the scrape and the footfall, loud like the ping of a sonar, and with a single movement, I turned my head, saw him behind the fog, fired off a single round and rolled to the left as I heard the splinter of bone.

"Fuckit!" Moro screamed, and I heard him flatten.

Two more flashes split the gray darkness and I fired again right into the muzzle. This time the round ricocheted and I heard Moro spitting dirt. That's then I lunged at the dark shape and landed on top of the sonovabitch. His eyes were wide open in terror—scared to shit as I was at that moment. He was one muscle—old and tough like yesterday's grizzle—and he fought back with his fingers, teeth, forehead, and knees. But I grabbed his wrists, ducked my head, and held on for dear life as he bucked like a rodeo bronc. He busted my nose with a head butt and I felt blood running into my mouth. I spit it right back into his face and he coughed and heaved. Then I brought my knee up into his balls. Once, then twice, and he screamed and threw his head back to gasp for air. Then I caught my teeth on his Adam's apple and I bit in as hard as I could. His fingers dug into my ribs and I thought for a second he would rip me apart, he was so goddamn strong. We rolled over in our own blood, him squeezing the air out of my lungs and me ripping at his throat with my teeth.

Then I bit through, and I almost choked on the hot blood that welled up in my mouth. Moro released me and grabbed at his own throat, trying to staunch the blood even though he must have known that it was only a flesh wound. I spit his blood out onto the gravel, reached for the knife on my ankle, and with one quick upward thrust, I shoved it right under his ribs. He screamed and bucked, kicking at me and pushing against my busted nose with his hand. I felt my nose traveling all over my face, but I kept pushing the knife blade in a large semicircle under his ribs until I finally heard the bubbling of air that told me I had ripped open his lung.

The old Jap gave a final heave and collapsed, blood surging out of his mouth as he fumbled for his gun. I rolled off, kicked our two guns away with my hand and pushed the point of my knife right into Moro's eye. He froze, not daring to breathe.

"I can still live, Milan, if you let me," he gasped. "Li Chin will never let you off this island alive if I die. He's coming now. Knows where I went. Life for life, Milan."

"This is for Bataan, Moro," I spit at him. "This is the revenge of a thousand men, the lives of hundreds of children." I'd never felt such fury. My blood was boiling with hate, even as it spilled out over the ground. "This is your life for theirs unless you tell me now who gave you protection after the war. Who got you back to Hawaii?"

"You mean you don't know?" He tried to scream, not believing what he was hearing. "Bataan? That's what this is all about? Not the Mafia? You stupid dago fuck, I'm CIA."

His breath was coming in sharp rasping sounds now, and he was drifting in and out. His eyes, now that I could see them in the advancing light, were getting a glassy and far-away look. He was going into shock. In a few minutes he would be dead. I still wanted to get his information and put the final round into his head myself. I wanted him to feel the pain before he died.

"What does the CIA have to do with this?" I asked. "What does Li Chin know? Tell me and I'll get you back alive."

"Li Chin worked for us before Pearl Harbor. How do you think we knew where your battleships were?" He laughed as best he could. "Now he's CIA like the rest of us." He spit up blood from deep inside his lungs. "Your Army Intelligence turned him during the war and he got me . . . in exchange for information about the Red Chinese. We've been operating a listening . . . post at this substation since the war." Then he he turned his head and looked at me as hard as he could. His eyes got back some of their expression and he looked at me with what I thought was understanding. "You're one of Hoover's little fags," he said. "I should have known."

I cocked the hammer back on my .38 and stood away from the bastard's head. I didn't want to get his brains all over me, even though the way I was bleeding it wouldn't have made any difference.

"Last time: who killed Frankie if Frankie worked for you?"

"Hong," Moro whispered. "Hong thought he was just one of the bellcaps that you'd bought. Li Chin never told anyone who was really working on the inside. He'll be mad as hell that Hong killed him. You'll tell him that before you die."

"Wrong!" I screamed at him and squeezed the round right into his eye.

The top of Moro's head exploded like one of the volcanos that ring Hilo and his pulpy brain ran over the ground like the mash from inside a rotten pumpkin. I reached down, cut off the dead man's shoes, threw them over my shoulder like a pair of skates, and took his gun. The sun hadn't risen yet, and I still had time to get back to Li Chin and get on the plane, even if I had to get on it with a nose that was jumping around every time I tried to breathe.

But despite the pain, I knew I had to dispose of Moro's body, just to keep this whole thing on the up-and-up. So I dragged the corpse back to the clearing where Frankie's secret swamp was hidden and rolled the body over into the dark pool. That would be his final resting place—an unmarked swamp that someday somebody would drain for another hotel or movie theater or police station. Maybe they'd find this rat's carcass. But by then I'd just be a bad memory in a lot of people's heads. Then I retrieved my traveling bag full of dough from where I'd stashed it and slung it over my shoulder like a Boy Scout knapsack.

I was bone weary but nevertheless tried to jog back to the hotel. My nose began bouncing so much that I thought it would fall right the fuck off my face. I had to tape it up and stop the bleeding. The pain was intense and I began feeling the onset of shock myself: lightheadedness, weakness in the knees, and a nauseating cold sweat that makes you want to fall down and die right where you are. But I got back to the clearing without falling down and crept through the bunches of trees that surrounded the hotel. No one was up yet and from the outside it looked like Li Chin wasn't expecting any trouble. I knew he had lookouts posted. He had to. He hadn't stayed alive this long without covering all his bets.

I circled around the perimeter of the clearing to see if I could spot anybody and with the exception of one or two bellcaps peeking through the glass, it seemed deserted. The bellcaps were the lookouts, all right, and I had to get at one of them to get rid of the other. First I reloaded my heater and put it back in my pocket with the safety off. Then I crawled along the stubble of grass, keeping as low as possible, until I had a clear run to the side of the hotel beside the glass doors. Keeping low, below the sill of the side window, I made my way to the base of the hotel wall. Then I crept towards the front where I'd last seen the bellcap. I drew my .38 and continued along the outside wall to the corner of the building. Then I took a handful of lava gravel, and like I was rolling a hand grenade into a Jap machine gun nest, I rolled against the bottom of the door. Nothing happened. I did it again, and this time I could see one of the bellcaps stick his head out and look around. I took a bead on the guy's head.

"Psssst," I hissed and pressed my back against the wall.

The bellcap leaned out of the doorway even further but didn't come around to my side of the building.

"Psssst," I hissed again as loud as I could.

This time, when the bellcap walked the whole way around the corner and stared at me with the stupid look of a Chinese waiter who doesn't understand your order, I motioned for him to turn around and walloped him across the top of his skull. He staggered backwards, but I grabbed him before he fell into the other bellman's line of sight and dragged him behind the building. Then I put on what I could of his uniform, tucked my .38 in the tunic, stuffed Moro's gun into my wasteband, extra slugs into my pocket, and slung Moro's shoes over my shoulder. Then I walked up to the door.

The other bellcap was looking at the dozing desk clerk when I walked in quickly and put the muzzle of my gun at the base of his neck.

"Not a sound or you're dead," I warned as I grabbed him by the collar with my left hand and marched him behind a set of potted palms. "Where's Li Chin?"

"Not . . . not know, boss," he stammered.

I put my hand over his mouth and kneed him sharply behind his thigh. He grimaced and shook.

"Now I'm going to cut out your right kidney," I hissed in his ear.

"Li Chin have room behind office. Have two guards watch all time."

"Get on your knees," I whispered.

At first he hesitated, but I made it even clearer as I forced him down.

"It's the only way you'll see breakfast," I said as he dropped silently to the floor.

"Hands over your eyes," I told him again, and belted him across the back of his head with my gun butt as hard as I could.

The sound of his falling woke up the desk clerk, sure enough, but my gun muzzle between his eyes convinced him to stay quiet. "You shut up and you'll live," I said, now not as worried about being disturbed. "Li Chin's door locked?" I asked.

The clerk nodded and pointed to a set of keys near the switchboard. I scooped them up with my left hand.

"Li Chin all tucked in?" I asked again.

"Boss sleep in special apartment behind office. He there all night," the old man whined.

"Where's the house phone wires?" I demanded.

The clerk pointed to a set of wires leading from the little switchboard under the desk to a wall plate behind him. I grabbed them and ripped them out of the wall. The lights on his switchboard went black. Then I belted the desk clerk with my gun and stuffed him behind his desk as well. Now the lobby was as deserted as it looked and I quietly walked to Li Chin's office door. I listened near the keyhole but couldn't hear a thing. Then I peeked inside through the lock. The two guards were dozing against the wall. I put the key in the lock and slowly turned the tumblers, hoping that the guards wouldn't wake up. Luck was with me—the lock and door hinges must have been brand spanking new and oiled to keep them smooth because the door swung open without a sound.

The only noise came from the snoring guards. I walked in and they didn't even stir. I put the muzzle next to one guard's ear and clamped my hand over his mouth. His eyes opened and he jerked, but when he felt the gun against his head, he froze in place. I reached over and took the gun out of his waistband and motioned for him to lay flat on his face. I did the same with the other guard and motioned them out of the office and into the deserted lobby. We took the elevator up to my room where I told one guard to tie the other up and gag him with a pillowcase from the bed. I checked the ropes and tied and gagged the second guard. I checked the clock. Almost seven. The morning mail plane wasn't due for a half-hour, but I still had to pay my respects to Li Chin and finish up my business.

With Li's men out of the way I washed the blood off my face, grimacing because the pain from my broken nose was throbbing through my entire head, and tried to tape up my face the way we taped fighters in the gym after a sparring accident. It was all I could do to keep from going into shock and passing out. But I knew what to do from having seen some of the best corner men in New York tape up the faces of beat-up fighters for the final round that would turn their brains into meatloaf. I managed to steady the floating cartilage by crisscrossing the Red Cross tape across my face and around my completely blackened eyes. I looked like I'd been in the fight of my life, and it still wasn't over yet. I turned my attention back to the guards on the floor.

"Do I have to plug you bums or split open your skulls to keep you from gettin' loose?"

They shook their heads "no" as hard as they could. Then they nodded and smiled behind their gags, their slanty eyes arching up to tell me "no worry, no worry." The careful thing would have to been to plug the both of them right then and there, but I was a contractor on company time pulling a job. The contract only called for one man: Kyoshi Moro. He was dead and my contract was fulfilled. Hong was an accident—self-defense. Frankie was done in by his own stupidity. Li Chin was the wild card.

I repacked my bag and lugged it down the lobby. A lone bellboy was looking around to see what was wrong and the desk clerk was just getting to his feet. I ducked inside Li Chin's door before anybody saw me, parked my bags, and peeked in his keyhole. I heard a toilet flush. Then loud Chinese. More Chinese.

"You fuck*uhs* still sleeping!" He finally called out in English from behind the door.

I heard the rattling of a telephone button and the slamming of the receiver down on its cradle.

"Hey, Sammy!" Li Chin called out. "Phone's out again."

No answer at the door.

"SAMMY!"

I positioned myself behind the door as Li Chin yanked it open.

"Where the fuck are you two boons?" he yelled as he stepped into the room, stark naked with water dripping off the smallest dick I'd ever seen in my whole life. I pulled out my revolver and pointed it directly at his head.

"I woulda shot the *moyl* if he'd done that to my dick," I said as Li Chin turned around, saw me, opened his eyes as wide as I'd ever seen anyone do, stammering like he was Lou Costello who'd just seen a ghost in his closet, and shot a spurt of pee in my direction. "If I shot that thing off," I said, motioning to his dick, "you wouldn't miss it. In my neighborhood they call that a *putzela* when they're being nice."

I threw Moro's shoes across the floor. Li Chin recognized them immediately.

"Where Kyoshi Moro is now he don't have no use for 'em," I said.

"I can see you had a hard night, Mike," Li Chin finally managed to say when he recovered from the shock of seeing Moro's shoes. "Did my associate offend you in any way? Was there a breach of Las Vegas etiquette?" He was very bitter now, but still didn't know the story.

"You don't pick your associates with care," I told him. "Colonel Moro had a questionable background. The people I work for were displeased that he was walkin' around."

"That so?" Li Chin said.

"Now he don't walk so good."

"So I imagine," Li continued. "What next?"

"Up to you," I told him. "You could make it very easy for me by calling for help, trying to take this gun way, or just getting me mad, and I'd plug you where you stand. Then I don't ever have to think about you again."

"But I don't think I'm gonna make it be that easy. Do you, Mike?" He asked. "As far as I'm concerned, you can walk outta here right now, say aloha Hilo, get on that mail plane that's circling overhead, and wait for the repercussions. And there will be repercussions."

I could hear the noise of engines over the sound of the ocean as the mail plane swung in for its early morning landing.

"Got a robe?" I asked Li Chin.

"Whatever for?" he answered, smiling a very strange smile at what he thought was my predicament.

"You're either gonna walk out to that landing strip in your birthday suit with that toothpick sticking up like somebody put a cigarette out on your balls or you can wear a bathrobe," I told him. "I don't give a shit because one way or another either you're takin' me out to that plane or you're dead where you stand."

"My robe's in there," Li Chin said, motioning with his head into his bedroom.

I held the gun on him and followed him into the bedroom where he pulled a towel-cloth shaving robe off his door and threw it around his shoulders. He tied the belt, stepped into a pair of rubber slippers that I saw everybody wearing around the hotel, and walked out into the lobby. The desk clerk's jaw dropped open as he saw us walk through. Then Li Chin's jaw dropped open as he saw his bellboy crawling out from behind the plants in the lobby and his other bellboy leaning in his underwear against the glass doors. The guests up and about were also astonished to see the disarray in the lobby and the bellboy holding the gun on the bathrobed hotel host.

"You've put a crimp in my business, Mike," Li Chin said. "I've got a lot of explaining to do to my people."

We made it out to the landing strip where the mail plane was just turning its nose into the wind. I could tell this would be a painful flight home.

"You've been doing a lot of explaining for years," I shouted to Li Chin over the droning of the engine. "That's what's been keepin' you alive."

The door to the cabin of the plane opened and Li Chin called out to the pilot. "You have one very important passenger. Take off right now, bring him where he wants to go, and forget you ever saw his face. Those are orders!"

The pilot looked at me, shrugged his shoulders, nodded to Li Chin, and went back inside the cabin without even saying a word. I looked at the plane and motioned with my gun for Li Chin to back away.

"One question," he called out, cupping his hands to his mouth and not even waiting for me to answer. "Why Moro?"

"We know who you are," I screamed out to him as I stepped onto the wing. "You don't know who we are."

I closed the door behind me as the pilot gunned the two-seater down the grass runway and lifted her nose off the ground. He circled low over the Hilo Hotel, and I could still see Li Chin standing there, his robe flapping away in the propwash like a flag on the Fourth of July. He just stood there looking at the plane as he grew smaller and smaller in the distance, until he was smaller, even, than his own pathetic dick.

The Klan

Late in the summer of 1953, I was told that Mr. Hoover wanted to see me in person. Things had become different now that the Old Man was feeling the pressure from the CIA. The jobs in New Orleans and Hawaii had made too many people mad. Mr. Hoover had stepped on their toes, ordered hits on one too many of their deep cover agents, and now they were putting on the brakes. The days of "shoot first and ask questions later" were being replaced with "write reports and send them off to Washington." It was as if the Old West was finally getting civilized. I didn't like it one bit.

All of a sudden we had to prepare special disguises whenever the Old Man came to town wanting a personal meeting with one of us on the Squad. It was still a rare occasion whenever we saw him. Hoover was such a near fanatic about maintaining security that he almost never met with any of us, but when he did, he was becoming a fanatic about disguises. On those few times we met in person, I'd receive a call from Washington that a "certain gentleman" was coming to New York. The first thing I would do would be to find a disguise to meet him. Usually, I'd fade into the woodwork as a busboy, a waiter, a cab driver, or someone he'd give orders to during the normal course of his day.

It was in August when Mr. Hoover checked into the Hotel Carlyle on Madison Avenue. I was told he was expecting me early in the evening and to arrange some kind of routine cover for the meeting. I called an old friend, Howie Kupperman of the All-City Cab Corporation, and told him I wanted a personal favor and to keep his mouth shut about it. I went down to his place, an old warehouse off Tenth Avenue in the forties. I needed a cab, a beat-up cab that no one in New York would notice from all the other beat-up cabs on the street. I also needed a quick hack photo license and some rough and tumble clothing. Howie made a few phone calls while I stood there, and half an hour later a character in a leather overcoat brought over a green hack license issued by the City of New York. Nobody asked any questions. Howie gave the guy a fifty-dollar bill, and he left without a thank you or a good-bye. Howie, who had carrot-colored hair and a long grin just like an alligator's, turned to me and said, "That'll be a hundred bucks."

"A hundred bucks?" I said. "I just saw you slip the guy a half a hundred.

"Hey," Howie said behind one of his grins. "I gotta eat. Besides I know it ain't your bread."

"So what?"

"So what! So, you might use the cab in a stick-up and I'd be left holding the bag. That's worth fifty bucks, ain't it?"

I didn't answer. Howie always knew I was into something clandestine, but he didn't know I worked for the government. We were friends from the Lower East Side days, and he was aware of one side but uninformed about the other. I gave him the hundred bucks. He gave me the hack card and the keys to the cab.

"Hey Mike, make sure you get the cab back by midnight so I can make some money with it," he shouted as I stepped inside the old Checker.

I laughed, started the cab, and pulled it out of the lot and onto the street. It was a hot, muggy, hazy afternoon—the kind of day New York is famous for. Visitors to the City often think they can actually see the heat waves rising from the pavement. It's not that at all. It's the sewers turning to steam. I headed east along forty-sixth toward Fifth Avenue. I had spent more time at Howie's than I expected to, and the cross-town traffic was very heavy. I was going to be late. You're not supposed to be late when you're meeting J. Edgar Hoover. I stopped for a red light at the corner of West 46th and Sixth Avenue. A middle-aged woman opened the cab door and stepped in.

"Jesus Christ," I thought. "Now I'm supposed to be a real cabbie." Suppose this broad wanted to go to the airport or Brooklyn? I'd be in deep trouble with the Old Man if I missed my appointment with him.

"Mishtah," she said in a thick Boston accent. "I want you to drive me to a hotel that my deah friends suggested. Do you know Jack Kennedy of Massachushetts?" she asked.

I knew who he was, all right. I also knew who his father was. Ask Meyer Lansky about Joe Kennedy and you'd see one of the few times that Mr. L. would actually get conniptions. What they said back during Prohibition was that you can't trust Joe Kennedy to keep his word. He stole from his friends so much that he had no friends. And right before World War II, the sonovabitch turned around and said that we should all get on Hitler's side, that the Jews could go to hell. Meyer was ready to bust a blood vessel. His temples were actually throbbing when Sam Koenig told him what Kennedy had said. And then Meyer, almost like he was a born Sicilian, swore a blood revenge on the entire family. "The sins of the father," he kept on saying to himself, mumbling like an old *zeydeh* vowing revenge. "The sins of the father."

"Never heard of him, lady," I answered.

"Oh, what a pity. He has such a lovely wife and she always stays at this hotel," she babbled on. She still hadn't told me where she wanted to go. The light had changed, cars were blowing their horns, and a cop was walking deliberately over toward me, sweating last night's Irish whiskey out all over his collar.

"Which hotel, lady?" I barked.

"The Carlyle."

I slapped the accelerator down and raced across the intersection. The cop just stared as I shot by him, and I could see his eyes following me. I only hoped he didn't copy down the plate number. But then he turned away, hollaring at another cab, and I started to relax a little. He was off my back and the lady with the accent was going to my rendezvous hotel. Even the traffic seemed to thin out a little as I headed uptown.

This broad was giving me a real ear job, talking all about the lovely Jackie Kennedy who had met her at the Boston Park Plaza Hotel and how handsome her husband Jack was and the rest of the whole stupid family. I thought of Meyer and smiled under my cap. Wouldn't Miss Fancy Pants have a cow in the backseat if I turned around and told her what I knew about her precious Kennedys. I pulled up in front of the Hotel Carlyle lobby and a doorman stepped up to the cab to open the the door for the lady with the accent. I glanced around me to see if I could spot Mr. Hoover, who darted out of the lobby when he saw me.

"Taxi, Mr. Hoover?" The tall blonde doorman asked. I swear he looked like an SS officer in a white dress uniform. The Old Man nodded yes and the young Nazi steered him toward the hack ahead of me.

"No. I'll wait for this one," Hoover said.

"But the other is free, sir."

"I'll wait," he said, his eyes glaring in a silent burn. No one ever says no to the Old Man even if he tells you that the moon rises at dawn.

The old broad finally got out of the cab and Mr. Hoover got in. He was still a little steamed. I glanced up at the rear view mirror and he nodded.

"Yankee Stadium," Hoover said. I nodded and pulled the cab away from the hotel. He always wanted to make a little small talk until he felt it was safe to really get into things.

"Those Yankees look like they're going to win again this year," he said.

"No stopping 'em."

"The White Sox have a pretty good team. And so do the Indians," he said.

"Yeah, but the Yanks got Mantle, Skoworon, Ford, and Yogi. They got the Peanut." Hoover always laughed when I talked about the Yankees.

"Watch out for the Senators," he slyly whispered. Then I knew his mood was changing and he was feeling more relaxed. We'd soon be down to business.

"Yeah," I said. "Say, why do they say Washington is like a Hershey Bar?"

"Why?" he laughed.

"Because it's full of chocolate and nuts."

Hoover didn't laugh this time. He looked very sullen and serious. "That's not funny," he said.

"I'm sorry," I whispered. I was very embarrassed. I even blushed a little.

Sitting in the back of the cab, Hoover explained to me that he was sending me to Atlanta, Georgia, where the Ku Klux Klan was beginning a new round of activity. They had been attacking black civil rights groups for the past four years, but had now turned their attention to Jewish organizations and the Catholic Church as well. Mr. Hoover was concerned, he said, that the Klan would set off a chain reaction that would provoke violent retaliations from both Jews and blacks. He said that intelligence reports had revealed that men like Jacob Druckman were planning demonstrations all over the South, and a highly respected and formidable black minister from Atlanta, Martin Luther King, Jr., was organizing black congregations in Mobile. The Klan had targeted King as a major threat, and Hoover was worried that the whole situation would flare up into violence unless he could get his people inside the Klan to gather intelligence and disrupt their activities. He was starting another counter-intelligence program.

"Mike, I want you to go to Atlanta and infiltrate a local group," the Old Man said. "Get me names and plans. I want to know what they're gonna do so I can get some indictments fast."

I just listened. You didn't interrupt J. Edgar Hoover when he was giving orders. He finally finished and looked at me through the rear view mirror.

"When do I leave?" I quietly asked.

"Tonight. Okay?"

Neither one of us said another word for a good ten minutes. I drove up toward Yankee Stadium while he just stared out the window.

"Mike," he grunted after a while. "This job might take a long time, so tell whoever you gotta tell not to expect you back for a few weeks. Tell'em it's a business trip. When this is done, I have plans for you to come to Washington. One of our mutual friends also has some plans for you. So handle this Klan business carefully, watch yourself, and get back here alive."

I nodded. He went back to looking out the window. I dropped him off at Yankee Stadium. He didn't even give me a tip.

I returned the cab to Howie and raced back to my apartment. I called my mother to tell her that I was leaving for a few weeks on a business trip. I told her I was buying a bunch of used cars from out West. What she didn't know she wouldn't worry about. It was always better that she didn't know where I was going.

After I landed in Atlanta, I hopped a cab at the airport and headed for a hotel in the center of the city. I phoned my recognition code to the Old Man's private line in Washington to let him know I had arrived, and then I went to bed. I would have to be on the job early the next morning.

I got up the next day even before sunrise, changed clothing, and went out looking for work. I found that it was always pretty easy to find a nominal job maybe as a bus boy, a waiter, or a bell hop somewhere. In those days, everybody seemed to be hiring people, and you could keep a job as long as you didn't spill any booze on old ladies or guys with silk ties. I found work as a counterman in a truck-stop diner in Marietta, a suburb of Atlanta that's pretty well travelled. The place was a typical truck stop: an old weatherbeaten shack at the end of a dry-as-dust parking lot just off an old state route. They served large portions of greasy food swimming in brown gravy with an ice-cream scoop of bone-colored grits heaped on top. Truckers would shovel grits and ham into their mouths before sun-up and wash down their meatloaf sandwiches with coffee until after dark. By afternoons it got so hot inside that all the fans did was blow the dust in from the parking lot. And every time the screen door opened and slammed, more flies would circle in and light on the pot of grits heating on the edge of the stove. By evening it was time for the mosquitos to eat. And you were the dinner.

I was quiet the first few days I was there, trying to get the feel of the place and the people. I had to learn their attitudes, their habits, and the way they did things. There were some big guys who ate at the truck stop, larger than any people I'd ever seen even in the ring. They wore stinking shirts smeared with oil and tied wet bandannas around thick bulging necks that were chafed bright red from the heat and road dust. Many were mean sonovabitches who'd bust open someone's head just to pass the time of day.

Late one afternoon, a bunch of regulars were sitting at the counter complaining about some new federal regulation to tax independent owner-operators at a higher rate than fleet owners. These were four guys you wouldn't want to meet if you were unarmed. Timmy Daunt, a tall twenty-eight-year-old who had been an independent trucker from the day he got his chauffeur's license, was the most vocal and the leader of the conversation. He trucked cheese, a commodity which was shipped in three-hundred-pound cases. I had seen him toss cases around like they were candy bars.

Timmy hated blacks and Jews with equal vigor. His cronies, Don Maisel, a good old boy from the Florida 'glades, Charlie Carrick, a roughneck rowdy from Georgia, and Ray Brannel, a "mighty mouse" with a quick temper from Greensboro, were equally tough and durable. They roared that Washington had really stepped on their asses this time with a road-usage tax that cut their margin of profit considerably. I wouldn't want to be a tax collector facing down these truckers by the side of the road.

I hadn't gotten into the talk of the trucking industry, so I kept myself out of the conversation. I just hung back by the coffee pot, re-filling their cups and emptying their ashtrays. Every now and then, I'd make a comment about the pussy-whipped pencil-pushers in Washington who couldn't tell the tail-end of a truck from the front, and I was answered with an approving grunt. It went like that all afternoon: drinking coffee, dumping ashtrays, and bullshitting.

Just before six, five young black guys parked their new Freightliner rig in the lot and came into the diner. Timmy Daunt and his crew stopped talking the minute they saw them in the doorway. The blacks sat at the other end of the counter and stared down into the grease and coffee stains that I hadn't yet wiped up. Daunt sideled over to them.

"Where all you boys from?" he asked in an almost soothing manner.

"Chicago," one of them answered.

"Ah, that's why. You boys don't know there are white truck stops and colored truck stops. Y'all see there's a difference here. This is a white truck stop. I suggest you boys best look for a colored truck stop before someone comes in and starts some trouble.

There was a long period of silence that just brimmed over with tension. One of the blacks turned toward him very slowly. His eyes narrowed right in on Daunt's face just before he opened his mouth.

"The U-nited States Supreme Court says . . ." he started to explain, overemphasizing the "U."

Daunt didn't even wait for what the court said. He grabbed him around the throat and pushed him right over backwards toward the floor. The other blacks jumped up, more to separate the two men than to mix it up, but Daunt's crew was on their feet in a split second and tore after the blacks at the other end of the counter.

The guy who Daunt had grabbed must have studied judo some-where because he broke the stranglehold, chopped Daunt across the side of neck, and had him on the floor. He was giving him short, sharp kicks to the bottom of his rib cage with the heel of his foot. Daunt was completely defenseless and his mouth was gushing blood.

The other blacks were just as tough and knew how to fight. Brannel was getting his redneck kicked across the floor, Maisel was bleeding from over top his eyes, and Daunt was barely conscious. My feelings were for the five black kids trying to make a living down there, but this was the opportunity I was waiting for.

I grabbed a baseball bat from behind the counter and waded into the thick of it. I swung the bat around as if I were at the plate and caught the "judo expert" right in his ribs. You could hear the crack above the sound of the yelling. He turned toward me, his hands up in a peek-a-boo style. But his body was wide open. I stepped right in, dug three quick jabs right under ribs where I I had hit him with the bat, and watched as he lowered his hands. Then I hooked to the side of his jaw and he went down on his knees. I grabbed his head, slammed it against my kneecap which I brought up into his nose, and bounced it off the floor. He just lay there glassy-eyed and didn't move.

Then I turned around to the guy who was working Ray Brannel over. He was as big as a gorilla and threw Brannel through a doorway as if Ray were a Raggedy Ann doll. I gave this guy a shot in the kidneys and saw his knees buckle. But he turned around and came at me. I threw a three-punch combination to his midsection which would have stopped anybody in the ring, but it didn't faze him. I backed up, peppering him with jabs to the face as he charged, but it was like trying to shoot an elephant with a BB gun. Then I unloaded a haymaker on the side of the guy's head. Nothing. I was about to get killed.

Brannel recovered, shook the fuzz out of his head, grabbed one of the metal ice cream chairs that the diner used, and crashed it down on the gorilla's head with all of his might. As he staggered under the blow, I hit him with another roundhouse right that snapped him straight upright. Then, as his eyes rolled up, I pounded the heel of my hand square up into his nose like I'd done to Fat Hong a couple of years before. We all heard the break, and the guy spun down to the floor in a puddle of blood. The three other blacks looked around the room, saw the four of us surrounding them, and ran out of the diner before Daunt and his crew got to them. Then Ray Brannel and Don Maisel dragged the other two kids out the front door.

We sat around the counter, wiping off blood and working bruised muscles and joints. We watched silently as the the black kids pulled their rig out of the lot. As soon as they were gone, we looked at each other and laughed out loud. Timmy Daunt threw his arm around my shoulder and grinned.

"You little bastard. You saved my ass," he said.

"Mine, too," Ray piped in.

"Where did you learn to use your hands like that?" Tim asked.

I told him I had been a boxer and won a few fights in my time.

"You know something, little buddy? You're aces by me," Carrick, the usually quiet member of the group, drawled. "I can't stand them fuckin' niggers."

"There's only one thing worse than a nigger," I said. "And that's a goddam, fuckin' Jew." If my father could have heard me, his *tallis* would be spinning.

"You're damn straight," Daunt chimed in.

"Hey, what do you call a Mexican fag?" I asked. "A señor-eater," I answered my own question before anybody could pipe up. "What do you call an Irish fag? A gay-lick. And what do you call a Jew fag?" I waited for an answer from the three, slack, hanging mouths in front of me. They all knew there was a punch line, but they'd be damned if they could figure out what I was going to say next. "A fuckin' Jew cock-sucker," I said, and they roared and slammed the counter top.

We sat around one of the tables drinking coffee and telling Jew jokes for the rest of the afternoon and evening. When my shift was over, they brought me to to a roadhouse to meet some more trucker friends and to see how I stood up to a night full of boilermakers and boasting.

I realized I had been right about seizing the opportunity as soon as we had gotten to the roadhouse bar. There were lots of other independent truckers, warehousemen, factory workers, and guys who thought cheap black laborers and Jewish bankers were responsible for the financial pinch they were in. It never occurred to them that blacks were hurting just as badly as they were. That night I went back to my furnished room, wrote a full report on what had happened and drove to FBI headquarters in Atlanta where I filed the report. It was sent, under an eyes-only clandestine cover to Mr. Hoover in Washington.

For the rest of the week, Daunt and the others came in for coffee and bullshit after their late noon routes were finished or whenever they didn't have a night load to haul. Once in a while we would get into a "nigger-and-Jew" session, but it never got beyond complaining.

One Friday afternoon, I was sitting in the diner by myself. It was hot but not hazy—a brilliant sunny day—and things were extraordinarily quiet. Not a customer had come in since lunch. It was late afternoon and I was amusing myself by watching the sun turn into a large ball of melted butter. I was bored and had nothing else to do. It was so quiet that all you could hear were the flies buzzing around the kitchen and through the holes in the screen door. That's why I almost jumped out of my skin when I heard Ray's voice from behind the bright sun.

"You're gonna go blind lookin' at the sun that way," he said. "Got nuthin' else to do but daydream?"

"It's been damn quiet out here all day," I said. "You guys don't work and I don't work."

"You should take up a hobby," he said and ordered a cup of coffee. I grabbed a clean cup, filled it from the pot, and shoved it in front of him.

"I had a hobby once," I told him. "I used to like to play with horses. Watch them run around a little track."

"What happened?"

"Some of the horses I played with didn't make it around as fast as the others."

Ray laughed as he slurped at his coffee. He drank it as if he were snorting it through his nose.

"I got a great hobby for you," he said between slurps.

I leaned over the counter to hear him better.

"What?" I asked.

"Huntin' coon."

"That's okay during the daytime," I said. "But you can't see them at night."

Brannel bellowed his big bull laugh. "I'm serious," he said. "We shoot 'em two or three times a month."

I was hitting paydirt. If I could report on an actual murder attempt, the Old Man would have his indictments and I'd be out of this sweat box of a diner.

"It sounds to me like some sort of a club," I said. He was finally getting around to giving me the kind of information I wanted. I had to get more.

"Yeah. It's a club, I guess. We have meetings and then go out and show them niggers we ain't gonna let 'em run roughshod over us." He was dead serious now.

"When's the next meeting?" I asked.

"I'm gonna take you just as soon as you finish your shift and hustle your ass outta here."

That wouldn't give me any chance to contact the Bureau. I had very little choice but to go along with the arrangement and file my report the next day. When I left the diner, he told me to leave my car in the parking lot. We were going to ride in his ancient pickup. We traveled for more than a half an hour over back country dirt roads that I could have never found on my own. Then we drove through an area thickly covered with pine trees and red clay. Ray came to a clearing, shut his headlights, and pulled onto a small meadow. There were eight to ten other vehicles there, and they put their lights out at the same time when they saw Ray's truck. I guessed it was some sort of a signal. We got out of the truck and he ushered me around a circle, introducing me to fifteen or so other guys as "one tough little bastard." A few of the rednecks threw punches at my stomach or jaw to see how I would react. My instincts told me to just lay back or weave, letting them slap at fireflies buzzing around in the darkness. This was a very playful bunch. They wrestled with one another, clubbed at each other with their big forearms, and fingered their revolvers, deer rifles, and shot guns.

Eventually we settled down, sitting on the hood of Ray's pickup, chugging down six-packs of bear and quietly staring at the stars. Then a giant Freightliner Autocar, bobtailing all the way, pulled into the meadow and all of the other truckers roared some kind of cheer. An enormous man in his late forties stepped out of the cab. I could tell this guy was their leader before he ever said a word. He wore work jeans and a red plaid shirt. His carriage was ramrod erect, as if he had been in the military. All the truckers turned their headlights on and converged on the man in the center of the clearing. He stepped into the light and announced to the group:

"Boys, we got us a buncha niggers over in Smyrna who are askin' for trouble. But we got us a new problem tonight, too. Them fuckin' niggers are getting help from a bunch of goddam Jews. Now which group you boys wanna go after tonight, the Jewboys or the niggers?"

"The coons," two or three faceless men from behind the headlights responded.

The big man jumped into his Autocar and just as quickly the others got into their vehicles. There was an excitement that everyone was getting caught up in.

"Who is that guy?" I asked as soon as we climbed back inside Ray's truck.

"You might say he's the president of our little hunt club," Ray said as he rolled down his window and spit out a wad of tobacco juice.

"Don't you know his name?"

"Sure I know his name. But I ain't gonna tell you. He'll tell ya if he wants to."

I was squelched. He was going to be a difficult person to get information from, I knew that from the start. But, up until we got back in his truck, I had supposed I had his confidence. I was dead wrong. I tried another path.

"Do the Jews always help the niggers?" I innocently asked, the words gagging inside my throat.

"Jews are damn smart people, little Mike," Brannel said as if he were lecturing. "They control everything. Hell, they control niggers and spics like dancin' puppets on strings. They fire 'em up about takin' jobs from white folks, lend 'em money, and rent 'em houses. If it weren't for the fuckin' Jews the niggers 'd just pack up and sail away to Africa. But the Jews are gettin' rich offer the niggers. When we finish with our business tonight, we're gonna go right after some of them Jewboys. That's why I wanted you to join up with us. You look hebe."

"Should I be insulted?"

"Hell no. Lots of hebes look like decent white people. That's what makes 'em so dangerous."

We drove into Smyrna, a little spit of a town between Marietta and Atlanta. And that's the most you can say for it. There are a few symmetrical streets in Smyrna that run perpendicular to Main Street; there's a large bank, a gas station, a white Baptist church, and a black Baptist church. That's the entire town. That night, the only lights in town were coming from the black Baptist church, and I immediately knew that that was where we were heading.

The New Canaan Baptist Church had recently elected a pastor, Ray told me, an aggressive young black man from Pittsburgh. In the three short months since he had come to Smyrna, he had organized his congregation into a solidified group of citizens, aware of the economic opportunities in Atlanta and of their rights in restaurants and on public busses. He was a harbinger of what was to come in the next decade.

The herd of trucks barreled into the church's parking lot. They ringed it so that no one could escape, and then the drivers exploded into the church through every possible entrance. They kicked in doors, broke through windows, and even punched in the side of a wall by backing a truck through it. I followed Brannel into a small auditorium adjoining the sanctuary where twenty young black men and women were holding a seminar on what seemed like voter registration. Brannel gave a rebel war-hoop and the truckers with us began swinging tire irons and chains after the black men. The entire scene revolted me. It reminded me of the movies I had seen about the Jews in Austria just twenty years earlier.

Ray Brannel, who I had pegged as a coward, was beating a young black woman he had pinned to the floor by straddling her body. As he slapped her face, her eyeglasses danced across the wooden planks and he looked up and shouted to me:

"Hey Mike, grab one and join the party."

Other eyes were on me, so I had no choice. I took off after the biggest of the men, brought him down with a tackle, and hit him a chopping uppercut just under his chin. He went out without even fighting back. The chaos lasted about ten minutes. That's all the time it took to force the congregants to drag themselves out of the church. Then the big man gave the signal and all the truckers ran out and into the parking lot. Brannel and the big man began pouring gasoline around the church's foundation and then lit it. It went up with a woosh like a bonfire at a pep rally with sparks flying into the night sky and igniting small fires in the adjacent woods.

Ray and I jumped back into his pickup and tore out of the parking lot in reverse, hell-bent for leather. This time the trucks didn't follow one another in any organized fashion. Instead they scattered in every direction. Ray laughed happily as we rode along the country roads back to Marietta.

"Mike, you little bastard," he said as he lit a cigarette with one hand on the wheel. "I saw you take on that buck all by yourself. You're somethin' else, little buddy."

"I can take care of myself," I said, trying to hide my disgust at what I'd had to do.

"Somethin' I always wanted to know—do you little guys always take on the biggest sonovabitch in the place?"

"Sure," I said. "It makes us feel big and important."

He laughed again and just kept driving as if he'd never heard of a speed limit. We pulled into a roadhouse, parked, and he leaned over to open the door on my side.

I followed him inside where many of the others had already begun drinking and bragging. The more rounds they finished, the more heroic their feats became until you wouldn't know that all they'd done was beat up a bunch of church-going families who they outnumbered almost two to one. And some of those were children.

Don Maisel wasn't bragging. He sat off in a corner sulking in a beer as some of the others gathered around him. They were shouting, but it was difficult to understand what the commotion was about. Ray, who was like an old washer woman when it came to an argument between his cronies, ran into the middle of the ruckus.

"What the hell's the matter, Don?" he shouted.

"I don't like beatin' on women and preachers. And I don't like burning down places that belong to God," he answered.

"They ain't women," Ray said. "They's niggers."

"A woman's a woman and it ain't right. I ain't gonna do it no more. Heah?"

"You gonna have bigger trouble than them niggers, boy, if you don't fly right," the big man said as he pushed his way toward Don. "We all here to fight for what's ours. And no Jew, no nigger, no nobody's gonna come down here and tell us what's they's. You best get your butt inside that nigger church the next time we set a match to it and burn with the rest of 'em 'cause like as all you got some nigger inside of you."

Ray and the others bore in and eventually Don caved in. You could see he didn't like it, but he sure as hell didn't have the backbone to stand up to anybody in that crew. He just kept drinking. They all kept drinking and carrying on. And at four in the morning, Ray dropped me off at the diner where I just fell asleep for the next few hours.

When I awoke, I phoned another "eyes only" report to Washington through the field office in Atlanta. Maybe these guys in regular FBI didn't know my name, but they sure knew how to respond to the recognition codes. It was always "yes sir" and "no sir" and "right away sir," and they never even knew who the hell I was. I had been used to working completely alone. This new routine the Old Man had set up was beginning to get on my nerves.

That morning, the *Atlanta Constitution* made the beating and fire in Smyrna front page news. The minute I saw it I knew Ray Brannel was probably crowing about it. On page two I read another story that sent a chill of anxiety right down my spine. Mark Cooper, a young rabbinical student from New York who was working at a local synagogue, had demanded an investigation and offered his offices to the black preacher and his congregation. I knew this young man was in for trouble.

The way things worked in Marietta, the truckers, who were all owner operators, became busy whenever the mill had lumber to haul to Charleston. The only person who didn't run that haul was Don Maisel. He spent a lot of time in the diner, and I got to know him. He wasn't at all like Brannel, Daunt, or Carrick. He had some education, but he was also sensitive and just too damned intelligent to swallow everything that Brannel and the others were feeding him. But Don depended on freight brokers to get him loads to haul. The brokers demanded and received a full twenty-five percent of any job a trucker did. And that was off the gross. The trucker still paid his own expenses. Even with plenty of work, Don couldn't make a living. He complained once about the system and the brokers saw to it that he received as few loads as possible. He went hungry for a while. And in his place they used a young black man who had an old but servicable rig. To Don Maisel, prejudice had boiled down to simple economics—a black man had taken food out of his mouth. In saner moments, he realized that both he and the black trucker had an equal right to make a living and that it was the greedy broker who was the villain who left nothing on the plate for anyone else. They were just fighting over the scraps. But Don kept saying, "Your folks is your folks," and he never would open up about the organization he was in or the Klan at all. Every time I asked him about the big man who gave the orders, he just clammed up.

I had suggested to the local field office in a telephone report that one of the regular special agents contact Maisel and offer him a salary in order to get him to turn informant. They had even met with him secretly, I was told, but he wouldn't give them any information. One afternoon, when we were alone at the diner, Don—pretending to talk about a friend of his—told me about his visit with the FBI special agent. You could see that Don didn't know what to do: he hated himself for beating up women and preachers, but he also hated the blacks because he believed they were taking away his work. He knew what he was doing was wrong, but he told me that his friend thought it was even worse for him to inform on his cronies. Deep inside, I felt pity for Maisel. I knew he could use the money the Bureau was offering and I suggested that he take it. He simply shook his head.

For the next week, it was like being on a treadmill. I didn't learn the identity of the leader. I hadn't convinced Maisel to turn informant. I was no help at all to the Bureau, and the situation was getting worse all over the rural parts of the state. I read the *Constitution*. Other black churches were being burned, blacks and whites were turning on each other, and the whole situation looked like it was being planned by someone at the top of an organization.

I just had to get inside and get some names, but I was depressed and feeling like a failure. Maybe I was feeling handcuffed because the times had changed. The shoot-em-ups in Hawaii and New Orleans felt like they were in another century. The paperwork aspect of the job was throwing me off my game.

I realized I was losing my prize-fighter's edge because late one night I was sitting in my furnished room trying to tune in the Yankee-White Socks game being broadcast out of Chicago. It was unusually quiet, and I should have been more aware of what was going on. Suddenly, I looked up from the screen and saw Ray and the Big Man standing right there in my room. Somehow they had gotten in without my having heard them. I felt at first like whatever happened, I deserved it. Ray was just standing there grinning his big, stupid grin. But the Big Man was dead serious.

"Ray and Don tell me you been askin' a heap of questions about me," the man said in an accent that was more Texan than anything else.

"Just who are you?" I piped up, taking it right to him. I was never one for sitting back on defense.

"That mean somethin' to you, boy?"

"Not especially. I like the way you work. I admire the way you get people behind you. I like to see how the other guys listen to you and believe what you say." I was looking for any chink in his armor and thought flattery might do it.

"Mister, you sure can throw shit. Even I can tell that's pure shit, hot and smokin' right out of the goddamn bull. If Ray hadn't spoken up for you, I'd swear you were a Jew rat down here from the government."

"Ah, come on. Little Mike ain't no government man. He's just got a big mouth," Ray said.

"Keep out of this, Ray," the Big Man ordered.

Ray became stone silent. The Big Man moved over and shut off my little television set.

"They tell me you helped these old boys get outta a jam with some niggers," he continued. "Ray said you whipped a black stud real good. He says you ain't too bad with your hands. I like that. But I don't like people askin' too many questions about me. You hear that, boy?"

"Sure," I said.

"I don't know that I can trust you like they do, and you already know more than you should," he said.

If this were my old neighborhood, this guy would already be dead. But I was here on the Old Man's clock, and he needed information.

"You can trust me," I said.

"You'll have to prove it."

"How?" I asked.

"You keep on askin' questions, boy, and you're not gonna have much future," he warned. "I'll tell you how when I'm ready." He paused and looked at me with his eyes mean and narrow. "You're gonna use your hands on somebody and I'm gonna watch."

"Okay," I said. "You'll just tell me when it's time."

"It's time, boy. You're gonna use your hands on a Jew—Cooper—the Jew priest whose lettin' the niggers use that church he's runnin'."

"Mark Cooper, that guy in the paper?" I asked.

"That's right. We showed those niggers a little that night in Smyrna. They were ready to do what we told 'em and then this Jew boy spoils it all. He's gotta be taught a lesson and you're the man to teach it."

The Big Man walked to the door, and Ray signalled for me to follow. We went down the back stairs, got into a big Ford station wagon, and drove to Westgate, a fashionable section of Atlanta. The car stopped across the street from Temple Israel. I began to pray to myself. I didn't want to do this. I knew God was watching me right at that minute. We got out of the car and broke into the temple through a window in the sanctuary. It was dark inside the temple, and we groped around like blind men at first.

"I heard these hebes wrap their papers in silver," Ray said.

Almost instinctively I wanted to say *torah*, but I caught myself. That would have given me away for sure. We went to the ark and Ray opened it. I waited for the bolt of lightening. Then, there was the *torah* right in front of me, wrapped in its silver crowns. I wanted to reach out to touch it and kiss it as I had been taught to do. I remembered how the rabbi loved the *torah* and how he lifted it high above the congregation. I remembered how my father and brother carried it proudly through the aisles of the synagogue while my mother held out my hand to touch it. I had learned to read it and revere it just as I was taught to revere the memories of my father and brother. Now they were both dead and wrapped in their prayer shawls. And now I was spitting on their graves and despoiling the very object they loved most in their lives. In my own mind, I could hear the *Kol Nidre* chant playing over and over as I realized I was committing the gravest of sins.

Ray took the silver crowns and carried them away as booty. But one of them dropped to the floor, resounding like thunder in the cavernous sanctuary. Then a light came on in the adjoining hallway and we heard footsteps. A large door opened, and Mark Cooper was standing there looking bigger than life.

"What's going on?!" the rabbinical student demanded.

"We thought we'd pay you a little visit social-like. See if they's anythin' in those books of yours about lettin' niggers into your church. 'Cause if they is, you ain't gonna have much of a church left," the Big Man said.

"I'm calling the police," Cooper said as he turned.

"Get him, Mike," the Big Man shouted.

I knew this was my test, a real test, and a test I was not getting just from the Big Man alone. How could I possibly know what was right? How could I hurt a rabbi? How could I have gone this far?

Cooper turned around and hit me. I felt blood on my lip. "Good," I said to myself. "Slap me again, priest." But Cooper had turned to run up the stairs and Ray began running after him. I knew that if the Big Man got his hands on the rabbi, Cooper would die. I jumped ahead of Ray, caught Mark Cooper by the back of the neck and spun him back down the stairs. He was strong for his size, deceptively so, and I hoped I could subdue him easily.

I jumped on him quickly and gave him a few sharp jabs to his ribs, just to let him know that I knew what I was doing. He tried to cry out for help, but I put my hand over his mouth. Then I gave him a sharp rabbit punch to the back of his neck and whispered in his ear as his knees sagged: "Rabbi, please don't fight back. Be quiet and let me get this over with."

He didn't listen. He turned and swung wildly at my head instead.

"If you can't handle him, boy, I can," the Big Man said as he stepped in to get his shot.

Without waiting, I threw a hard right to Cooper's stomach, doubling him up, and then a short left hook to the side of his jaw. Cooper went right down to one knee. I grabbed him by the collar and stood him up. Then I put more body shots into his ribs, places where he would feel pain, but where he would recover quickly.

As he dropped to his knees again, I heard him chanting a *Kaddish* softly to himself, our prayer for the dead. When I heard the Hebrew and the melodies that I had heard from my earliest days, I eased my punches. The Big Man looked at me sharply and grabbed Cooper by the hair.

"God forgive me," I said silently and threw a right straight to his jaw. Cooper's head snapped right out of the Big Man's grasp, and he flipped over backwards. He lay there on his side, unconscious but breathing easily. The Big Man stood over him.

"That's only a warning Jew boy," he said to the rabbi who was just begining to stir.

He turned, and we followed him out of the sanctuary back into the street. We got into the station wagon and took off. No one said a word. For once, I didn't feel like talking and I guessed that even Ray didn't want to brag. I just kept asking God for forgiveness in the same breath that I cursed J. Edgar Hoover. But when we got back to my room, the Big Man seemed more friendly.

"Mike," he said. "You did fine. Real fine. I like the way you whipped that hebe's ass, quick and without too much shit. I'm Elliot Blair," he said smiling and offering his hand.

I shook it all right, but I felt like scum. I was one of them that night. Just another filthy bigot no matter who was giving the orders. Elliot and Ray left, but I couldn't sleep. I kept dreaming of my father and his *tallis* and *yarmulke*. I dreamed about my Bar Mitzvah, and I dreamed that David and Solomon had ordered me away from the Temple forever. I was a disgraced Jew.

The next morning, the *Atlanta Constitution* carried a story about how Mark Cooper had surprised some thieves in his temple and was beaten. The story hinted that the men who beat him might not have been thieves at all, but members of the same gang who had burned the Baptist church in Smyrna. The story quoted Cooper. He wasn't giving up, he said. He was going to hold an interfaith prayer vigil until the gang was stopped. Even some members of the city council were expected to show up.

That same afternoon, Elliot, Ray, Timmy, and a few of the others stopped by the diner. Elliot was particularly upset about the newspaper article.

"You boys don't realize that Jews are a million times more dangerous than niggers," he said. "You gotta understand that this prayer thing is pure bullshit. It's Jews gettin' sympathy from the white middle-class assholes who don't realize they's only helpin' niggers take their jobs and fuck their daughters. We gotta put a stop to it now even if it means blowin' off this Jew's head."

Blair ranted on for twenty minutes and all I could do was listen. I wanted to call Atlanta to tell them to pick Blair up on a murder conspiracy, but that wasn't a federal crime. Only the state of Georgia could arrest him, and they weren't about to lift a finger. Besides, they needed a witness other than myself. I was trapped until a case could be built against them. And that was something I could never do.

Blair told us that we would hit the temple again that night. It would be the last warning. The next time, Cooper and a lot of other people would die.

"They'll be more than just us there tonight," Blair promised. "You boys get as many eggs as you can, and fruit. Shit that we can throw. We're gonna send a message to all the church-goin' people to stay in their own churches. These Jews is mine."

Ray and I left in his truck, picking up fruit, eggs, garbage, and just about anything else he could get from the refuse piles of roadside diners and bars. By the time we reached the temple in Westgate, it was dark and many of the other truckers had already arrived. They were shouting obscenities at the religious Jews who had gone to *schul* at sundown.

They had set up a huge cross in front of the temple and set it aflame, its sparks shooting off and dancing like fireworks. I could see faces peering out at us from inside the temple—black faces and white faces huddled together behind glass, but strained in fright. Then other truckers arrived and began throwing rocks and bricks. Soon the giant windows in the sanctuary began to shatter and it was *Kristallnacht* all over again. Only this time, I was throwing the bricks, cursing at my own people, and cursing at the name of the God of my fathers.

Some of the truckers wanted to throw torches and light the whole place on fire, but Blair held them back. He might be mean, but he wasn't stupid. Burning up the good, white, God-fearing Christians who might be inside was not the way to turn Atlanta against the blacks and Jews.

"Just keep dancing around with them torches," Blair called out. "We'll kill us some next time."

More people joined the mob outside the temple: bus drivers in their uniforms, construction workers, farm hands, even people who looked like white-collar workers, and children as well. Everyone in Atlanta was there, I thought, and all of them poured out their hatred on the Jews. The demonstration became more and more ugly as the crowd pressed toward the temple. Then the police arrived and I waited for them to break up the mob. But to my astonishment, the police at first just stood there. Then some of them joined the demonstration. I decided to put a stop to it my own way.

I broke away from Ray Brannel and took a lit torch from one of the truckers. He didn't want to give it up, but I convinced him with my foot. When I was sure he wasn't watching, I tossed the torch through the open window of an empty police car. Nobody saw me do it, not even the asshole cop who was standing in front of it and screaming "Jew, Jew, Jew."

That was all it took. Before five minutes had passed, the car was on fire. Then the fire engines came rolling in, and then the television news crews begin pointing their cameras at the truckers. That was the signal for the police to break up the mob. And then the whole police car exploded. Ray and I heard the gas tank go as we tore down the street.

"I'd like to get my hands on the cocksucker who lit up that police car," Ray said as he chewed on a cigarette.

"Stupid fuck," I agreed. "Ruined the whole damn night."

The flames, the broken windows, the curses, and the violence all spun around in my mind as I drove back to my room from the diner. I didn't know where it would end, but I couldn't go on much longer without shooting one of them myself. And I didn't relish the thought of another sleepless night.

There was a message waiting for me at the desk when I arrived. A Mr. F. Boylston Ingersoll wanted to talk to me in Atlanta. That was a recognition code—corny but effective—that Hoover of the FBI had a message for me. I phoned my contact at the Atlanta field office. To my relief, he told me that Don Maisel had come forward to work with the Bureau just that evening. His grandfather was Jewish, he told the special agents, and Blair had pushed him too far. Now the Bureau had the witness they needed and would soon have other informants. Maisel would gather evidence, the FBI would arrest low-echelon members of the organization and would turn them into informants as well. It wasn't pretty, but we were in a war and had to win it any way we could.

My assignment in Atlanta was finished. I packed my bags and headed straight for the airport. I heard weeks later that the FBI had completely penetrated the organization and was even getting some local indictments against Klan members throughout the rural South. I knew Hoover wanted me in Washington, but I went to New York first. I didn't even stop to see my mother but . instead I went directly to the Lower East Side to where we used to live. I didn't even know what I was looking for. I knew I had to walk those streets again just to hear the voices that were so familiar. I walked by the temple where I was Bar Mitzvahed, and I felt the weight of thousands of years on my shoulders. I had done a terrible thing. No matter how noble the ends, I had violated the commandments. No matter what I had done before, this was a sin that I understood. Maybe I would be forgiven for what I did, I thought. Maybe God would see it differently. I knew, however, that I had to make my own restitution for Cooper someday and ask for forgiveness. And in the creepy, out-of-nowhere chill of that September afternoon on the corner of Ludlow Street, that was the vow that I made.

When I was working as a contract player and stuntman on the Warner lot, I was up for a tough-guy role in a gangster movie. Jack Warner ordered this publicity shot.

I saw Mr. Hoover age as the years took their toll on him. When he was younger, Mr. H. liked to pick up a Tommy gun and pose for the cameras, as he did in this publicity shot for a Hollywood movie. As he got older, his fights with Truman, Eisenhower, the Kennedy brothers, LBJ, and Nixon wore him down. But he was still a fighter even at the end. (Wide World)

The Old Man hated Allen Dulles (center). He called him a "Harvard pantywaist" and blamed him for everything the CIA did wrong. In Mr. H.'s mind, the CIA was the biggest mistake Truman ever made. (Wide World)

The Old Man carried a grudge against President Truman because the president created the CIA and put Allen Dulles in charge. Although he showed the president respect, as in this news photo with Attorney General J. Howard McGrath (right), Mr. H. never forgave the president. That was one of the reasons he turned the Alger Hiss file over to the young Richard Nixon. (Wide World)

After all the things the Old Man did for Nixon, Nixon tried to oust him from the Bureau. His aides hounded Mr. H. until the day he died. (Wide World)

Frank Costello was the head of the Commission, the most powerful don in the country. I didn't know that he was also the Old Man's personal friend and associate. Mr. H. respected Mr. C. and allowed him to work his territory in peace. (Wide World)

Mr. C. was one of the only dons I ever knew who lived to retire from the business. He eventually died of old age. The Genovese Family had ordered a hit on Mr. C., but the bullet only grazed him when Frank turned around to look his assassin in the eyes. The cops searched Mr. Costello after the hit and found a list of the Vegas casino skim in his coat pocket. That was what tipped them off to how Meyer handled the dough coming out of Nevada. (Wide World)

The Old Man called Meyer Lansky "the nicest criminal I ever knew." Mr. L. was a gentleman. He was my benefactor from the time I was twelve years old. He was a loyal and patriotic American who helped us win World War II. (Wide World)

Everybody loved Bugsy Siegel (left). It broke our hearts when the Commission revealed the evidence that he was pocketing his own skim from the Vegas operation and depositing it into a Swiss bank account. Bugsy always had stars in his eyes from the time he was a kid. He loved the movie stars and they loved him. George Raft was also a stand-up guy. (Wide World)

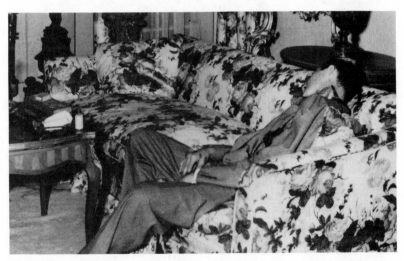

Benny had to go. That was what the Profacci Family told Mr. L. after they caught his girlfriend Virginia Hall on her way to Switzerland. Meyer reluctantly went along. What else could he do? Business was business. Meyer cried the night they plugged Bugsy at his girlfriend's place in Beverly Hills. I cried too. Bugsy always took care of me. (Wide World)

Lucky Luciano was already in the joint when I was coming up. Dewey had framed him on a bum vice rap, but turned to him to help the Allies win the war. Lucky set his people up in the OSS to police the New York waterfront. That was my unit. Then he helped the Army make contact with the old Moustache Petes in Sicily that Mussolini had put out of business. Dewey pardoned Lucky after the war and deported him to Sicily. (Wide World)

Lyndon Johnson hated the Kennedy brothers. He thought they were a pair of spoiled brats whose father put the fix in for them. When he heard that Bobby and Jack were about to throw him off the ticket because of the Bobby Baker scandal, he blew his top. After President Kennedy was killed and I got back from Dallas, Mr. Hoover said to me, "LBJ, no doubt!" (Wide World)

Dallas, November 22, 1963. Everybody told the president not to go to Dallas because he was going to get hit. I always figured that JFK knew the hit was coming and simply sat for it. Maybe he knew there was nothing he could do and was trying to put his brother in position. How was he to know they would hit Bobby too? I was sent to Dallas the day after to mop up witnesses. The white arrow shows the president and the black arrow points to Governor Connolly who also took a slug. (Wide World)

To look at President Ford and Vice President Rockefeller together, you'd never think that some of the people behind the Company wanted to get Ford out of the way so Rockefeller could take over. Years later, Rockefeller died under mysterious circumstances. Did they get to him, too? (Wide World)

After everybody turned down the contract, the boys had to go to the Manson family. They got Squeaky Fromme, a real amateur. But I put the kaybosh on the whole deal by turning up the heat on the Secret Service. They let Fromme get into the hollow square, but shut her down at the last minute. That way they could blame her for the whole thing. (Wide World)

The USS Ranger, the world's most beautiful lady and my first love. She could pack a punch, too! I'd give anything to walk her flight deck one more time before I die. (Wide World)

The Court of Life

I didn't feel so good for a long time after I got back from Georgia. I got into a lot more fights than usual, busting up guys at the gym I had horsed around with for years just because they made some stupid joke about Jews with big noses or laughed at the funny-looking rabbis down on the Lower East Side. I even went to *schul* once or twice on a Friday night, making my momma happy, but making me feel very funny about it for weeks after. Once I tried to talk to the old neighborhood *rebe* about what I was thinking, but he just stared at me with his ink-dot eyes peering over the rims of his thick glasses as I if I was trying explain why two and two equaled five, and I looked back at his expression and only asked him about his daughter and her plans for the future. You can imagine the rumors that started around the old neighborhood when he met my momma by the fruit stand.

There was nobody I could talk to the way I used to. Sam Koenig was dead. Meyer Lansky was spending more time in Las Vegas with Benny warning him about his *shiksa* showgirl friends than he was with his associates in New York. And I only saw Mr. C. once in a blue moon on a Sunday afternoon before the weather turned really cold in the fall of 1953. He was getting out of his limousine in front of what he called his "Civic Association" on Kenmare Street. He had told me once it was the only place he could go to have a quiet afternoon of anisette, heavy Italian coffee, cards, and the stilleto-thin black Sicilian cigars that even the younger *gumbas* had long since given up in favor of American cork-tipped cigarettes from the "L.S.M.F.T." ads.

The immigrant bocce ball players I used to talk to along East Houston Street had also gone. Most of them had come from farms and towns and never really took to the city streets. But they worked hard and sent their kids to school and raised them to fight in the war. Then these children started their own families, moved out to

Queens and Long Island and took the old men with them to wait out
their years on one of the quarter-acre tracts Uncle Sam promised
to each returning war veteran who still had enough fingers left to
sign his name to the mortgage. There the children penned the old
men up in little bedrooms off the backyard where they looked out
their windows with hollow eyes, listened to their children fight in
the bedroom down the hall, nodded off in their memories, and told
themselves they had been successes in their time.

The old prizefighters from over on Grand Street who used to
run the amateur tournaments weren't around too much either
anymore. Many of them had gone into the service early in the war
and were left on the beaches of Tarawa and Iwo Jima. Others were
buried outside of Palermo or in the little graveyards along the
slopes of Monte Casino. And I was already living the life of the man
who wasn't there. At Mr. Hoover's insistence, I had dropped out of
the actor's workshop and moved back to New York after spending
a couple of months in Los Angeles looking for stunt work with Steve
McQueen, who everybody was telling me I resembled.

"You're too visible there," Mr. H. had said. "In your job you act
for real, not for the movies." He'd also said that all actors were
either fruitcakes or Commies, but since I'd never met any fruitcakes or Communist actors myself, I didn't know what he was
talking about.

He'd smoothed it over with Mr. Warner so there'd be no hard
feelings. The head of the studio wanted me to work on the lot as a
prop boy and contract extra for pocket change and all the lunch I
could eat at the Warner Brothers commissary. "You'll break in,
kid," Mr. Warner had said. "You'll make it; you're still young." But
Mr. Hoover would have none of it, called Jack Warner himself, and
told him, "He's not for you." The phone calls from Mr. Warner
stopped and I flew back East where I looked for a job in any line of
work where I could set my own hours and come and go as I pleased.
The Old Man had made it clear that he didn't want me to have to
make excuses to anybody about my absences.

Then Mr. H. decided that he wanted someone to keep an eye
on the makes and models of cars that the foreign missions to the
United Nations were ordering from New York car dealers. The Old
Man had some calls made to people who'd sold cars to the police and

government agencies and got me a job as a car salesman in Brooklyn. I knew the business from having sold used cars when I got out of the Navy. But this time I was *on* the books.

"He wants you to learn the business," I was told through the grapevine. "It's steady income and you get a new car every year. That way nobody don't ask no questions about what they call 'means of support.' "

And I didn't ask any questions either, especially when I was working for Flatbush Buick but getting paid by Bay Ridge DeSoto and spending most of my time in the fleet sales office of Atlantic Avenue Pontiac. It took me only about a month to understand how the people in the government moved cars through the used-car sales lots, changing color and serial numbers and reissuing the title, registration, and plates so many times during the course of a week that a single car became five cars and allowed the police to forget about a warehouse job without embarrassing anybody. Besides, the insurance companies paid anyway.

But the job also taught me how foreign diplomats got their cars, especially when clerks at the consulates made private arrangements with car dealers to overcharge the diplomatic missions and pay themselves dealer commissions under the table. We also kept tabs on what cars went to the police precincts, especially the detective squads. In fact, during the first three months, I knew where every fleet car was located out of all the Brooklyn Buick dealerships. I could recite it to you like I was standing in front of a class. I made it a point to know because the one message from Mr. H. after he set me up in Brooklyn was, "Know who's drivin' what!" One of Mr. H.'s people gave me that order after work one evening when I had gone over to Gleason's gym on West 30th Street for a workout on the light bag. That's all that was in the message, but that's all I needed.

Mr. H. never said a word to me directly, and I didn't attempt to reach him either because I was told never to try to reach him unless it was an emergency. I just played dumb, stayed visible, letting the stupid precinct cops see me on the street, and waited for my messages. None came. It was as if I had just dropped into a hole where no one saw me and no one heard me. I started going out with a black-haired Greek girl who was still a teenager, and that settled me down a little bit. I couldn't talk to her about what I was doing, though, and I had Friday-night dinners with her parents in Williamsburg where we all talked about the automobile business and my future as a car salesman.

"So, Mendel, you think someday everybody will have a car?" the *zeydeh,* Maria's old grandfather, would ask after we had said our *baruchot* over the wine and *challah.*

"Someday, *zeydeh,* people are going to have two cars in their families and the rich people might even three," I would answer.

"Tsk, tsk," he would cluck, "how can you drive two cars at the same time. So where would you go? Kids don't know what they got today. When I was your age in the *shtetl* you was lucky to get a goat." And he would slurp his soup and gum his chicken and think about what I said. Then he would look up at Maria's father and say, "Shmuel, the boy's got a future."

I found myself getting into fewer fights. I had to wear a tie and jacket everyday, even though I was kicking tires and climbing under the hood to show chauffeurs from the United Nations Missions that our motors were clean, our used cars didn't burn oil, and the brake fluid reservoirs wouldn't leak as soon as the car drove off the lot. Sometimes I had to split a sales commission with a greedy undersecretary from some country the size of the Bronx, but I didn't care. I cashed my paychecks, gave momma as much money as she wanted, saw Maria at dinner on Friday nights, and stayed out of trouble.

I stopped waking up in the middle of the night. Even the cops stopped giving me the once-over along Delancey Street as if they were going to pick me up, toss me in the can, and give me a message from the Old Man. There were times when I even half believed that the past ten years, especially my time in Georgia, had been part of a nightmare. But then I would spot Mr. C. looking at me from the tinted window of his black limousine as it passed by and I would know that for whatever reason, I was being rested. I was between fights, maybe putting on some weight to move up to the next division, but it would begin again.

I was sitting in Marshioni's, just over the Brooklyn Bridge on the Manhattan side and just like I'd sat there on hot afternoons since I was a kid, on a long lunch break in late August. It was only a few days before we were supposed to begin clearing out the last of the '54s for the new '55 two-tone Buick Specials with the windshields that wrapped around to the side vents. I was waiting for my boss's big executive demo model to arrive with the leather seats and the eight-cylinder engine so I could show it off to Maria and take her family for a drive out to Far Rockaway for one of the last warm summer weekends of the year. I'd already eaten and was sitting back at the counter, looking at who was coming and going and making believe that it really was before the war and I was playing hooky from school. But like the aftertaste of a memory you feel when you wake up on the edge of a bad dream, I felt an uncomfortable chill when these two figures appeared in the doorway, silhouetted against the afternoon sun.

"Some strawberries and whipped cream for my friend at the end of the counter," I heard one of them say in a voice too young to be afraid of. Then he looked at me and I tensed my shoulders, waiting for them to watch me eat the strawberries and acknowledge their presence.

Part of me would have liked to have stayed anonymous, to be like other people who live on the surface and don't have to respond to private codes and hand signals. But part of me was just like the guys standing at the door ordering up the strawberries. I was thirty-one, fast and strong, and I lived the most vital part of my life completely in the shadows. I walked with fear and I used fear as a tool. When I paid a visit to someone's office up on Seventh Avenue, it wasn't to do business like the guys who had gone to FIT on the GI bill and were selling designs out of their sample cases. It was to convince him that no matter how many other bills he had to pay, his weekly vig payment was the most important. I wasn't supposed to care if his daughter needed braces or his mother had cataracts. I wasn't supposed to care about his payroll or his union contract or the Fuller Brush Man who was making a delivery that day. The vig had to be paid.

You see, most of these guys were in debt to one of Mr. C.'s shylocks up to their ears. They had borrowed to build their businesses up from a single bank of machines and a cutting table to fancy showrooms with *shiksa* blonde models that floated over to the customers and made them happy. They were so hungry to fill the department stores and new shopping malls with merchandise that they borrowed against everything they owned, including the orders that they had yet to manufacture. And when it paid off, they called themselves successful and moved out of Brooklyn to raise their kids in ranch houses and split-levels with basement playrooms in places like Cedarhurst and Woodmere. When it didn't pay off, they had to look me in the eye when I stood behind their desks and tell me about the unions and the truck drivers on strike. I still lived on the Lower East Side where Yiddush and Polish were giving way to Spanish and Sicilian to Chinese. I didn't like seeing these old men cry and blow their noses in their ties, but I had my bills to pay also.

The men by the door kept on looking at me as the counterman pushed the bowl of strawberries across the counter. I was sorry I ever said I liked the damn things, but it was better than staring into a bowl of eggplant or something. I just hoped I didn't get an allergy to them because the way Sicilians cured you of allergies was to slap your face until the next slap raised more welts than the allergy. The men were waiting until I took my first bite. Then they moved down the counter, stood on either side of me and whispered, "Someone wants to see you." They didn't have to say anything else. I nodded and went along with them. You don't say no to Mr. C., ever. He would make it even with my boss. One of his people would call him on the phone and say that I had an errand to run. My boss would understand. He wouldn't say no to Mr. C. either.

With the two messengers sitting on either side of me in the back seat, the car headed north for a few blocks and pulled up in front of Garfein's restaurant where I could see through the window that there were more than the usual pair of button men lolling about inside. Mr. C. wasn't like the other dons. He didn't travel with an army of people wherever he went because he didn't want to draw any attention. Most of the time, he only had two bodyguards. If it was really an important sitdown where someone's life was being decided, he'd bring an extra man along. But this day I counted at least four button men on the inside. The three men with me in the car brought the number to seven, a two-car safari from Mulberry Street to the Lower East Side.

The driver just pointed at the restaurant after he set the foot-brake and motioned with his head. There were no words. They opened the door for me and escorted me to the door. I wasn't even sure that they knew what was going on inside. I walked in to find a completely empty room. At 3:30 in the afternoon, Garfein's should have been a busy place, even this late in the summer. There was a button man standing by the back door at the entrance to the banquet room. He took off his hat and and pointed it at the door. Again, I didn't need any words to understand his message. I walked past him through the heavy wooden door and into Garfein's main hall.

The lights weren't on—not unusual for a summer afternoon when the hall wasn't being used—so at first I couldn't see very well in the shadows. I only heard the sound of the closing door echoing off the high ceilings. I figured the hall would be as empty as it sounded and that I'd have to wait for Mr. C. to show up. He liked to stand on ceremony that way. He always kept you waiting; you never kept him waiting. But I was surprised to recognize the outlines of two men off in the corner, only barely visible underneath the large drawn shades. They hardly moved at all and made no sound, and the hall was made even quieter by the dying echoes of the door. I knew that they could see me because I felt the pressure of their eyes as I walked across the polished floors.

The stouter of the two men extended his hand and grabbed me by the elbow as I reached him. The little man took me by the other arm, pulled me towards him, and kissed me on the cheek. I could feel the stubble around his mouth on my ear as he whispered, "This is special for you, Mendel. We did this for you."

I didn't know what was up, but I had the presence of mind to whisper, "Thank you, Mr. Lansky" into the darkness surrounding Mr. L.'s eyes. Mr. Costello kissed me on the other cheek and held me by the wrist. He took my hands and put one of them on his wrist and the other on Mr. L.'s. We all stood there with joined hands.

"We wanted to make you one of our family," Mr. Costello said in his raspy voice. It cut through the darkness like the sound of a file. "But we knew it could never be. You will have to be content with knowing that you would be a made member of *La Familia* if you could be."

"This is the closest you will ever come, Mendel," Mr. Lansky echoed. "It was the closest Benny and I ever came to Charlie. It was what Sam Koenig wanted for you."

"Tommy Lucchese would stand up for you," Mr. Costello said. "Because it was for him that you performed your first service. And he would present you to me, swear to me an oath of your loyalty which he would guarantee with his own life, and in my religion I would stand godfather for you. And you would hold your right hand over a candle while it burned the flesh of your palm and I would say, 'This is the fire you will feel if you break your sacred oath and trust.' Then I would place a gun into your left hand and say, 'This is the gun you live by.' And I would take a knife and cut into the flesh of the palm of your right hand until the blood quenched the flame on the candle and say, 'This is the knife you die by.' And you would swear a vow of loyalty and *silencia*."

"*Omerta*," whispered Meyer Lansky, only half believing in the ritual itself, but not wanting to show the slightest sign of disrespect to either Mr. Costello or his traditions.

"*Omerta!*" I echoed as loudly as I dared in the darkness. And I swore the vow of loyalty and silence to Frank Costello and Meyer Lansky and was made without being made. I had my family at last. I was protected for life, for as long as I kept my oaths, even though it would be known only among the three of us in that hall. I was still in the shadows like the man who wasn't there.

I didn't even go back to work that afternoon. You can bet that my boss over at the car lot didn't even raise an eyebrow when he got the message that a certain Mr. C. required the services of his friend Mr. M., which was me. And my boss, anxious to show Frank Costello that he knew how to perform a service, volunteered to pay me for the afternoon and give me a raise as well because I was selling so many cars, which, between you and me, was bullshit.

We ate big that night. Down on Mott Street, Mr. C. stood us all to his favorite Sicilian veal in the party room of one of his most private restaurants. I had to watch my manners, though, because even while I wanted to stuff myself on the hot veal and fiery marinara sauce, I saw Meyer Lansky watching me from behind his smile. "Never forget who you are," he used to say. "Or what you are." And I knew what he meant, especially when dealing with Sicilians, who were very different from the Jews. Benny Siegel learned that lesson the hard way just a few years later when Meyer, his back against the wall, couldn't defend him any longer. He had to give the

OK for the hit after the Profacci and the Genovese families showed that he was skimming for himself off the top of the syndicate's cut. Meyer Lansky never recovered, but business was business and what the Commission said was final. Even the Old Man himself had to concur and told everybody to stand away. He sent Meyer Lansky his personal condolences, however, because he had liked Benny, and Benny had showed him a good time whenever he went to the Coast.

I could call myself made even though I wasn't. It gave me an identity of sorts in the Family, but it wasn't anything I could brag about. After all, the only people in the room with me at the time were Meyer Lansky and Frank Costello and neither of them were the talkative types. They were also the only two men ever to retire from active business with their heads still on their shoulders. And, of course, I couldn't tell Maria anything about anything. Her family would have thrown me out the door if they'd even had a hint that I was connected to the Families in any way. They wouldn't have even been happy about The Squad. So whoever I was, I had to keep it to myself and be happy about it. But Mr. Hoover had other plans.

I was driving my boss' demo into work one Friday morning a few weeks after the meeting at Garfein's when I noticed an unmarked police car swing in behind me as I made the turn onto the Williamsburg Bridge. I could see in my rearview mirror that the driver of the black Plymouth was talking into his radio as he sat about two or three car lengths behind me. I still got nervous when cops tailed me because you never knew what was on their mind. They liked to follow rumors just like the next guy, only in their position they were able to act on them by pulling you in for questioning and making you sweat out a whole day sitting in a squad room and giving names and addresses of people who could alibi your whereabouts on any particular date. I didn't want any of the local dicks nosing around Maria's family because they were immigrants and would get nervous about their daughter's boyfriend who was "in trouble" with the police. I was especially concerned about that since Maria and I were gonna get married. I was already practicing how I was gonna break the news to Mr. H.

I drove nice and slow, keeping the needle at twenty-five and letting angry cab drivers pass me and shake their fists out the window as they rode by. The cop stayed right on my tail. He certainly wasn't looking for speeders. I kept to the local streets until I reached Flatbush Avenue, the cop cruising along behind me, where I turned into the showroom lot just before Albermarle. I sat in the car and watched the police car continue on and make a turn around the block. As I was getting my paperwork out for the day's deliveries, I noticed him come up on the other side of the street and park. I was under surveillance. Did the cops figure I was made? I asked myself. I didn't know that was a crime. In the old days, I might have walked over to the cop and baited him into making a pinch just to find out what he was after. But I wasn't a troublemaking kid anymore. I had a job and a girlfriend and I was working at my new job on Mr. H.'s orders. I'd play it by the book. Maybe, I said, this guy was carrying a message from the Old Man—better make myself available.

So in the early afternoon when I would normally drive the boss's car back into town for lunch at Marshioni's, I told the floor manager that I'd walk down the street for a sandwich and coffee and eat at my desk. I had too many orders to fill out, I said, too many registrations to file for diplomatic plates, and I didn't want to get behind. I walked real slow, trying not to be too obvious as I passed the police car, but letting the cop know I'd made him and was giving him the chance to give me a message if he had one or make his collar and get it over with. He didn't waste a minute. By the time I crossed in front of the car, I heard the engine rev, the transmission drop into gear, and the tires crunch as the cop edged out into the traffic on Flatbush Avenue.

"Get in here fast, Mike," he called from window. "We're only gonna go around the block."

I kept pace with the car, but didn't cross the street.

"This a roust?" I asked. "I'm just a workin' guy who's gotta get back to my desk."

"Don't play games with me," he snarled. "If you want, we can do this like the old days, and we both know someone who's not gonna be happy about that."

I obliged, satisfied that I wasn't being picked up on any bum rap just to keep some lieutenant happy that his racket squad wasn't sitting on their asses all day in a doughnut shop in Brooklyn.

"So how do you like workin', Mike?" the cop asked, extending his hand for me to shake and nodding that he wanted me to do it.

"Beats not workin'," I said, taking his hand and feeling the piece of paper he had concealed in his palm.

"We just like to keep tabs on the neighborhood kids," the cop continued. "Like to see you boys makin' good in the world and becomin' taxpayin' citizens like the rest of us. Anyplace I can drive you?"

"Naw. I'm just gonna pick up some coffee and get back to the showroom. Got a lot of cars to deliver."

He stopped the car, reached across me, and opened the passenger door. "Think I could get a good deal if I came to you for a car?" He asked, nosing around for whatever was floating near the surface that he could pick off on a lazy August afternoon. I knew that if I was willing to cut my commission down to chump change, I'd have a cop for life. He'd come in handy some day.

"I'll put something aside on a corner of the lot that you can use to take the family in," I told him. "Make sure no one buys it. When the new models come in from Detroit next month, I'll get it for you at a price not even the dealers in Jersey can match. You come to me in a week and you'll drive out in one of my boss's demo '54s with the special paint job."

"Good boy," he said. "And they told me in the squadroom you was a punk. Ya learnin' how to play ball, Mike. Ya been listenin' to somebody smart."

I put the slip of paper in my pocket, got out of the car, grabbed my lunch and went back to the showroom. Afternoon business was already beginning to pick up. There were customers milling around the showroom and through the window I could see some of the typical used-car kids kicking at the tires of a '49 Chevy two-door manual coupe rusting through its frame on the back of the lot. The sign I'd painted on the windshield—First $150 Takes It!—was drawing them in. The boss was promising to stuff an extra sawbuck into the envelope of whoever could move the heap off the property and I really needed the money these days. I wanted to get married and show Maria's father that I could take care of his daughter. I would have rather stayed on the showroom floor to pick up a customer, but I had to read the note before doing anything else.

I slipped out to the bathroom where I locked the door behind me in a stall and opened the folded paper. It was only one sentence carefully printed in pencil: 8/28—6:29 frm Penn Sta to Union Sta DC. EYES ONLY! That meant I'd miss work on the next day, Saturday, but I'd explain to the boss that it was an emergency. Mr. H. would make it alright with a phone call, I hoped, but there was nothing else I could do.

I flushed away the note down the toilet and got back out to the floor fast. I was in time to see one of the kids walking around the Chevy in circles as if mentally counting the money in his pocket. He turned to go and then turned back. Then he turned to leave again. This called for what Mr. L. always referred to as a grand gesture. I pulled twenty-five bucks out of my pocket and walked up to the kid as fast as I could. I tapped him on the shoulder and held the twenty-five bucks in front of his face. Then I pointed to the car and stuffed the money in his hand. The kid nodded emphatically and stuck out his hand, and we had a deal. I put my arm around him and walked him back to my desk in the showroom where I pulled out the salespad and wrote up the order. He handed my twenty-five bucks back to me and carefully counted out the money in his pocket as if it was his life savings.

"It's all yours," I said. "We'll even throw in an engine tune-up, oil change, and a wax job and you can drive it away on Tuesday." Then I waved to my boss across the sales floor and pointed to the Chevy in the lot.

When the kid had left, I handed the saleslip and hundred and fifty bucks to my boss who pounded me on the back, peeled a twenty from the money I'd just given him, and told me to take Saturday off. Sure, the deal had cost me five bucks out of my own pocket, but it saved my having to make any excuses. And in my boss's eyes I was golden.

It was Maria's grandfather who was most impressed by my deal when I told the family about it that night. "You have a knack for sales, Mendel," the *zeydeh* said over and over again. "Doesn't he, Zev?" he asked his son. "You could use him in the business." And he winked at Maria who was too red-faced to answer. He had just given us his blessing and I knew I'd never forget the little-girl smile she smiled at me across the table. It was the smile that stayed with me while I was dozing on the train the next morning all the way down to Washington. And it was the smile in my mind that I woke up with when I heard the conductor announce Union Station, the last stop.

I rubbed my eyes and stumbled out onto the platform, the effects of the Sabbath wine still making me feel a little groggy at that hour in the morning. The station was deserted; nobody traveled to Washington on a Saturday, especially right before Labor Day. I headed directly for the ticket counters, not really knowing what I was supposed to do next but knowing also that the Old Man never left loose ends dangling. When I saw the lone cab driver by the closed information window pacing back and forth, I figured that was my message.

"Lookin' for a fare?" I asked.

"Not unless you're goin' to the used-car dealers' meetin' in Arlington," the driver said as he pointedly looked away from me.

"I'm your fare," I told him, and without turning around to make sure I was following him, he led me outside to his checker cab waiting at the stand.

The driver didn't talk at all as we pulled out of downtown Washington and headed across the bridge to Virginia. Nor did he start the meter or look in the rearview mirror. He might have been as tired as I was, but the ride took only ten minutes so I didn't have to make any conversation. I'm sure he was happy about that, too. When we pulled up in the driveway of the dormatory-sized house set back on a very green, very trimmed lawn, I fished in my pocket for some bills, but he said, "Been paid," as I pushed the money through the window. Then he turned away from me as if he was afraid of looking directly at my face.

I'd seen people act that way before, of course. And I knew this cab driver had at one time driven for a don or at least someone high up in the Families. The rule was that unless you were made or had been granted some special favor, you were never to look a don directly face-on. That way you could never be forced to identify him. It was an old custom that nobody ever talked about any more, especially outside the Families, and I wondered if Mr. H. knew about it. Since he knew about everything else, I assumed he probably knew this custom too and had picked the cab driver especially for this meeting.

The front door opened as soon as I stepped onto the porch. I couldn't see who was behind the door because he closed the door after me at once and stepped into another room before I could even turn around. From the sidewalk, you couldn't see inside. The curtains were drawn and there were no lights at all from any of the windows. Only the closely cut lawn would have indicated that the house was neither abandoned nor condemned. I didn't see any FBI-types roaming the grounds. That was unlike Mr. H. because he normally liked to have at least two men lurking around. He always believed in security.

I sneaked a look around the vestibule while I waited to be shown inside. The interior of the house was very empty, with almost no furniture of any kind except for a large conference table with chairs around it in what could have been a dining room. A door opened down the hall and I could see Mr. Hoover lean out and wave me towards him. I nodded and walked towards him.

"Come in," the Old Man said. "This won't take long at all."

The small room where Mr. Hoover was waiting for me reminded me of his typical room at the Carlyle on the very few times I had seen him there. He was sitting in his shirtsleeves alongside a small writing table by an open window. There was an empty drinking glass on the table. He stood up to greet me, shaking my hand and staring me right in the eye, and then sat down. There was no other chair in the room. Mr. Hoover opened a narrow drawer in the table and pulled out a what looked like a dossier in a file folder attached to the back sheet by one of those metal fasteners that I'd seen in legal folders or in police files. It couldn't have been my police folder because it was too thin.

"They tell me you're selling a lot of cars," he began. "Are you keeping your eyes out for who drives what?"

"Yes sir," I said. "I know what each mission has been buying and the types of cars that the different consulates like to use."

"And you've kept records of all the registrations?" he asked.

"Just as you asked me to," I said. "And the serial numbers also. I can trace any car to any mission."

"And nobody knows you're doing it?" he ordered. "It's gotta be on the q.t. because if it ever gets into the papers, the damn ambassador to the United Nations will scream bloody murder."

"Don't worry, sir," I said. "The records are safe. Not even my boss knows that I make extra carbons of all his deliveries to the foreign missions—"

"That's not what I asked you down here for," Mr. Hoover broke in, satisfied that I was doing what he wanted. "I want to start a new system and I wanted to tell you about it face-to-face." He opened the dossier on the desk, revealing a old military portrait of a black-uniformed SS officer. Attached to it was a recent passport photo of what was obviously the same man. "I don't have to tell you what this is, do I?"

"Someone who got through after the war?" I asked, more out of politeness than anything else. I already knew what he was showing me.

"He didn't get through. We let him through," he said. "His name is Hans Diedrich, another one of G2's special cases. He was a medical aide at *Tereisenstadt* who amassed a small fortune in confiscated property and cut a private deal with Army Intelligence. He's in New York now."

I bit my lip when I pictured how easily I could get to this man, and balled my hands into fists. The Old Man must have seen how red my face was becoming.

"We're going to start a new system now," he said. "Too many of these people have begun to come out of hiding, and we want to do what we have to do systematically. We're going to do this like a court of law."

I looked at him in disbelief. Before, it was just like any other contract. You get your orders and your dough and ba-da-boom. The man's dead and you go home. Anything that had to do with a court sounded too complicated for me.

"It's not hard to understand, Mike," he continued. "In these special circumstances, I simply can't go on ordering that certain people disappear. Some of these people are such perverts, you and the others have to understand what you're doing." He paused. "There are ten of you now, you know."

Ten! That hit me like a left hook. This thing was bigger than I thought.

"Still, nobody knows about any of you. In fact, I even call you the Unknowns to myself," he said. "There are rumors, of course—

there always are. People suspect—the CIA assumes I got my own personnel, especially after Li Chin's meeting with the Company boys in Los Angeles, but they don't know. That's what's important. Now I want to start acting on these pervert cases like we were a court. I show you dossiers and if you think the man should die, you turn over a glass. Just like you-know-where."

If these had been any other circumstances, if I hadn't been getting orders from the head of the FBI, I would have laughed. Unless Mr. Hoover was a personal friend of people he shouldn't have been, there was no way he could have known about one of the oldest hand signals of the Moustache Petes from the *Unione* days. If one *capo* wanted to know if another *capo* at a sitdown concurred on a hit, the first *capo* would push forward an empty glass across a table. The second *capo* would give his assent by turning the glass upside down. If he disagreed, he would pick up the glass and put it down rightside up. If the man was hit anyway, the peace would be broken until compensation or other satisfaction could be given. But how did Mr. Hoover know all this?

"I believe you understand the meaning of this," the Old Man continued. "When we convene, and we will from time to time and only under the most special circumstances, we will sit in judgment on people beyond the reach of our government and our court. They are felons our law enforcement cannot possibly touch." He was getting agitated like I'd never seen him before. "We can't allow these people to walk around as if they are human beings. They have to be eliminated. But I want to do it right. I want to call this the 'Court of Life.'"

I only nodded and turned back the pages of Diedrich's dossier so I could read his record. I was filled with a fury I hadn't felt for a long time. I reached out and held the glass before Mr. Hoover's eyes. Then I turned it upside down over Diedrich's picture.

"Not yet," he said. His voice was very solemn, like he'd come to a fatal decision. "I still have to make more plans for the other Unknowns. But I'm pleased to have your concurrence in this. Now go back to New York. Get ready for your next job. You will get your next message from me very soon."

He grabbed my hand and shook it hard, clearly pleased that I would go along with whatever he wanted. Then he said, "You know, Mike, I understand that you wanted to stay in Los Angeles and work for Jack Warner. I understand that. Sometimes you just can't have exactly what you want, especially when you've already made other choices that can't be unmade. I just hope there's no hard feelings about what I had to do."

Now I was feeling moved that the Old Man realized that it really was a sacrifice to have to leave California and turn my back on what Jack Warner said would be a career that anyone in his right mind would want. It was the career I'd dreamed about when I looked in the mirror and thought I saw a movie star like Jimmy Cagney staring back at me. But I wanted to let Mr. H. know that I was stand-up no matter what. I was loyal to the people I worked for, always.

"I'd like to think that I'm a born actor," I said, speaking seriously to him in a way I'd never done before. "It's what I want to do. But maybe now, instead of being like other actors who perform only when they're in front of a camera, I'm acting for real, twenty-four hours a day. They're acting for money. I'm acting for my life."

Mr. Hoover nodded. He understood. He had taken lots of publicity photos with actors during his career because he liked to keep his name in the newspapers, but his expression told me that he knew what acting meant to me. I think he appreciated what I said to him.

"Then your next job will really give you the chance to act," he said, a very slight smile breaking out between his bulldog jowls. "I'm going to hang a detective's shield on you and turn you lose in the Police Department." His smile quickly faded. "Watch the line," he said. "Stay right in the middle. You'll be protected from both sides as long as you watch the line."

I had to bring up Maria. I had to tell him that I was making plans. I didn't know how he'd take it because he'd always been pretty strict about the regular FBI agents who'd gotten married without telling him. "Maria and me," I blurted out. "You know Maria, she and I . . . well, we plan . . . " Mr. Hoover just turned around and walked out of the room without saying a word. I didn't know what I was supposed to do. Then, after what seemed a couple of minutes, he came back in. He stuck his hand out. "Best to both of you," he said. "Remember what I said about that line."

I knew what he meant, of course, and thought about it as I got in the cab to take me back to Union Station. But Mr. Hoover was pretty dramatic himself when he wanted to be and made his point just a week after our meeting in Virginia. I'd gotten taken to dinner by one of Mr. Costello's button men who kept me out until well after four in the morning, when every bar in the City should have been closed. But he kept saying, "One more place," until he finally dropped me off at Grand Central Station where, in the empty waiting room, I saw Frank Costello himself motioning to me.

I was so tired and so bleary-eyed after a night of bar-hopping that the scene itself seemed almost like a dream: Frank Costello standing under the big clock in Grand Central Station. But as I walked toward him, obeying orders as always, I saw him turn his head toward the long incline that led to the 42nd Street entrance. And there, only half stepping out of the shadow for a minute so I could see him, was the Old Man. J. Edgar Hoover and Frank Costello in the same place at the same time. They looked at me; they looked at each other. No one spoke. No one needed to speak. Then each of them turned and went in a different direction. It was crazy, but the message was clear. They had let me see them together; they had given me the message. I was right in the middle, just as Sam Koenig must have figured I'd be.

Hessian Tavern

I'd been working the night watch out of the Number Six Precinct's homicide division in Lower Manhattan off and on for over a year and a half by the late spring of 1957. On paper, I was attached to the division's major crimes unit. And even though I'd gotten used to the police routine, I still couldn't believe the gold detective's shield that I was carrying in my pocket. Sometimes, when no one was watching, I would just take it out and stare at it. Other times, I would sit in the can and shine it up with toilet paper until it gleamed. And once and awhile late at night, when I was really alone, I would run my fingers over the starpoints like it was Aladdin's magic lantern. And in a way it was. I was posing as a cop, just as Mr. H. said I would be, working undercover in the NYPD, watching for the names of individuals on the Old Man's private hit list, and reporting their whereabouts to Washington. All of this, you got to understand, while I was still hustling cars parttime in Brooklyn and disappearing for up to a week at a time every couple of months or so to locate people for the Court of Life. You had to find 'em before you could pass judgment on 'em, Mr. Hoover used to say. Before anybody could turn over any glasses.

I was a mystery to the other detectives in the squad room. I didn't roll on the routine calls and I wasn't paired up with a permanent partner. I just showed up at selected crime scenes while the forensics crew was taking photographs, lifting latents off surfaces, or collecting other types of evidence. Some of the cops at the Number Six thought that I was working for Internal Affairs; others might have assumed I was a regular FBI agent attached to the Department for joint operations. Not even the watch commanders knew who I was, but they'd been told by their precinct commanders to look the other way whenever I showed up in the station house. I kept to myself most of the time, didn't go drinking with the other dicks in my unit, or do what cops did with other cops. I didn't have any experiences I could share with anybody, and, of course, I couldn't talk about what I did in the war. I knew police procedure even though I hadn't attended the Police Academy or spent any time as a uniform. I knew how the cops worked from the other side, and I'd learned how to conduct an investigation during my years in intelligence and on the Squad.

I also knew why Mr. Costello hadn't been asking me to pay any visits for the past eighteen months. Now that he was retiring from the Commission's business he sent me my strawberries only when he wanted a sitdown or when he had something special that needed a particular type of discretion. Ever since that night in Grand Central Station, which I still only half believe to this day, I realized that Mr. Hoover and Mr. Costello worked together. Not that they were partners, you understand, but that they seemed to stay within their own territories. It had all begun to make sense after that night. I knew that Mr. H. liked to play the horses and turn up at fancy joints with show-business dames hanging on his arms, but I never knew where he found'em. Now I knew where. I also knew that he and Meyer Lansky sometimes broke bread together. Mr. L. was never rousted, was rarely served with federal subpoenas, and was generally left alone to conduct his business. Mr. L., on the other hand, didn't go around shooting anybody like people in some of the other Families, and making life embarrassing for the cops and the feds. So in this way everybody got along. Mr. H. could worry about his fifth column, Mr. C. could worry about keeping peace among the different Families and looking forward to retirement, and Mr. L. could worry about the cash flow in his Las Vegas casinos.

Like the guy on TV, I was leading different lives. I was a used-car salesman in Brooklyn, driving to work in the morning with a cardboard cup of coffee in my hand, touting junk heaps to hard-headed Joes with shallow pockets who wanted to impress the wives with their abilities to spot a bargain, and going home in the afternoon just like the rest of the crowd. People who knew me from the old neighborhood said I'd finally settled down. I'd been married to Maria for over nine months. We'd moved out of Lower Manhattan and into Brooklyn and had begun to save what we could for a private house on Long Island. On the surface, nothing could be more normal.

Maria, of course, didn't know where I went on my business trips and she knew that there was a part of what I did that she couldn't ask about. From my relatives, she'd heard all the stories that I was a *schlammer* for the East Side money-lenders and the Sicilian roughnecks and that I'd been seen in the company of people wanted by the police. But neither Maria nor anybody else knew that by 1957 I was an independent contractor for most of the Families in New York, that I was protected by Frank Costello, and that I was working for J. Edgar Hoover. And since 1956, I was part of Hoover's plan to infiltrate the Unknowns into local police details in cities around the country to look for the thousands of people in Hoover's private files. These were my lives, and I walked a tightrope, keeping them separated from one another while I tried to appear as normal as possible on the surface.

But tensions broke the surface. There were times when I came home from work with the kinds of bruises you don't get negotiating the price of a car across a desk. And there were times when I kept particularly late hours, especially when I was following a suspect for the major crimes unit that not coincidentally was on Mr. Hoover's list. More often than not the suspect disappeared before he could ever be picked up by the other detectives. There were neighbors of ours who saw me with a squad of detectives surrounding a building in Brooklyn, my gold shield hanging out of my jacket pocket, and said to Maria, "We didn't know your husband was a cop—we thought he sold cars." They weren't our friends after that, and Maria complained about the hard stares she got from our neighbors in the supermarket for the months that followed.

Husbands and wives share friends, but my real friends walked in a world of fear that no one who did not walk there could ever understand. Husbands and wives share family, but what could her family ever share about me? Her grandfather still thought I sold cars for a living, but her parents suspected different. Maria was alone too much, they thought. Why did I have to go on so many business trips? they asked. They knew I wasn't certified kosher, but what could they do? They were orthodox and had to live with the bargain they had made. I myself had no family for Maria to share. My mama was dead; papa had died at the end of the war and my older brother had been killed during the war.

The balancing act that I'd learned to do over the years had become a part of my life. Like the Spanish guy who could keep all those plates spinning at the same time in the air on the Ed Sullivan Show, I had learned how to run from plate to plate in my life and keep each from falling as soon as I spotted it wobbling on the stick. But each year there were more plates, and it was getting trickier. Soon I'd need more hands. With the balancing act, I'd developed a kind of surface tension. Maybe you can say it was because I was an instinctual actor, but I'd also figured how to sit in one place and go through the motions of what I was supposed to be doing, but in my head I'd be somewhere else. That used to drive Maria crazy until she got used to it, but after she did, she realized that there was a part of me she'd never know. She couldn't know it because it was too dark, too dangerous, too much held in place by the thinnest sections of mental boilerplate. And it was always under pressure.

There would be weeks at a time when I wouldn't show my face at the Number Six. Then I'd be there every night for a month working the shift just like any flatfoot. Maybe some of the other dicks wondered why I was standing around a used-car lot during the day and going through current major crime files and missing-persons reports at night, but they didn't ask me. They asked about other precincts I was supposed to have worked out of, members of my supposed Police Academy class who, coincidentally, never seemed to be at their phone or get their messages, or superior officers who conveniently had forgotten my name or didn't have my records in their files any more. It was safest, the squad room detectives thought, to assume that I was from IA and as much their enemy as the bad guys on the street. So they left me alone.

At first, Mr. H. was keeping his eye on me, too. Each week I'd find a sealed DOJ eyes-only folder in the top drawer of my desk. In it were the names of people the Squad was tracking: war criminals, Soviet military attachées assigned here during World War II who were never quiet repatriated after VE Day, Eastern Bloc United Nations delegates who had habits of dropping out of sight, and other individuals who were otherwise immune from official FBI investigations. I would check Mr. Hoover's list against the names of individuals in our police investigations and trace the addresses. When I found any information Mr. Hoover could use, I sent it back to him in an eyes-only pouch. Ninety-nine percent of what I was doing was just like holding down a stolen-properties desk. In the beginning I was only checking the lists. And by reporting the results of what I'd found back to Washington, I was the return echo on Mr. Hoover's sonar.

But as the months wore on and I moved from selling used cars to filling special orders full-time for the UN missions and consulates, the cross-references became more and more complicated and interesting. From time to time Mr. Hoover would become especially concerned about what types of vehicles the Eastern Block missions were buying. If the Albanians or the Poles wanted dark tinted glass for the rear windows of their Cadillacs, that was information I'd forward to Washington. If the East Germans ordered a Coupe deVille instead of a Sedan deVille, the Old Man would want to know why. If a new name turned up on a purchase order, that, too, was information he found important.

Toward the end of 1956 right after the Jewish holidays, Mr. Hoover began sending me straight-out contracts in the list of names from Washington. I didn't question him; I simply cross-referenced the names against the ongoing files of the major crimes units in Manhattan that circulated by Teletype every morning and when I hit a match, I dispatched myself to the investigating unit. I knew that I had the clearance to do this because no one questioned my presence at the surveillance. Sure there were a few stares and glares from the veteran gumshoes, but by the next night they stood off and let me do my work. And when it was time for the name to disappear, I notified Washington in advance, and someone somewhere on some Teletype cleared it with some local precinct captain or a a nameless deputy chief inspector in some office in the police building. I never knew who and I never asked any questions. The official surveillance was pulled off and my surveillance began. The person that was Mike Milan disappeared and I became the mark's shadow, the phantom ballet dancer who would slip out of view the split-second the person looked over his shoulder in apprehension. I'd watch the man's routine, when he went to bed, where he ate, what subway he took to work, how he held his dick when he pissed, and what side of his bed he slept on. I would know how his car was wired, where he stood when he plugged in his razor in the morning, or whether he took a flashlight to the basement to change a fuse. I stepped into his life and lived it until a moment would come when he and I almost became the same person. In the darkness I would take his hand. And then he would simply vanish as if he'd never been. A few days later, I would notify Washington that theirpackage had been delivered, the subject of their investigation had disappeared. And in the most routine of fashion, that name would simply not appear in its alphabetical order on the following week's list.

The worst part of it was that it was all so easy, like I was pulling tubes out of TV sets on an assembly line. Each face, each life, was like another unit that rolled up on the conveyor belt, got packaged, and rolled off out of view. You didn't have the luxury of thinking about them. You just executed your contract. That was your job and you did your job. Afterwards you took your wife out to Lenny's for some scungilli over linguini and maybe a little Lambrusco to wash it down, winked at the boys from the old neighborhood, and drove back to Brooklyn with your honey in the still of the night along the Shore Parkway in your boss's executive demo 1957 Chevy convertible with the top down, Meussurry the Keussay on the radio, and your gold detective's shield pinned safely to the inside of your wallet in case some flatfoot stopped you for weaving back and forth too much.

There were at least fifteen people who disappeared in this way and I guess you can say they'd be listed as unsolved homicides. That's why any names I might give you from that list would be completely false. If you need to satisfy yourself about the legality of what I did, let's just say that they were bad people doing bad things. They were threats to all of us, but they were beyond the law. Fortunately, they were not beyond Mr. Hoover's law. Before the Kennedys came to power, that's how things were done.

In May of 1957, the Old Man stepped the pressure up another notch. On my usual list of people to watch out for, I found a name I recognized from three years earlier: Hans Diedrich. This was typical of Mr. H.'s very perverse sense of humor. He liked to match a job with a person who already had an emotional reaction to it just so he could watch the show. I'd gone through that experience in Georgia back in '53, and I knew that Mr. H. thought it the measure of a man to do a job under emotional pressure. He liked to push people, especially people he trusted, because he wanted to see what would happen if he upped the ante of that trust. It was like a horse race to him. If you could run on a dry fast track, he'd want to see you run in mud. If you ran the track OK, he'd put you in the gate with quicker mounts so you'd have to run faster just to keep up. Then he'd add weight to your jock. He'd keep piling it on until he saw that you couldn't do it any more. And the trick to staying alive with him was to get him to take the pressure off before you broke. It all seems clear now, just as if I'd known it at the time. Unfortunately, I didn't realize it until years later after half my brains had been scrambled by the CIA or the KGB or both in a VA hospital in Manhattan, and the Old Man had let himself be pushed into allowing it to happen.

Hans Diedrich. I told myself you can never figure what names'll turn up on a hot list. It'd been over three years and I'd been mired in a routine of detached executions, selling cars, and putting on weight. When I saw his name I wanted to drop everything and look for him. I wanted to get a close-up look at the man in person. But this was not a hit. The Court of Life hadn't sanctioned it. The Old Man was only looking for him. Maybe the FBI wanted him to lead them to other former concentration camp guards who had gotten into the country with him or maybe they just wanted to keep tabs on him until the day he died. I didn't know. But I ran the name down to R&I and found out over the Teletype that a Hans Diedrich was one of the names on an application for a liquor license which was eventually sold under the name of a bar up in Yorkville called the Hessian Tavern. Jeez, I said to myself as the machine tapped out the information like a drummer keeping time in a marching band, I wonder who eats there?

Later that afternoon on my way home from the precinct, I drove one of the major crime unit's cars up to Yorkville, 89th-and-1st, for a looksee. The neighborhood was as I'd remembered it from the early '40s when old Sam Koenig walked me through there once right after we'd entered the war. "There are Nazis who live here," he'd said. "Spies!" They'd even had Bund meetings up in Yorkville during the '30s when Hitler was first coming to power, and they fought every attempt Roosevelt made to get us into the war. After the war, Yorkville had changed somewhat, but to anyone who'd grown up in New York in the 1940s, Yorkville was enemy territory. And that's how I felt that afternoon as I cruised passed the Hessian Tavern and parked the car across the street.

It looked like a family place from the outside and there were plump Germans walking in and out, husbands and wives sitting down to an early Friday night dinner at the local restaurant. On Broome Street this would have been a little family bar, maybe with a few sidewalk tables placed around for a summer Sunday afternoon dinner. There was nothing about it that would make anybody especially crazy, except that somehow a Hans Diedrich had been connected with it. I had seen his official Nazi portrait, read his dossier, and turned over his glass four years ago. I wanted to see what he looked like in the flesh.

It was already getting late when I checked the clock on the dashboard—clocks in police cars almost always worked—and decided to bring the unit back to the precinct and return later in the evening with my own car. I wanted to go inside and eat some dinner, but it seemed like a real family restaurant and anybody single would have stuck out like a sore thumb. Not the way to appear inconspicuous. Besides, I had Maria to worry about. Things had been getting tense between us recently because of all the time I'd been spending at the station house and on surveillance. Maybe, I told myself, we'd just have dinner at the Hessian Tavern. Certainly be a change of pace. I was only gonna look the place over, see if I could recognize anybody that looked like Diedrich. And once I saw him there, I'd stake out the place until I could pick him up and tail him to where he lived. I was only filing a report. So, without thinking about any of the consequences, I told Maria we'd be going out that night to a new place, somewhere she'd never been. And I congratulated myself on my ingenuity as I turned the key in the ignition; just another plate that needed spinning 'cause it was getting wobbly on the stick.

I already ordered too much beer and was looking around the smoky room. There were pictures of men in lederhosen and Tyrolian hats all over the wall, portraits of German *frauen* carrying trays of huge steins smiled down from over the bar, and a big Black Forest cuckoo clock ticked away on the far wall. Maria ordered a glass of white wine and tilted her head back and forth to the oompah band playing on the jukebox. She was having a good time. I was trying to control my temper and realized this was a mistake. But what could I say to Maria? "Sorry dear, but no mixing business with pleasure." She didn't know a thing except that my fuse was shorter than usual and that I was spending too much time out of the house.

I kept searching the joint for anyone vaguely resembling Hans Diedrich; at least that would have given a purpose to the evening and allowed me to stand down. After all, I kept telling myself, if he's here once, he's here often. Maybe I'd ask at the bar. No! No conversations—this was only a looksee. I'd be back soon, probably even the next day. That was when I heard the laughter in the far corner. Then *Lili Marlene* from another table. And everywhere the sound of German: hissing, spitting, cursing German and choruses of *"ja, ja, ja, ja!"* That's when I heard a loud *"jawohl!"* and snapped my head over to the bar. It wasn't Hans Diedrich, but certainly someone who'd been in the military. He was big, probably over two hundred pounds, and swaggering like he was used to giving orders. His voice, heavy from drinking, seemed to rumble from deep in his lungs as it rolled out over the room, a *basso* to the laughter of the old men and women at the tables.

"'Was ist loess?' ich sagt, 'Nicht war? Sie sind Juden! Wir haben fiele Juden im Tereisenstadt. Und kindern."

He was obviously enjoying his story, bragging about something in German and English for a small audience at a corner of the bar. Maria was saying something, but I tuned it out. I had to hear what this guy was so proud of. There was something ominous about him hanging in the air, something terrible, something that he would reveal only once and never again. He held up his hand, waving off a question from someone in his group.

"Nein, nein," I heard him say as a he laughed off another question. I waved frantically to the waitress who made a beeline for my table when she saw me. Maria seemed startled by my sudden movement.

"Send a pitcher of whatever he's drinking over to that gentleman," I told her. And as the bartender drew it from the tap and handed it across the bar, I caught the big man's eye, smiled, and waved my hand. *"Danke, guten abend,"* he called out, poured a round for the people sitting near him and drained the rest of the pitcher without even taking a breath. I pointed to the bartender and raised my thumb. He drew another pitcher and handed it over the bar.

"Honestly, Mi-*kul*," Maria said. "What are you doing?"

"Just trust me," I told her, my blood beginning to rise as I pressed her hand, left the table, and walked over to the bar.

The man drained the pitcher again and blinked his eyes. They were red and bleary, rheumy from age and beer.

"So what happened?" someone asked him through a thick Bavarian accent.

"*Nein,*" he waved them off. "*Ich kenne nicht.*"

"Come on," I joined in. "You've got our interest, you can't stop now."

"Michael!" Maria's voice was sharp.

I laughed and pounded the big man on the back. "I know you want to tell it," I said.

"*Awrrrright!*" he said, something like anger and horror together rising in his voice. "I pickt tzem up. Ze two if zem, *über meinen kopf!* Und zey vas schtill konnektit. *Verschteistu?*" he screamed. "Konnektit bei ze schtring!" And he forced a terrible laugh, his eyes now wide with fear as he told of a crime so chilling, so terrible, that even the people at the bar were transfixed and revolted at the same time. He was near tears now, but still unrepentant, his full confession spewing across the bar like a putrid bile from deep within his soul. "*Und die Doktoren mitt grosse eigen, mitt grosse stimmen,* zey shouted like zey wass ze *Juden.* 'Wass machstu, ist eine mutter!* Put zem down *JETZT!' Aber ich was, was einne vilde,* lik a crazy mann. Und I carried ze mutter und ze konnektit bebe to ze vindoh und . . ." He was reliving the moment now. All of us were. Standing there right there: in the doctor's office at the special concentration camp at *Tereisenstadt,* watching a guard heave a mother and her newborn child, still attached by the umbilical cord, high over his head and bring them to the window. "Und I srew zem auht. Und zey bounst vunce. Only vunce." He paused to let the effect of his confession sink in. "*Keine Juden!*" And he shrugged his shoulders and laughed through his tears.

He bolted from the bar and ran to the back of the restaurant. I was oblivious to everything around me except him. I couldn't let him get away. I saw him close the bathroom door behind him and even before I forced it open I could hear the sounds of heaving and wretching from one of the stalls. I ran to the jukebox, pulled it away from the wall, and turned the volume up as high as it would go. Then I burst through the door and saw him bent over the toilet, the stall door still open. He turned briefly to look at me, vomit oozing from the edge of his mouth, hiccupped, heaved, and turned back to the toilet to spew another load. I couldn't control my hands. I hit him a two-handed chop to his left kidney with all my might. He groaned as he heaved, his knees buckled, and his head banged hard against the porcelain of the tank and split open in a bloody gash as he fell forward. I picked him up by the hair and plunged his head directly into the bowl. He struggled but I held him down hard, crushing his nose against the bottom of the toilet. Blood and vomit bubbled up to the surface of the water as he struggled to breathe. But it was too late. He was too weak and too drunk. In his soul, he was already dead. I held him down as he thrashed for air, water and blood splashing over the edge of the toilet rim and across the floor. Then he stopped moving and the last bit of air gurgled out of his lungs. I still held him down, though, not wanting even the hint of life to remain; not wanting there to be even the remotest chance of reviving him in emergency room somewhere.

When I left the bathroom, I could see that the people in the bar knew that something terrible had happened. They averted their eyes from my face, as if I was now wearing the mark of Cain; as if I, having taken judgment upon myself, now bore his guilt. Even Maria looked at me in a way she never had before. And we left the bar without speaking, the air all around us turbulent with the echoes of violence and rage and heavy with presence of death.

Years later, shortly before he died, Mr. Hoover would call me to account for that action. In private, where no one could hear us, he would remind me of what I did, pick up a glass from the table, and turn it upside down. The Court of Life would give its judgment, and I would be absolved, at least in this world.

Dallas

Friday was a sunny day, I remember, and warmer than usual for November. In fact it was so sunny that the whole morning had seemed like a holiday with people leaving work at odd times or taking early lunch hours just to get home earlier and start the weekend. All I could think about was work. I had been managing used-car and special sales for Atlantic Avenue Chrysler Dodge since late 1961 and had three guys under me working the outside lot while I handled the sales of customized Imperial stretch limos to the foreign missions personally. Our own body shop did a lot of the custom body work, window installation, and special paint jobs, making my job even more complicated. You can imagine the tons of paperwork I waded through every week just to be able to tell the boss how we were doing. And I wasn't even at the showroom everyday because I had been doing so much traveling for the Old Man since '61 when his new boss took over at Justice.

Suddenly the pressure on the Squad had increased. Everybody had to be light on their feet and even more cautious than before because of the Ivy-League creeps that were pouring over every scrap of paper coming out of Mr. Hoover's office. We were playing by new ground rules now. The McClellan Hearings had forced all of us to look over our shoulders and be extra careful about speaking bluntly about who said what to whom. No more dossiers in airport luggage lockers; no more handwritten notes slipped to me in the back seats of police cars; no more brown envelopes waiting for me at the One-Three's criminal intelligence unit where, since '62, I was referred to as Detective Sergeant Milan. I wasn't really a detective and I wasn't a sergeant, but the ID was real, there was a civil service list somewhere showing that I'd placed ninth on the sergeant's exam, and you couldn't bite through the shield. Now I was receiving inquiries from the Old Man over the phone through an intermediary in Quantico code-named Pencil.

I'd been seeing a lot of Florida recently, bumping into the CIA's field people in every bus station and airport waiting lounge between New York and Miami because the Old Man was in a race to pull together as much intelligence down there as possible in the wake of the Bay of Pigs. Rumors about who was doing what to whom were being passed back and forth over midnight Margueritas and Cuba Libres between agents of rival intelligence services who would confab in the back booths of Miami bars as their paths covertly crossed. What made matters even more confusing was that the people hobnobbing and bragging about being in the know didn't really know what was going on at all. First of all, there were so many independents involved and local contract players out of Chicago and Detroit that you couldn't tell who was who without the official score card. And nobody—I mean nobody—was keeping an official score card. You couldn't keep the names straight.

In my opinion, everybody was getting sloppy because most of the old-timers were gone. When Lucky and Frank ran the show, you knew who was People and who wasn't. When you had a sitdown, the guy across the table was only interested in the dough. There was none of this ego shit and political influence. Nobody cared about Senate committees and snotty little lawyers. People kept their mouths shut and their flies zipped. The Bobby Baker scandals that were breaking out in the newspapers had an unsettling effect on everybody, and newspaper reporters carrying wads of dough were hiding behind every toilet stall in every restaurant. Even in New Orleans, a town usually known for its subtlety about such matters, information on the street about "the Cuban connection" was fetching top dollar for anyone who could concoct a story wild enough to be believed. None of anything was true, as far as I knew, but then I was officially "out of the loop," which is how the CIA *goyim* translated "being in the dark." In fact, the pressure on the FBI to clean house and cooperate with Bobby Kennedy's Harvard lawyers at the Department of Justice was so intense that the Old Man hadn't even ordered a Squad hit in over a year. I, at least, had become a recording clerk, finding out who was where and passing it along to Pencil.

But I was making good dough and it was all on the up-and-up, too. I was selling cars like nobody's business and even doing some professional prizefight promotion on the side at the Island Garden and Sunnyside Garden. I had long since been promoted out of putting the muscle on Seventh Avenue deadbeats to arranging contracts for up-and-coming fighters. This was the kind of work I knew best—scouting talent and putting together fight cards. And the managers respected my ability not to overmatch a young fighter with older pros who would beat the shit out of them so bad they'd be pissing out their brains in gym showers for the rest of their lives. Of course, boxing was changing, too, especially with heavyweights like Sonny Liston who could take a man out with either hand in the first round before the fans had had chance to swig down their first beer. That's why the precard was becoming so important. Unless you had a couple of crazy bantam weights and a middleweight bout or two to whet the appetite, the show would be over before you could take off your coat. And the best places to bring lower-weight classes up to Madison Square Garden status was in rings like Sunnyside Gardens where the fans wanted action and plenty of it.

In fact, if you want to know the truth, I was even thinking about retiring from the intelligence game. I mean, I was forty years old, I hadn't even fired a single round at anybody in over a year, and I was doing more mediation of disputes between the Good People than anything else on the other side. Mr. C. was gone, Mr. L. was spending his time down in the Caymans trying to resurrect what he'd lost in Havana and protect his interests in Nevada. My old friend Li Chin had mended his fences with Washington and was doing business in places where ten years ago he would have been shot on sight. He even had the stones to gripe that I'd been too rough on him down in Hilo. Go figure!

I'd also been anxious to get legit because I was a family man now with kids who would soon go to school and have to say, "My daddy works for so-and-so and does such-and-such." What would my kids say? They certainly couldn't hold up a toothbrush at show-and-tell and say, "My daddy drills people." You have to think about these things sometime, and I was no exception. But cars: it was the American way. Everybody wanted one and was willing to pay big. It made sense to work as many hours as I could, ride herd on my little group of salesmen, and look to the future. Maybe with some money from people in the right places, I could open my own dealership someday, I thought, and call it Milan Chrysler Imperial. I was dreamin' the big dream along with all the other civilians.

So when Friday morning broke bright and sunny, I got to the showroom as early as possible to go over the used-car inventory with my salesmen. Then I would try to get out of the showroom as quickly as possible in the afternoon so I could spend some time at the One-Three checking names before I headed home to Queens to spend the weekend. By eleven in the morning, that was exactly how the day was shaping up. College kids, already filtering home before the Thanksgiving break, were looking over the 1957 rustbuckets that were rotting on the back lot. The push-button jalopies that I couldn't pay people to haul away the year before were suddenly coming into their own as the little snotnoses kicked the tires and wanted to know if those old clunkers could make it down to Fort Lauderdale. "Sure," I would say. "Just don't put it in reverse." That was what that morning was like. By 3:30 that afternoon, everything had changed. Forever.

The first thing I noticed along Atlantic Avenue was that traffic had slowed to a crawl. Cabs had pulled over to the side and turned on their Off Duty lights. There was no truck traffic like there usually is. People—total strangers—were talking in the streets. Even bag boys at the supermarket down the street were walking around like they were zombies in a trance. Walk-in business had stopped. It was like there had been a total eclipse of the sun or something. I wasn't listening to the radio because I was too busy pouring over the papers on my desk. But without even looking up, I had an icy feeling that everything around me had changed. You know the feeling you have when you sense that someone has just walked over your grave? That was how I'd started to feel.

I tried to shake it off at first. I said to myself that what was happening on the street was just the phases of the moon. People were getting stir crazy because the weekend was coming and it was too warm out for November. Maybe they were already tasting the turkey. But that wasn't it. There was something really wrong. I walked over to the showroom windows directly on Atlantic Avenue and saw an old black lady with shopping bags crying big wet tears as she stood alongside a parked cab. Then I heard a buzz around me; people talking in voices louder than they should. No one came over to me, they were too busy talking among themselves in little groups. There were people I didn't know, people who weren't customers milling around the showroom as if they lived there, talking to the salesmen and to other people I didn't know as if they'd known them for years. Maybe we were at war and I was so buried in paperwork I hadn't heard.

"Mike, get over here," I heard my boss call out. "Maybe you wanna get home to your family."

I looked at him like he was gonna tell me the world had come to an end.

"President Kennedy's been shot," my boss said in a voice that was truly paralyzed with fear.

"He'd dead," an old woman who was standing beside my boss said. And she snorted back tears and pointed to the street through the showroom window. "I heard it on the cab radio."

At first I was in shock. Nobody hits the president. And I was speaking professionally. At least one person has to be invincible, and that should be the president. It disturbs the whole order if you think the president can get rubbed out. My next thought was about Maria—should I try to get home? Would anybody try to contact me? Should I lay low until the heat from this thing died down? I mean, I didn't have anything to do with this, and already I was worried about the repurcussions. After running through a list of possibilities in my mind, I figured the best course of action was to call Maria and tell her to stay put—which is what I did—and hightail it over to the One-Three if only to see what came over the wire. If anybody needed to contact me, the precinct would be the logical place to do it, especially for Pencil or Mr. H. himself.

More to save myself from having to explain where I was going in the middle of the afternoon, I talked my boss at the showroom into closing shop for the rest of the day. "Out of respect," I told him. "Nobody's gonna go out shopping for a new car when any minute the whole place might get bombed by the Russians. What if the whole assassination is the first step in the Third World War?" I asked him.

He just about shit in his pants and didn't even answer. Instead he called over to Raymond who did all the cleanup and maintenance work. Raymond was crying also, bemoaning the fate of the poor people's president to whoever would listen to him.

"Raymond," he said. "You start closing up shop. Tell the men."

And within minutes, the iron shutters were dropped, the lot gates were closed, and the garage doors were locked. I lettered CLOSED FOR THE AFTERNOON IN MEMORY OF THE PRESIDENT signs for the door and the lot gates, and ten minutes after that, I was headed over the Manhattan Bridge, through my old neighborhood, and up to West 30th where the precinct station was located. I was able to sort things out more carefully as I drove, dodging stopped cars and trucks in the lanes ahead of me like I was on an obstacle course. I knew that Kennedy had a lot of enemies, more than anyone else I could think of. People always said that his father had been a double-crosser most of his life, expecially during Prohibition, but his connections to Boston's politics made him too valuable to rub out. Besides, he was protected by most of the New England Families even though most of the New Jersey Families had hard-ons for him as big as your arm. The two sons, especially the younger one, had been putting a lot of pressure on our People for the past couple of years, and had stepped on a lot of toes doing it. Mr. H. would have liked to knock Bobby Kennedy off himself, I can tell you that. He almost pissed in his pants with delight when he got his hands photographs of John Kennedy and Marilyn Monroe because it gave him a tiny bit more leverage in dealing with the clan. Between the Cubans, the Teamsters, the boys in Chicago, and even people in his own backyard, Kennedy was one of the most disliked presidents I had ever known. Even Truman knew how to protect his ass better than Kennedy did. To tell you the truth, I wasn't surprised that Kennedy was shot at. I was more surprised that it didn't happen sooner.

I expected the precinct to be in a state of confusion, like if we suddenly declared war and expected an invasion any minute. But instead, the desk sergeant was presiding over a tomb. Cops were standing around listening to radios or watching the one TV set that they had brought up to the desk. Almost nobody was being booked, and the few civilians in the station were there only to find out information and maybe learn something before it came over the TV.

"Sergeant, your phone's been ringing off the desk for the past hour," a uniform said to me as I reached the detective squad room on the second floor.

Before I even nodded to acknowledge him, a guy I'd partnered with on surveillance once or twice whispered in my ear.

"Washington's been asking for you. There's a number on the desk for you to call."

Whenever J. Edgar Hoover called you directly, you could expect that it was soemthing like a national emergency. When I called back, however, I was patched directly through to Pencil who didn't waste any time in ordering me down to Dallas on the late-night flight.

"You will need a handgun and silencer for this assignment. You'll find tickets in an envelope with your name at the American Airlines counter at LaGuardia. Your instructions have already been sent down in a briefcase which will be waiting for you at the luggage counter your name tag on it. Follow those instructions and follow those instructions only. Confirm your completion of the assignment with me at the usual phone number and take the next flight back to DC National airport. I don't have to remind you to tell no one where you're going and no one where you've been."

I tried to ask Pencil some questions about who I was looking for and how long I should expect to stay down in Texas, but he was as tight-lipped as any person I've ever tried to talk to over a phone. He seemed genuinely worried, as if things were really out of control and he couldn't see how they would be put back together again. He finally got testy and told me in no uncertain terms that I had better stop asking so damn many questions, get my ass to the airport, and complete the assignment.

"I understand the message," I said. Then I heard a click on the other end of the line. I called Maria back to ask her to pack some of my things for a two-day business trip.

"Pack a couple of suits for me," I said. "It's a last-minute sales conference for all the fleet managers. I can't get out of it."

"I understand," she said slowly into the phone. "Just suits?"

"Yeah, yeah, just a pair of suits, ties, you know."

I could hear in her voice that she suspected I was already part of the story that was unfolding on TV, but she said nothing and I wasn't about to reveal anything. There was a real feeling of panic infecting everything. I could also hear that in her voice. What if missiles started coming in any minute? What if army tanks started

rolling down Broadway? What if this was the beginning of something bigger than we had ever seen in this country? I know she was
more concerned about the kids than anything else, but it was hard
not to worry. Somebody had gotten to the president. That meant
anything could happen next. Even Pencil was nervous. And for the
first time in a long time, I was going to be very glad that I was
carrying a weapon.

As I hung up the phone, I could see one of the other squad room
detectives eyeing me very closely. But before he could walk over to
ask me any questions, I deliberately ducked out the squad room
door and was down the stairs in a flash. I knew he was following me.
Maybe he saw me peel out of the parking space, maybe he didn't.
But I wasn't taking any time to worry about it. I just eased into
traffic, hung my gold shield over my jacket pocket, and flattened the
gas pedal to the floor as I shot right across 34th Street towards the
Midtown Tunnel and the Long Island Expressway.

I had a cup of coffee with Maria in the kitchen before I left and
told the kids that I would be going away for the weekend, not that
they knew what I was talking about. But I could see in Maria's eyes
that she was afraid. "It's a business trip," I kept telling her. "Only
business. I'll be back before you know it." I said that more for my
benefit than for hers. And with the look in her eyes staring at me
in my rearview mirror, I drove to LaGuardia and found my way to
the American Airlines counter amidst the confusion and panic that
was all around me.

The Dallas Airport had already been turned into a something
like a military staging area by the time the plane landed that
evening. Televison camera crews and reporters from God knows
how many newspapers were all over the place, crashing into each
other and shoving microphones into every face that paused long
enough to look at what was happening. The police had set up
barricades to control the crowds at the entrance and exit stations,
and at least one military unit was patrolling a corner of the arrivals
terminal. I guessed that the entire place was still under some form
of federal jurisdiction because of what had happened, but I wasn't
about to ask any questions to find out.

I pushed my way through the crowd to the luggage return
counter, looking like any harried traveling salesman anxious to get

home. No one stopped me. I waited in line at the luggage counter and when I reached the desk, I asked the pretty girl behind counter to look for a suitcase with the name Mike Milan on it. I gave her the claim check that was in my ticket envelope, and she found it in about two minutes. So far so good. Then I took it to the bathroom, sat myself down in an empty stall, and opened it up.

Whoever had packed the information had done a good job because all I found was an itinerary for Mike Milan that listed a series of meetings at car dealerships and a reservation form for the Dallas Yellow Cab Company. The contact name on the form was Gerard Brinkman and next to his name was one of the recognition codes that Mr. H. had first used when he began giving me assignments years earlier: my military serial number with the last digit changed from a three to a four. Whoever Brinkman was, the number next to his name had sentenced him to death. There were to be no questions, no decisions, just a number that meant he would be disposed of. At the bottom of the itinerary was a final appointment for me at a Faracce's Disposal Company. I didn't recognize the name, but I recognized the meaning. Whatever I did with Brinkman, I was to deliver the body there and leave it. The disposal boys would do the rest of the job.

I placed a phone call to the cab company and told the dispatcher that I had reservation for a cab the next day, but that I wanted a special driver: Gerard Brinkman.

"Yeah," the female voice said at the other end of the line. "He'll be working tomorrow. Where do you want to be picked up?"

I didn't have any hotel reservations or anything, so I simply told her to have him meet me at the airport when he began his shift.

"That'd be at seven in the morning," she said. "Where can he find you?"

"Have him wait for me at the taxi stand," I told her. "I'll find him."

I hung up. I didn't like the catch-as-catch-can nature of this whole deal, but I didn't have much choice in the matter. If it'd been up to me, I would have taken at least a week to find this guy, study how he lived and what his patterns were, and then snuffed him out without involving anybody else. I had already made myself uncomfortable with this assignment—not to mention the fact that the whole city was as jangly and as broken-edged as if a bomb had fallen, which, of course, it had. I could only hope that he was dumb enough to show up as if it was business as usual and put himself where I wanted him. I was getting too old for this racket, I told myself.

It was already getting late by the time I found an empty table at the coffee shop and ordered up something to eat. Even though I'd only had a cup of coffee since the morning, I really wasn't hungry. This wasn't like the old days when I was in control of the hit and could take my time. I tried to read the papers while waiting for the waitress to bring the food over, but I couldn't settle down. There was something that was so wrong about this assignment, so flukey about the suddenness of the whole thing, and it was taking all my self-control just to keep from pacing back and forth around the terminal. The worst part of it at this stage was that I had to appear completely normal. With all the cops and Texas Rangers walking around, anybody who looked crosseyed in the crowd was likely to be picked up and questioned. You can believe that I didn't want to be caught with a loaded nine milimeter automatic in an ankle holster and a screw-on silencer in my pocket. Not even my detective's shield would have protected me if that happened. Since a cop had been killed that afternoon, anybody from out of town walking around with a gun and no FBI badge was probably fair game.

The hamburger was cold, the onions were rancid, and I didn't even finish the coffee. Instead, I went to the airport shop, bought a pocket-sized bottle of Pepto-Bismal, and had that for dinner. I figured it might settle my stomach and if I got out of this place in one piece, I promised myself, I'd celebrate down at Lenny's on Mulberry Street.

By the time I finished the papers and taken the Pepto, the crowds at the airport had started to thin out. Even the cops had dispersed and all the news crews that had been setting up earlier had pulled away in their vans. I assumed that whatever the military unit had been guarding must have left also because there were no soldiers around any more. Even the cops seemed to have found other places to go. I realized just how tired I was and set about looking for a place to sleep. That also proved futile. The reporters and TV crews had booked every room they could get their hands on so rather than make myself crazy, I found a couple of empty chairs in a far corner of the lounge and tried to doze as best I could until dawn. With any luck, I figured as I nodded off, I could deliver Brinkman first thing in the morning and be on a plane before anybody realized he was gone. That was the only thought that allowed me to get any sleep at all in the most uncomfortable new-fangled, orange-plastic airport lounge seats I had ever seen in my life.

When I woke up a few hours later, I knew I'd been in the middle of some pretty disturbing dreams, although I didn't remember any of them. My back was stiff and my stomach was still upset. I was completely disoriented. The coffee from the machine had tasted as if was made a week ago, but what little sleep I grabbed had done me some good. I was at least able to think about what I had to do without getting sick to my stomach.

As it got closer to seven, I kept watching the cab stand where the drivers were queuing up for the first commuter flights of the day. The morning newspapers were out, with thick black headlines describing the assassination the day before, and the reality of what had taken place gradually sank in. Shock had given way to resignation—somebody had gotten to the president—and things would never be the same again. Sure, I told myself, the police were announcing that they had the shooter, but anybody who knew anything realized that that was plan bullshit. I'd been in the business long enough to know what a hit looked like. And even though I didn't know who did it, it was too professional to be anything but. However, I couldn't let any speculation get in my way. I had a job to do, I was part of whatever bigger picture was going on, and I had to get out of town. Maybe I'd sort it all out later, but right now, I was either a part of the problem or a part of the solution. Unfortunately, I had no idea which was which.

I finished the coffee and peered out at the taxi stand. At least one of the drivers was looking around like he was expecting somebody. Worth the first shot, I told myself, and took my bag out to the cab stand where I caught up with the driver who had just gotten back in his cab.

"You're here to pick up a Mike Milan?" I asked him.

"Don't know any Mike Milan," he said. "Dispatcher told me she had a reservation for a cab at seven. Didn't give me a name."

"You Gerard Brinkman?" I asked.

"Are you the seven o'clock fare?" he asked sharply in an accent that was more midwest than it was Texan.

I threw my luggage in the back seat and caught a look at the hack's license before he said, "Hey." It was Brinkman all right, there in the flesh.

"I said, HEY!" he shouted. "I got a reserved fare."

"I'm the fare," I told him. "I called yesterday." I got in and closed the door behind me. "Get going, we got a long day."

Brinkman got behind the wheel and turned around to stare me full in the face. "You asked for me, special?" he said. "Why?"

"Heard you were a good hack." But he wasn't buying it. The deep scowl on his beetle brows and the set to his jaw were only growing more rigid as he continued to stare. This guy was like a mule.

"Look," I said, trying to soften the tension up a little. "I been in Dallas before and I know that cabs is tough to find when you wanna go a little bit outta town. The girl at your dispatch was givin' me a hard time about makin' sure the driver will take me where I gotta go. Finally I asks her, 'Which driver will go a little extra out of the way for a big tip?' And she says, 'Ask for Brinkman and he'll take care of ya.' Now ya wanna go back on her word or ya wanna take me where I gotta go so's I can take care of you and you pick up a nice piece of change for the weekend?"

He slammed the door, put the cab in gear, and pulled out of the taxi line. He had his hand resting on the meter flag when I said, "Before you turn the meter on, here's where I'm going. You take me outta town to a place I bought into called Faracce's. It's off . . ."

He stared at me in the rearview mirror. "I know where it is. It's half the way to Fort Worth. It's gonna cost. It'd been cheaper for you to get your own car."

I pulled out a wad of dough and slid a pair of twenties across the front seat. "That's for starters. I don't want to worry about anything but my meeting. Now you drive where I tell you to drive, wait for me, and get me back to the airport before lunch."

Brinkman fingered the dough behind his ear like he was listening to see if it was real. Then he flipped the meter flag with his thumb and picked up the radio microphone. "Yeah, 4-7 to dispatch. That fare never showed. I'm goin' 10-86 for some break-fast."

"10-4, 4-7 you're 10-86," the female voice squawked, and Brinkman cut the radio off. "You're gonna make this worth my while, right?" he asked as he turned around over the seat.

"You'll get more than you ever got before outta this fare," I said to him with a smile. "Take you a long time to spend it."

I could see him raise his eyebrows in the rearview mirrow.

"You don't know what I spend, buddy," he said finally, as if it had taken him that long to think up some snappy rejoinder to keep the conversation going.

Up to now this had just been dumb luck, or maybe the people in Dallas were in such a state of shock—even those behind the hit—that they were just doing what they were told. It's been known to happen. You could tell a guy who's just pulled a trigger on someone to march straight to the cops and they'll take care of him and the guy goes and does it. I've heard about situations like that. Brinkman pushed the cab onto the entrance ramp for the main Fort Worth highway. We would be at the place in about forty minutes, I guessed, mentally converting the mapline distance between Fort Worth into hours.

"So yesterday was a busy day down here all around," I finally said after Brinkman had worked his way over to the left lane and settled down.

At first he didn't answer. It was like I'd hit a dead zone in his brain or something.

"I say," I said in a louder voice, "When they told me I had to come to Dallas today, I wasn't happy about it. You guys had a busy day yesterday and I didn't know if you recovered from it."

"Who's *they?*" Brinkman asked.

Smart boy, I said to myself, I better stay alert. "The lawyers. They want me to get these papers signed by Sunday. Lawyers got no respect for anybody's time." I was only trying to break the silence, to stay alert so I wouldn't lose my edge.

"Lawyers, huh?" he said and drifted off into stony silence.

"So I said," I said after a while, "When they says I had to be in Dallas today, I wasn't happy about it. You people recovered yet from yesterday?"

This time I thought that if Brinkman had guns behind his eyes he would have fired them directly at me off his mirror, he was glaring so intensely. "Look, pal, for all I know you could be a reporter for some asshole smut newspaper looking for shit to print. I could wake up Monday and read my name somewhere and that's the end of me. So ask me about the weather, ask me about gettin' you pussy down here, but don't ask me about you-know-what or you'll be walking to Fort Worth."

I'd heard guys like this before. He was as ready as anybody to spill his guts to the first person who asked him. Only you had to know where the guts would spill and how to ask him. It was a challenge to get some real information, and I wasn't going to let it pass me by. It became a game for me. I wanted his confession before I foreclosed on him, no matter what Pencil said.

"So how do I get some pussy down here?" I asked.

"I thought you were gettin' out of here by lunch?"

"Next time I'm back," I said.

"Next time you're back, ask me," Brinkman said, obviously enjoying the game he was playing.

"No shit," I said. "You know where the best club in town is for that sort of thing? I mean some hacks say they know, but when it comes right down to it, they go by rumor as much as anyone else. But if a hack really does know how to make a connection with some people who can show you a good time, he's worth his weight in gold in advance. If you know what I mean." I fished. I fished for anything I could get because you never know what bobs up to the surface when the bottom's been as stirred up as this town's was.

"Carousel Club," he said.

"The where?" I asked, knowing that name from somewhere in my memory.

"Carousel Club," he repeated. "Where the elite meet to eat. I know the owner. You can get anything you want down there. Anything. If you're doing any business in this town, it's worth your while to drop down there anyway and pay your respects to the management."

"And who should I ask for?" I asked.

"I already said too much," Brinkman said, suddenly remembering where he was and what he was doing. "You heard nothing from me. Just go down there on your own and you'll find all the pussy you can handle in one night, maybe two." He pulled the cab off the state route and headed along some kind of feeder road for a while. I tried to pull more stuff out of him, but he dodged every question and stray comment like he was bobbing and weaving and playing peek-a-boo. Finally he pulled up alongside the wire gate of a junk yard, stopped the cab, and set the brake.

"This is where you said you wanted to go," he said. "Now what?"

"Now we go inside where I have my meeting," I said. "You wait. I give you money. You take me back to the airport."

"Yeah sure," he nodded. "You wanna open the gate?"

I got out of the cab and walked over to the main entrance. It was bolted shut but not locked. As I peered through the wire mesh to see if anyone was inside, Brinkman honked the horn and stuck his head out the window.

"If there's nobody here," he called out, "And you're playin' me for a sucker, I'm driving away." He was right. We were completely alone. I could ask him anything I wanted.

I waved the wad of dough in front of the windshield. "I told you I own this place," I said. "There's somebody here—me. There'll be somebody coming, too. Now I'm openin' the gates and you pull the cab through. How many times I gotta tell you I'm takin' care of you?"

I shoved the bolt back and swung open one of the gates. Brinkman eased the cab through and I closed the gate behind him. Then I walked over to the shack and motioned for him to get out of the cab. He was wary, but he walked over to the door where I was standing and said, "Now what's wrong?"

"This lock's stuck, I think. I need a hand here," I told him.

"I don't bust locks," he snarled. " Maybe you got the wrong person for the job."

"I didn't say bust it," I said. "I said it's stuck—take a look at it." And as he bent over the lock, I edged behind him and drew the automatic carefully and slowly out of my ankle holster. "See that?" I said. "Something with the bolt, needs more strength than I got."

"This ain't stuck," Brinkman said with a nasty edge to his voice. "It's plain fuckin' locked. If this is a goddam breaking and entering and I'm the fall guy, keep your dough and forget about it."

He was starting to turn around when I shoved the gun barrel hard against the bone behind his ear.

"Hey!" he called out.

"Just freeze right where you are," I said. "Don't even breathe." I could notice beads of sweat breaking out on the guy's temples and his knees started shaking. I pushed him against the door, bent his head over, kicked his legs apart in a spread-eagled position and patted him down. He was clean.

"A cop," he said to himself.

"You were a busy boy yesterday," I said. He was still facing the door. I kept the gun hard against his head and walked him over to the back of the cab where I spread-eagled him again over the trunk so he couldn't move without first turning over on his back to keep him from falling on his face.

"I . . . I don't know what you're talking about," he finally said, not understanding what I was doing but fearing the worst. "Everybody was busy yesterday."

I threw a sharp left uppercut into his kidney and he groaned as his knees buckled to the ground. I grabbed him by the collar and pulled him back up to the trunk where I slammed him face down into the metal.

"I can do this for another hour," I said. "By that time you'll almost be numb. That's when I'll start on the other kidney. Then when you're good and hurt and pissing blood down your leg, I'll blow your balls all over the cab. That's when you'll be beggin' me for a round in the mouth. You ever thought you'd beg somebody to kill you? It's gonna happen. Or you can tell me what I came to find out and drive outta here in one piece. My car's already here. I don't need you anymore. You walk away with your life and I walk away with what I wanna know."

"I don't know who who you are," Brinkman muttered, the pain just beginning to subside. "I drove a cab all day yesterday. I don't know anything."

Another left uppercut and he went down again. This time, I planted a knee between his shoulder blades as he tried to grab onto the rear bumper of the cab and I mashed him into the dirt. I grabbed him by the collar and threw him against the trunk again and dug another left directly under his ribcage. He sank down to the ground and I let him fall, staying behind him so he couldn't see my face or the gun. Then, as he started to spread his legs to get up, I kicked him square in the nuts from underneath and stomped the base of his spine as he writhed on the ground.

"I'll crush'em right where you're lyin'," I said. "And when they're paste in the sand, you'll still be beggin' for the one round. Give it up now. You ain't a pro at this and you won't last long."

At first Brinkman tried to shake away from my foot, but it was no use. I only put more pressure on his back.

"Who are you working for?" I asked, stepping up the pressure until he cried out, "I never met him."

"Who set it up?" I asked, easing the pressure just a bit to let him know that there was a way out.

"I didn't know his name. Never saw him before."

"This is fuckin' bullshit," I said. "Someone you never met before tells you someone you don't know wants you to shoot the president and you expect me to believe that?" I put all my weight on his back and he cried out again. "That's not the way it was." Then he paused. "I never met the guy before I was introduced to him by this broad at the Carousel Club. And I didn't shoot nobody."

"Oh yeah, and what did you do, spit peas at him?"

"No, it was nuthin' like that. There was me and two other guys. We weren't even after the president. We were supposed to shoot the governor, but things happened too fast. They were gone before anybody did anything," he said.

"Who put out the contract?" I asked.

"Like I said," he spit into the dirt and I could see that blood was coming out of his mouth. I'd injured something inside and he knew it. "I didn't know the guy. This broad over at the Carousel set us up. She knew I needed the dough and I guess I got the OK from her boss."

"Who's her boss?" I asked, but I had already placed the Carousel Club and I remembered who the owner was. He was in deep shit with some of the boys in Chicago and had been running around like a rabbit trying to come up with more dough than he had.

"Jack Ruby," he revealed. "I only know him from sayin' hello to'em all the time at the club. I bring fares there lookin' for a good time, know what I mean? Ooof. Just like you asked."

"How many others?" I continued.

"I think there were two other guys doin' what I was supposed to do. But I don't know who they are or where they was when the shooting started. We was just supposed to shoot at the governor when they passed and get out of there. That's all. But nuthin' happened. I mean, everything happened and I just got outta there fast."

"Open the trunk," I told him.

At first, he moved very slowly, but I pulled him up by the collar and that seemed to help him. He popped open the cab trunk, I turned him around, and made him sit on the bumper facing me. Then I cocked the hammer back on the automatic and put it against his nose.

"I'm gonna live, right?" he asked.

"That depends on the next answer," I said. "Tell me why" "Huh?"

"Why? Why'd you do it? Who do you really work for?" I asked him, hoping to find out some more information that I could send back to the Old Man. Even though Pencil had told me no questions, I had to know what made this guy tick, if only for my own understanding.

" 'Cause Connolly's rich and I don't have a dime," he said. " 'Cause I gambled a lot of dough that wasn't mine. 'Cause I owed people I couldn't repay. 'Cause I had a job and Connolly fired me. 'Cause, 'cause, 'cause. 'Cause anything you want, right?"

I stood away and aimed down the barrel at his nose. " 'Cause you do this one job and you walk away clean, right?" I asked.

"Yeah. I walk away, that's what they said. Now, you said I'd walk away, right?" he asked.

"Wrong," I said, and the sound of the single round I'd squeezed echoed out over the desolate, dry Texas landscape and sounded hollow in the emptiness of that junk yard.

The force of the round blew the top of his head against the underside of the trunk lid and spattered brains all over the fender. The sonovabitch didn't even twitch like most people do when you shoot 'em in the head. I folded his legs into the trunk, wiped my prints off the automatic, tossed it in after him, and slammed down the lid. Off on the edge of the junkyard, I found the giant magnet suspended from the crane and the autobody compression machine. The way these deals work, that would be Brinkman's grave. I drove the cab over to the wrecking pit and left it there. Then I went back to the shack, reached through the window to slide the door bolt back, and found the keys I was supposed to find, hanging on the wall. The car was behind the shack. I looked at my watch. I'd make my phone call from the airport, I told myself, and catch my lunchtime flight.

The Old Man himself was waiting for me in the VIP lounge at the Washington National Airport. The note on my passenger page ticket that the luggage clerk gave me when I picked up my bag only said that my meeting was in the lounge. It didn't say who or why. There was nobody in the room except for Mr. H. and me, and we exchanged no greetings.

"You already know too much," he said with a kind of resignation in his voice. "So I'll just say: Johnson. No doubt. We stand away. Do you get it?"

I shrugged my shoulders and nodded my head.

"Take a long vacation," he said. "Very long." And he left the VIP lounge by the ramp that takes you right to the plane.

Hate Incorporated

"Mi-*KUL!*" The voice split the darkness.

"Mi-*KUL!*" I remember it kept on repeating. Every time it repeated, the darkness grew a little lighter. One time it grew so light that I thought I even saw something moving behind a curtain. But then the voice stopped and it was dark again.

"Mi-*KUL!*" There it was again. I was thinking that I was supposed to get back to it. It wasn't a conscious thought like I had reasoned it out. It was more of an instinct, something I knew I should be doing. When I heard it, I knew I had to get back to it. But I didn't know where it was. The voice was like a stone dropped into a pool of still, black water. Its echoes rippled out in all directions, breaking up the surface of the darkness and letting bits and pieces of images break through.

I don't remember when I first heard the voice. I only know that there was the voice and there was the darkness. There was something that preceded the darkness. Pictures. But I only saw the pictures after I would hear the voice. One time, I remember, after I heard the voice I was on a plane—a jet—and it was circling and circling because it couldn't land. I was waiting for the voice so it could land. Then I heard a loud, wailing siren as if it were on top of me. And I thought I could see people standing over me. I was lying down and they were very close. Then the darkness opened for a second and there was a light. It was so bright it filled everything. Then suddenly it was gone, but the siren kept on wailing until it, too, faded away into darkness.

There was another time that I can just barely picture when I heard the voice and was aware that I had hands. I had feeling in my hands. I tried to move them but they wouldn't work. I kept trying for as long as I heard the voice. Then the voice kept saying, "Good, good," but my hands touched something and I felt unbearable pain, pain cutting through the dim light. I heard a scream coming from the distance. Then the darkness must have returned because I felt like I was floating in it for a long, long time. I remember waiting for the voice, but there was no voice, only rats in bellboy hats chasing me on motorcycles. The the closer they got the bigger they were until the voice and the sound of the motorcycles was gone.

Sometimes, I even knew what I was and the sound "Mi-kul" reminded me of things. But then I would feel a jabbing pain in what felt like my arm, and the voice faded and I was floating in darkness again. The sound of motorcycles would come and go and I would feel a terrible pounding from deep inside. The pounding would get heavier and more intense until the darkness would turn red with every beat. Then a jab of pain and the pounding would subside until it became more of a throbbing. The throbbing would last for a long time and the rats would come back until I heard the voice again.

"Mi-KUL!"

The motorcycles stopped.

"Mi-*KUL!*"

This time the sound was really loud.

"Mi-*KUL!*"

Suddenly white light was everywhere and I knew that I was supposed to *see* something.

"He knows we're here," I heard a different voice say. It was lower than the first voice. "I want to increase the glucose," it said again.

"Are you sure?" another voice said.

"He's been in shock long enough to wipe out the Dead Sea Scrolls. We can begin retraining him soon," the first voice said.

"Shall I bring in Mrs. Milan now?" the second voice asked.

I was Mike Milan. I couldn't see, but I knew something. In the darkness and in the light, through the throbbing and the motorcycles that would come and go, I knew that I was Mike Milan.

"Mi-*KUL!*"

"Uuhhh." I felt more than heard the sound. It was coming out of my chest.

"Is that good?"

"Strap down the IV before he yanks it out!"

"The vein's all collapsed; we'll have to move it anyway."

"Move it after he's back under."

I was lying down in a bed. I had sensation. I could feel something soft under me. Then I felt pressure from inside, sharp pressure. Then I remembered I had to piss. Then I was pissing.

"There's still some blood in his urine," the lower voice said.

"Could you wait outside for just two minutes, ma'am?"

"But he's wakin' up isn't he?" The Mi-Kul voice asked.

"That's why we need two minutes. You'll be right back," the lower voice said.

"She's gone."

"That's 'cause of all the pentathol, I think. You're overloading his system on sodium. His pressure's through the roof as is," I heard the second voice complain.

"It's only a little blood. I think he has a tract infection from all the insulin. I want to adjust his meds anyway."

"He's finished. I'll empty the jar and you can get his wife back in," the second voice said.

"Mrs. Milan? You can come in now."

Milan, Michael. United States Navy, Seaman Third Class. Serial number 80762546.

—We know all about the USS Ranger. It's 1945. You are onboard the Ranger. You are an ordinance mate. You are looking for a seaman by the name of . . .

Milan, Michael. United States Navy, Seaman Third Class. Serial number 80762546.

"Michael! Can you hear me?"

Maria was looking down at me. I could move my eyes. I was in a hospital room. Why was the voice of an interrogator ringing in my mind?

"Michael! Can you see me?"

"Uhh." The sound was coming from inside me. "Uh-rii-uh." There was something in my mouth pressing down on my tongue. I could barely move my lips.

"It's the tube we have in his throat, Mrs. Milan, to keep it from drying out. That's getting in the way of his speech," a man in a white gown was saying to Maria. But a tube wasn't always in my mouth. I remembered being interrogated. I was onboard the Ranger. There was no tube in my mouth. It was this same voice. What was he doing on the Ranger? Is the war over? Did we win?

—Mike, who is the president of the United States?
Franklin Delano Roosevelt.
—What year is it?
It's 1944. I know where I am.
—What was the name of the seaman you were looking for?
I am a Seaman Third Class, United States Navy, serial . . .
—We're not going to get anything this way. Use the insulin.
"How are you feeling, Michael?" Maria asked.

"Ask him what year it is, Mrs. Milan," a second voice asked.
I tried to move my eyes to follow the voice, but I couldn't. The voice
came from over my head, and I couldn't raise my eyes. "He took a
pretty nasty beating. There's a chance it may take him a few weeks
to get oriented."

I think I heard Maria gasp. She was holding her hand next to
her mouth. "Does he know me?"

"Uh-rii-uh." I groaned again. I tried to move my hand, but
something was holding down my arm.

"Just take the damn tube out for now," the voice in the white
gown said. "It's only getting in the way. I want to take another blood
samp tonight. We can reinsert later."

"Don't try to move, Michael," Maria said. "The doctors'll take
your tubes out."

I felt hands around my mouth and on my throat. I remembered the rats grabbing me. They held me by the throat and were
squeezing it closed. There was darkness all around me. I couldn't
breathe. I fought them off. They were pinning my arms to a concrete
floor and shoving something into my mouth. I was in a warehouse
and the rats were all around. There was loud music playing. The
vibrations from electric guitars filled my head until I thought my
brains would burst.

"Don't fight us, Michael," the white gown said. I was back in
the light. "Let us get this out, and you can try to talk."

Something was being slid out of my throat and I tasted blood
in my mouth. It was salty.

"Maria," I said. "Where am I?" I could hardly move my mouth.
It was like my jaw had been clamped shut. I was feeling the kind
of pain I'd feel after a heavy fight in the Navy those times I'd gotten
the shit kicked out of me in an exhibition bout that turned mean.

"You're in a VA hospital, Mike," the white gown said. "Don't try to move your jaw, it's been broken and for now it's wired shut. I'm Dr. Viguerri, your neurologist. You were brought to us from California. You'd been in an accident. We can talk about it later." Then he turned to Maria. "Only a few minutes today, Mrs. Milan. Help him get adjusted a little. You can spend some more time together tomorrow."

The man who called himself Viguerri left the room along with the other guy in a white gown. Maria and I were alone.

"Do you know me?" Maria asked very tentatively.

"Yes, I do," I said, " But not much more than that, I'm afraid."

I was trying to be cautious. The room was still spinning pretty wild, and for the first few minutes, I wasn't really sure what was a dream and what was real. The throbbing pain was helping me stay awake and focus on where I was. Maria was staring at me with a concerned look that meant things were very serious. I tried to shake off the dreams, but they were too real. I knew they were too real to be dreams. Why, I remember I kept asking myself, was I thinking about the USS Ranger? Was I interrogated after that incident? My real memory said no. I had just disappeared onto the New York waterfront and the whole "missing Soviet naval observer" incident was papered over. The sea records from the Ranger were destroyed shortly after the war. These were facts and I was sure of them now. But why was the memory of an interrogation still fresh in my mind? And who broke my jaw?

"What's today?" I asked her.

Maria seemed stunned. Maybe the question was too sudden, but I had felt there were gaping holes all around me that had to be filled. And the echoes of voices that kept replaying in my brain were the questions of interrogators.

"It's March 21," she said very tentatively. Then she added, "When did you think it was?"

"What year?"

At that point she seemed genuinely frightened, as if she was talking to a Martian that had taken over my brain.

"No really," I said. "I think I'm remembering something more than I'm supposed to or I may have been having some very bad dreams. Just tell me the year."

I could see her blanching, but my grip on things was just too fragile to worry about her feelings. If I got out of this alive, I'd make it up later. Right then, I was more worried about staying sane than taking care of anybody else.

"1965," she said finally.

"Thank God," I said. At least I knew I wasn't crazy then. Maybe it was all a dream, but it seemed too real and too persistent. Even as I was sitting there talking to Maria, I felt that I had been interrogated only hours earlier. It was just too clear. "What did the doctors tell you?" I asked.

"They said you'd had a bad shock, that your war injuries were acting up, and that you might have to stay here for a few months for treatments," she said, trying to hold back tears. She was clearly worried also, especially with the kids and all. "You have been gone for a while," she said as firmly as I'd ever heard her make a point.

"Did they say anything else like what was wrong with me physically?"

"No, they said you had broken your jaw and punctured your lung," she sniffled and rubbed her eyes. "They took X-rays." Then she broke down crying. "When we didn't hear what happened, I thought you were dead. You've been gone for three months." She threw her head on my chest and I thought the top of my head would blow off. She felt me tense and realized that I was in pain. "I'm sorry," she sobbed. "I was so worried. Nobody called. Nobody, except for Fishbein at the showroom. He said he was replacing you but that if you showed up, he'd find a job for you selling in the showroom." That sonovabitch, I thought. One phone call, just one, and they'd be raising his tombstone in Mount Hebron.

"Did anybody else call that asked for me but didn't leave a message?" I asked. Nobody from the Families would have been that careless. They might have stopped in at the showroom, not at the house. A man's own family was protected. Anything otherwise is an *infamia* and whoever commits it signs his own death warrant.

"Fishbein said you had messages at the showroom," she sobbed. "He didn't want to replace you, but he said it was business and he didn't know where you were."

Three months! All hell should have broken lose if I didn't turn up for three months. I was feeling the edges of panic rise up around me. I was still very shaky about where I was, and I had lost all sense of time. For me, I'd just come back from the past, from 1944. I thought I was being debriefed in a Navy hospital. Then I was being questioned by the Nazis. The two memories were almost the same except that I was never in a Navy hospital and I was never captured. Why would I remember things that had never happened? Then Maria was smiling.

"The doctors said you had a tr... trauma? They said you might not remember things right, that you might forget things. Maybe you'd think things happened that didn't happen," she said, trying to explain what the doctors had tried to explain to her. Maria was the daughter of a Greek merchant whose own father had fled Russia during the pogroms. What did she know of traumas? For that matter, what did I know of them? "They said you wouldn't act normal for a long time," she continued. In other words, the docs said I'd be a nutcase. That must have made her crazy in her own right. "They asked me to ask you that if you wanted to remember something, to tell them. They said that you could go home if you came back for treatments. They said . . ." and she paused. This sounded painful. "They said . . . you were *mentally* disabled," and she started crying again. "That you were really mentally disabled because of what you did during the war but that nobody realized it until now."

Bullshit! I got an honorable discharge from the fuckin' Navy hangin' on my wall that says I left the service in one piece. One piece. Nobody was going to change those records now except Mr. Hoover. And if he hadn't touched them, I'd go down to Washington and change them back myself.

"The doctors said if you cooperate with them, you can go home real soon," Maria continued. "As soon as your jaw begins to heal, I can take you home. But you have to come back here for treatment. And you have to take a rest from work. You have VA disability coming, they said."

If you were to talk to me about that day in the hospital now, I'd remember it as clear as a bell. It's one of the few things that I do remember. But now inbetween its what I remember. That's where the trouble is. If I tell you what I know and don't know, you'll see why. And you'll see why what I did made perfect sense at the time, even though it was an act of pure vengeance. You'd've done the same thing.

That first day I remembered knowing where I was. The more I asked Maria about how long I was there and how I got there, the more she was pushing me to stop worrying about what happened and settle back on my forthcoming veteran's disability. "They even said they'd get the VA to pay off the mortgage on the house because you're permanently disabled. And they'll pay the kids' college, too. All VA, the doctors said."

It was too good a package. Sure, what schmuck wouldn't go in the tank for that kind of dough? Set up for the rest of your life. You can sell cars, not sell cars, what did it matter? The house, the kids' college, a pension. All tied up nice and neat. But something smelled rotten just like, as Maria's *zeydeh* used to say, a fish rotting from the head. Somebody wanted me out of the way. And at that point in my hospital stay, I didn't know who it was. It could've been, and I'd've laid odds at that time that it was, the Russians. The KGB. To my absolute surprise, I found out later that they had nothing to do with it.

That afternoon in the hospital was like an island of light in a sea of darkness. I was just plain too block-headed, for a forty-two-year-old man, to realize what had happened. I was too worried about being perceived as one of the shell-shocked, mustard-gassed old geezers that roamed around Essex Street talking about going over the top with Wild Bill Donovan and the rest of the Fighting 69th. I wasn't a psycho-case or a Section 8, and I wasn't going to let them call me one either. First, I figured, I play dumb. Since I didn't know what was happening, I thought I should stick around awhile and maybe report this to the Old Man. What a stupid sonovabitch I was. If I'd had a head on my fucking shoulders I would've gone along with Maria and anything else they wanted just to get my ass out of there. Maybe that wouldn't have worked either and they would have made my act. In any event, I have to live with what I did and spend the rest of my life with scrambled eggs for part of my brain.

I told Maria not to worry, of course, and to get back to the kids. I figured that once I got my hands on a telephone, some of the Good People would have money at the doorstep and I'd have the Old

Man's ear. I also figured to scare the shit out of Fishbein so bad he'd have me selling cars from the hospital bed. What actually happened was quite different. When the docs came back, they just about yanked Maria off the bed. Then they asked me what I remembered about how I got there. I told them it was all blanks to me. I didn't even know how I got to California or wherever they said I'd been picked up.

I was telling them the truth. At first, I really didn't remember why I was in California. That part of it came back to me right away, though, and when it did, I was able to start connecting the dots, putting the puzzle pieces I knew were pieces into place. For the rest of it, I just have the disjointed memories—bits and edges of what the drugs and the shock treatments did—what the doctors told me to think, and the months when I just seemed to wander through the house on Long Island like some derelict or, worse, a lunatic talking to himself. I may never have the equation that will put it all together. I only know how I ended it, bolted it down with boilerplate again so that it held for a while, and ran like hell for the rest of my life so that if and when it exploded, it would explode only after I was gone. If you think that doesn't make any sense to you, realize how much sense it doesn't make to me.

In the fifteen or so minutes before the doctors came back into the room, I tried to suck in as much of the present as I could while assembling my memories. I'd figured that was the logical first step before trying to learn what they were after. What did I remember? The dossier. I remembered seeing a San Francisco Police Department internal memo on a group calling itself Hate, Incorporated. A California-based motorcycle gang. That would have been in 1964, June, less than a year earlier and right after I'd gotten myself transferred to the One-One-Two in Queens. My contact at Quantico was a voice I called Receiver. God only knows what happened to Pencil. I assumed that after Dallas there was a shakeup of the whole operation. It took the Old Man six months to contact the Unknowns and I was surprised that he was even doing that.

The SFPD memo said that the department had lost two of its officers, one uniform and one undercover narcotics detective, to the gang. The memo called the gang an underground terrorist organization that had released threats to law enforcement agencies in the state over local FM radio stations. The cops had disappeared. Then their bodies turned up. The SFPD had linked the gang to drug sales, kidnapping, and murder for hire. They even implicated the gang in a series of migrant worker murders. The Old Man was worried about it. He would be. Anything that threatened the established order was a threat. But he didn't give me any assignment. He just wanted me to watch the NYPD intelligence files for any similar series of crimes.

A month later, he sent me an LAPD internal memo about the disappearance of one of its narcotics cops whose body had not yet turned up and a Los Angeles County Sheriff's Department officer who had been found dismembered in a culvert off one of the freeways. Two months later, after the High Holy Days, Receiver sent me the Bureau's dossier on Hate, Incorporated, along instructions to get to Los Angeles. That's where my trail stopped. No matter what angle I approached it from, what little fragment of memory I was able to hold onto as it flitted by, I couldn't plug it into the rest of the puzzle. All I had, when I thought of Los Angeles, was the image of a motorcycle biker with a dark helmet and a leather jacket. And I had a sense of forboding and doom, a fear that there was no way out, the trap had sprung shut behind me, that those were my final moments.

I couldn't shake the feeling of dread that I associated with that figure on the motorcycle, the feeling that he knew something about me and I didn't know a thing about him. Wherever it came from, that fear was all I had. I needed that fear because it was my link to what had happened. For the first time in that hospital room, I understood what Cus D'Amato had meant when he said that you needed to use your fear to feed you, to make you alive, to give your life meaning. I knew that that fear would take me back to California and I would confront it there. Then the doctors came back.

"We want to get you home as soon as possible, Mike," Dr. Viguerri said with a very practiced laugh. "I don't know how you did it, but you're costing the VA a mint here."

"You can send me home today, Doc," I answered through clenched teeth. "I'll be as good as gold."

"Wish it were that simple," he said. "You know Uncle Sam. All paperwork and no decisions. You got to walk out of here as close to one piece as possible. Your jaw's got to be on the mend, you can't have any fluid in your lungs, and you have to be as sound as we can get you up here." And he pointed to his head temple as if he were shooting himself in the head.

I played along. "What's it gonna take?" I asked.

"Cooperation. You answer the questions we ask," Viguerri answered. "If you come to a dead end, that's OK, too. You tell us it's a dead end and we'll get back to it later. Once we know that you're on the mend, we'll send you home. Your wife can drive you back in once a week for talk sessions, kind of a debriefing if you know what I mean, and then you go home."

"That's it?" I asked as naively as I could.

"What'd you expect?" The doctor asked as he moved to insert the IV back in my arm. I didn't fight him. "Now you lie back and get some rest. You may have some strange dreams. After all, you've had a pretty hefty shock, but in a few weeks, now that you're memory's returning and you're out of danger, the dreams'll subside."

Viguerri clicked open the stopper on the catheter tube in my arm and I heard the jar above my head start to bubble.

"See what you can remember, Mike," he said. "Don't force it. Maybe you let it come to you as a dream. We'll talk about it later."

I remember feeling that I was tired again; I remember that very clearly. I remember feeling safe. I looked forward to seeing Maria again. I felt like I was home, like whatever it was that I was afraid of earlier, that it was gone. I remember I couldn't see the doctor anymore because everything was dark, but I knew where I was, I thought, and I wasn't afraid anymore.

Mendel

I remember I was hearing someone calling my name from a long way off. It echoed over and over again like it was in an alley between tall buildings on the Lower East Side. The sound used to bounce off those buildings and echoes would echo more echoes until you couldn't tell what the sound was.

—Mike, tell us about Quanset Point. Who told you the Japanese sailors were spies?

What Japanese sailors?

—That's right. What Japanese sailors? You are Seaman Third Class Michael Milan. You are an ordinance mate on the USS Ranger. You served on the aircraft carrier Ranger for the duration of the war. What did you do after the war?

I sell cars.

—That's right, you sell cars. You've always sold cars. Tell us about Mr. Hoover.

Mr. Who?

—Mr. Hoover. When did you first meet Mr. Hoover?

I don't know a Mr. Whoooov.

—You never met Mr. Hoover. You never worked for Mr. Hoover.

Never worked.

"This isn't going to work. He'll remember everything when he comes out of it," I thought I heard a voice say.

"Even if it does, it'll take years. We can't keep him out of circulation that long. They'll shoot us," another voice said, I think.

"We can take him downstairs for a short one just for starters."

"We won't overdo it, just a short one. We'll see how he responds."

"A short one."

I saw light. I remember moving. I was on my back, moving down a hall. Lights were passing by overhead. There were echoes in the hall. There were the sounds of hollow bells going off like dongs. Woosh, doors closing above my head. I can still see them. I'm moving. I'm moving down. I've stopped. Woosh, I can see doors open. Lights again. Hands on me, all over me. Pinches. I feel pinches. Cold on my chest. I feel shivers. I smell burning.

—*Michael, Michael, Mi-KUL! Where are you? Come home. Mike. Mike, you stay away from his left. Cover your chin. Wake up, Mike, he's killin' ya. You asleep? Box'em willya? Move left. Stick and move. STICK AND MOVE!.*

—Mendel, Mendel, Mendela. MEN-DA-LAA. Bring your father's lunch down to the store. Don't waste no time!

—Nu, Mendela, boychickl, wohin gehst so schnell?

—Aayy, Mikey, what's'ina bag? What'sa hurry? Donfuhget, latuh, duh game on Chrystie Street. Im'a waitfuhya.

—Ah, Mendel, home early. Did mama send my lunch? Thank you. My son. This is Mendel—excuse me, this is America—Michael, my son. Mendel, say hello to . . .

—Mendel, put'er there. Whaddya know whaddya say?

The Yanks is what I say.

—The Yanks, huh. You a Yankee fan?

U-bet.

—You know a lot about the Yankees.

I know everything about the Yanks.

—Now, Mendel, say good-bye to Mr. Lansky. He's a busy man.

—Not at all, Ben-Zion. I'm never too busy to listen to a kid what knows what he's talking about. Tell me some more about the Yanks, Mendel.

Yanks are unbeatable. Nobody in the league can touch'em now that DiMaggio's in the majors.

—That's swell. You think they'll win again?

You kidding? You see the Yanks today? Beat the Phillies on DiMaggio's homer. Wait 'till tomorrow.

—Tomorrow, huh? Care to make a sporting bet?

—Mr. Lansky please.

—Ben-Zion, how'za boy gonna learn? What about it, Mendel?

Yaw so shoowah, you gimme two-to-one?

—Two-to-one, yaw way.

Heah's my buck.

—Heah's my two. Ben-Zion, hold the stakes.

—Mendel! Where'd'ya get the buck?

Just got it, dat's all. Be heah tmorra, Mr. Lansky.

—Aftuh the game.

—*You don't have to worry about this, Mike.*

I ain't worried, Mr. Lansky.

—No, Mike, there's no Mr. Lansky here. You don't have to worry about anything. You'll be going home very soon now.

I don't remember the lights coming on. But suddenly I was sitting up in my bed. The bed tray was across my lap. I remember looking down at a VA benefits form. I remember signing it.

"This is important, Mike, because it means we can release you shortly," Dr. Viguerri said.

I must have nodded.

"Normally, Mrs. Milan would have been asked to sign it, but since she's not here, it doesn't matter. Do you have any questions?"

I must have shaken my head.

"Good, we'll schedule one more therapy visit tomorrow and then I think we can discharge you for the time being. You'll have to come back for treatment, though, and you'll keep receiving your medical benefits and pension."

I know that I shook my head because things were beginning to clear.

"What's that, I can't hear."

I leaned forward. "The date," I gasped. "What's the date?"

"It's September 23, Mike."

I heard a click by my ear. I recognized what it was just before I began to feel tired. I would have liked to have reached over and knocked the whole damn IV unit over or pulled the catheter out, but I didn't have the strength. I didn't have the strength for anything.

—*Maria will be here soon and you'll be going home.*

—MENDEL!!

—Where did you get that dollar?

—Tell your papa, Mendela. Where did you get the dollar?

I been savin' it. Savin' it fra long time.

—May I ask why?

Sshhh . . .

—OK, whisper it in my ear.

To buy mama a shawl for her birthday.

—I understand. Good boy, Mendel. But what will you do if the Yankees lose?

Don't worry, papa, they won't.

—How can he be so sure?

—*Don't shout around your father, Victor, he needs rest. That's what the doctors said. Rest.*

—But Mom, why does he just stare?

—Rest, Victor, he's tired.

—Now the whole block is talking about Daddy. Everybody. Nobody wants to come here. I don't have any friends any more 'cause of him.

—Susan, you don't talk about your father like that. He was hurt. He's getting better. Just a few more treatments the doctors said.

—Why do I have to mow, it's Susan's turn?

—Victor, please, it's hard enough with your father like this. Can't you make it just a little easier?

—This won't hurt, Mike. It'll make you feel better. Do they still call you Mendel? I can't believe that name. Who names a kid Mendel?

—It's what they used to do, Vig, I guess.

—Mendel, fucking kills me.

—Nu, Mendel? Jetzt, wohin gehst so schnell?

—Ah, Mendel.

They won, Mr. Lansky. Just like I said. You see the Clipper's homer? Outta the park.

—Take this, Mendel, you won it.

Oh no! Dat's a twensky. I won two bucks, I take my two bucks.

—You're not gonna take my twenty? Something wrong with it?

Nuthin's wrong, Mr. Lansky, only I didn't win it. If I won it, I woulda taken it just fine. But I didn't. Just gimme what I won.

—Ben-Zion, give the boy the money. Mendel, you run along. We'll see each other soon. *Ben-Zion, shhhh. I'll give you the twenty, buy him a nice Bar-Mitzvah suit from me. And be sure you tell him it's from Meyer Lansky.*

"MARIA!"

"Michael! What's wrong?"

I was sitting in the basement of my house in East Merrick. At least I recognized that much. My face was itching so bad I thought it would fall off. The room smelled of old men in hospital wards. It was a deep body-odor smell of stale piss. I looked down. I was in pajamas. Pajamas and slippers, and the sun was out. Why wasn't I working? I remember I looked out the window sort of to get my bearings. My dreams were burning in my head, burning like my brains were on fire. Where was I? Why was I thinking about Meyer Lansky? The last time I saw him was on the news. He had been trying to get into Israel or something. Where was my gun? My badge?

"Michael, what's wrong?"

"Look at that lawn," I remember saying. I was staring out the window into what looked like a meadow gone to field. "How did it get that way?" I asked.

"We were short of money with you not working and all," Maria said as if she was talking to a stranger about the problems of someone else. "And Victor hasn't mowed as much as I'd like him to. And Susan is in afterschool plays, you know and . . ."

"And no one offered to help?" I asked, still not realizing how long I'd been out of commission and how bad the money situation was. Maria didn't really know about the Families, so there was no one she could've asked. "Do I still go to the hospital?" I remembered that much about my situation.

"You were going regularly until last month when someone from Washington showed up," Maria explained, but she clearly didn't know what had really happened. I would only find out myself years later. "He said he was from the Navy and he wanted you discharged immediately. The two doctors said they hadn't finished, but the man from the Navy said that if they didn't finish with you he'd finish with them. He kept telling them. 'This is over as of now.' He said the Old Man personally wanted you released. They signed your medical papers right away, and I haven't taken you back to the hospital since. But you acted like you were somewhere else for the past two months."

"I'm back now," I said. I was feeling my oats. I didn't know why or where, but I'd managed to get out of something terrible alive, and the Old Man knew about it. He probably knew about it from the start.

I felt like there were a million things that I had to do at the very same time. There were people I had to see, phone calls to make, scores to settle, appointments to make. I wanted to talk to Fishbein, put the fear of God in that worm, send a message to Receiver, go down to the One-One-Two. But it would take days, even weeks to rebuild my network so that it worked.

"What hospital were you taking me to?" I asked Maria. "All these months?"

"The VA hospital on the East Side," she said.

I pressed my hands to my temples as hard as I could. There were so many things to remember, so many ideas flooding my mind all at the same time. Gradually, over the next few hours, as I would ask her specific questions, whole pieces of events would move themselves into place. I asked her about when I left for California. What I'd said before I'd left. How I'd been returned to New York. When she'd first heard about where I was and what had happened. I knew that in what she was telling me I would find the keys to what really had happened. There were loose threads just waiting to be pulled, and the whole fabric of my last year would unravel into separate strands, strands I could follow.

Every few minutes, I would have to stop and digest. I would fire up circuits in my brain which had been dead for months. It was like adding two and two over and over again, seeing if they still made four if you counted on your fingers, your toes, your eyes and ears, your elbows and knees. I tried not to become fanatic. That would have only scared her. But it was as if I was an empty vessel that needed filling. I could only go as fast as she could repeat things to me. But I began to make lists so I wouldn't forget. And then I remembered that I never made lists. I always kept everything in my head. Why was I making lists now? Why was I forgetting information I'd just learned? I'd hoped that would eventually change, but I didn't force it and I made all the lists I needed. I still make lists to this day. They changed me, those bastards. Jumbled up part of my brain, I think, so that now I have to write down what I used to be able to remember. That made me really mad when I first realized it.

Talking to Maria took hours, but I could see that she was getting more confident the more we talked. The kids came through a couple of times, saw me talking to Maria, and floated out again. I would have to make my peace with them, too, I knew, but for that immediate present, I needed to become whole again.

There was nothing Maria could really tell me about California. And to this day, there is nothing more that I remember about it on my own. Years later we found a member of Hate, Incorporated, in Brooklyn. He was a drug courier trying to make a deal in the City. The Good People found him for me because they knew I had a score to settle. We lured him to a funeral home we sometimes used for disposing of people who had to disappear. We had weapons to sell, we told him, and drugs to distribute. He showed us no respect— called us old men in a young man's game. But while he was still laughing, I discovered that my hands could still do some damage. Before he came to, I tied him up in the basement of the funeral home. This time I asked the questions. He filled in a lot of blanks before he died: how they were waiting for me even before I got to California; what agency got the Old Man to send me to California in the first place and then tipped the gang off; how I'd been caught in the warehouse, and who arranged for my transfer back to New York after I was drugged. That was all I needed. The punk also bragged a lot about Hate, Incorporated. Said that they weren't afraid to die. That was OK with me. I rounded up a couple of people I knew who weren't afraid to kill nice and slow. Then we invited the punk to his own autopsy. At first he said he would last longer than we would. But we'd done this before. Only this time we tape recorded every sound he made. We tape recorded every scream and every shriek as a new organ was exposed. We showed him his own spleen. Then we made sure that each name he gave up as he begged to die got a copy of that tape. We played it into their telephones early in the morning. Maybe they weren't afraid to die, but we showed them how long it was going to take when we got our hands on them.

Weeks after the autopsy, I drove to the hospital. I still had a final score to settle with the one voice that I remembered through all the darkness. I kept the hospital under my own surveillance, driving round and round the block at all hours until I saw the comings and goings of each doctor and orderly that I even vaguely remembered. I was looking for only one man. I stayed well out of sight, of course. I couldn't let anyone there know that I was back. I had to send my own private message that my friends at the Agency would know had come only from me, a message they would understand. I waited for just the right moment when the unmistakable face would be alone at an opportune hour of the morning. I savored it when it came, when he walked across Third Avenue, oblivious to everything around him. I was almost standing on the gas pedal when I turned on the lights and saw the reflections from Viguerri's eyes as they were caught in the glare. He was just like a leaf floating across my windshield. There was a thud, a bang, and I kept right on going into the night.

Kent State

The Old Man seemed to shuffle when he walked. He dragged his left foot instead of lifting it right away, and he breathed heavy whenever he took a step. Now he was walking across the room to shake my hand. He was doing it deliberately. It was his way of making his point, the closest he would ever come to admitting to a mistake. He'd let himself be talked into something he didn't want to do. They told him the Unknowns had to go. They argued that the Squad was only an embarrassment. Worse, it was outright homicide, conspiracy at the highest levels. His beloved Bureau would be humiliated, disgraced, if it ever became public knowledge. I know he dug his heels in at first, bared his teeth because he was getting mad. He became stubborn as a bulldog standing stock still over a bone in the dirt. He argued back without admitting anything. That was his way—never give in; never give the bastards a goddamn inch. Deny everything. But he was too old. The CIA was too powerful. It had grown like a hydra, just like he said it would.

Then there was the Kennedy thing. He knew he shouldn't've used the Squad, but who else did he have on such short notice? And these were hits. He couldn't use regular Bureau people, it would've leaked out all over the place before the first sitdown of the Warren Commission. So he tried to cover his tracks. Used people on the Commission. Dragged it out. Evidence was lost. The same drill we'd used a hundred times before when he had to hide the bodies. But the same voices kept saying over and over again, "Close it down." Then they showed him how. Retirement would be easy. One by one, pick up the Unknowns, pull'em off the streets. Let the Agency do it. They have doctors. They've been using the same tricks on KGB people for years. They're experts at this. Then they played the Kennedy number. "Bobby knows." "Frank's mouthpiece talked." "It's all gonna come out." Did they strike a bargain? Was Bobby part of the deal? I can't say anything for sure; even if I knew I wouldn't say.

I know he gave in, though. In the end, he stood away from us. It had to have been that way. No orders. No dossiers. No Receiver. The phone number was even disconnected. None of that would've happened if he hadn't turned the other way. So they must have picked us up one by one. Me they got in a warehouse in East LA. Beat the living, fucking shit out of me. Broke my jaw so bad I still can't talk right. Busted my ribs. Tore a piece out of my lung bigger than the hole in the goddamn Titanic. Then they turned on the juice until I glowed in the dark like a fucking searchlight. And they told me shit. Told me I wasn't who I was. Didn't do what I did. Didn't have a past. I sat in my basement for months, staring out at the growing grass. Walking down the street in my pajamas like an old rummy who shoulda been put away in a padded cell.

Word got back to the Old Man. Broke his heart right down the middle. We were his right arm. There was nothing he asked that we wouldn't do, and he knew it. He trusted us with his life. He knew what we were, but he knew that within limits there's room for everybody. He said to Frank Costello, "Do what you do and don't tell me about it." He called Meyer Lansky the nicest criminal he ever met. And we repaid him in kind. You didn't see drugs in this country until the CIA brought them in. Frank put his foot down and told the entire Commission: "No dope!" The Old Man respected that. He knew that his agents couldn't do what the Families, the Good People, could do. So the Old Man must have remembered the service that we performed for him. He pulled me right out of the hospital. Sent his agents down and took my records out of the doctors' hands. I know!

But the Squad was no more. He gave in and cut off his arm to make peace because he couldn't fight any more. And then he began to lose control. Everybody was making deals every which way. One minute you were working for the CIA, the next minute you were hit. Nobody was running the show anymore. And before you knew it, there was dope all over place. Dope was the Old Man's worst nightmare and he had to watch it overwhelm every law enforcement agency. Every deal he had cut with the families and the other intelligence agencies to keep narcotics out of the country simply dissolved into competition between rival drug organizations to push more and more dope. There was just too much money to ignore. This wasn't like the old days at all. Back then, Mr. H. knew exactly what to do to enforce the rules—he ordered hits. Drug pushers just disappeared, even drug pushers the CIA had put in business. You knew that if you crossed the line, you would pay a penalty. Now there were no penalties and Mr. Hoover had to watch it all fall apart before his eyes. Little kids were selling dope in school yards. College teachers were bragging about smoking it in front of their students. Mothers were giving reefers to their children like they were Oreo cookies. This wasn't like Prohibition when everybody wanted booze but couldn't buy it. Drinking booze was legal; you just couldn't sell it. Once you had booze, you could drink as much as you wanted. Dope was different. But because they talked the Old Man into turning away from his friends among the Good People, they gave up the control that kept this country from being torn apart. And by 1968, the chickens were coming home to roost.

The Old Man had known it was wrong to shut down the Squad when they started pressuring him about it in '64. But their logic got to him over the years. The Unknowns were just a bunch of old men. The old dons were dying off, too. They told him that it was a young man's game. Then there was Vietnam. The goddamn CIA got so powerful that the handwriting was on the wall. They got to LBJ. He couldn't protect Mr. H. anymore, so the Old Man had to give in. Then in the same year they took out Bobby Kennedy and King. The cities were burning up. The courts tied the Old Man's hands. If some punk shot a cop and said it was an accident, the courts patted him on the head and blamed the cops for causing the accident. It was the Old Man's nightmare come back to haunt him the minute he gave his inch. But he was gonna show them now. He was gonna show them that he could still call the shots.

That sonovagun was making it a point to shake my hand even if it took him all day to walk across the hotel room. He was going to do the right thing and square it with me in person. That was why he wanted this meeting, although he never came right out and said it. It was now my portion to be stand-up. You could feel the tension in the room as he moved. The two Bureau types at the door dared not turn around or, worse, reach out a hand to help him. He waved everybody away but me. Then he took my hand in both of his and shook it like he was pumping water from out of a well. His pop-eyes were large, rheumy, and runny. His bulldog jowls sagged badly. His clothes hung off him. He liked to be dapper when he went on vacations to Palm Springs in his snappy double-breasted tropical suits with big looping suspenders and his wide, California ties. But that was in the old days when he and Frank would go to the track and argue with each other about the ponies. His voice was gravelly now, not the sharp, whiplike twang he used when he stood up before Congress and told them how he was going to catch bank robbers and shoot'em down in the street like he did Machine Gun Kelly and Baby Face Nelson. Everybody knew he didn't really shoot them down, but they pretended that he did so he wouldn't get mad.

"There's not too many of us still around, eh, Mike?" He asked.

"No, sir," I said, agreeing with him even though I was only in my forties. "Very few of us left these days."

"You feelin' OK now?" He pressed. "I mean . . ." and he reached out and tapped on my head like he was feeling to see if it was still on straight. "You know, up there."

"They didn't get to me, Mr. Hoover," I said. "They tried all right, but they didn't get to me."

Mr. Hoover reached into his big pants pocket and pulled out a shiny twenty-dollar gold piece.

"You remember this?" He asked.

I smiled. Even if they had burned away all of my brain, I could never forget the gold pieces, one of the the the original recognition codes we used to use.

"I remember," I said.

He pushed it into my hand, forcing it into my palm with surprising strength.

"You keep it. For good luck," he said laughing a little. Then he paused and looked at me with a real serious stare. I remembered that look. "No one is here. Help me over to the table." And he leaned on my arm as I walked him back to the table by the window.

It wasn't the same table nor was it the same room. But from the way he was acting, it could easily have been twenty years earlier. He opened the top drawer of the desk and took out a thin folder and opened it on the desk top. Then he poured the water that was in a glass back into a pitcher. He read silently, skipping through the pages.

"Klaus Feuscher, Waffen SS, formerly a brownshirt, sneaked into the United States with false identification papers after the war. The NYPD found his body stuffed into a toilet in an uptown restaurant. An unidentified man and a female companion were observed leaving the restaurant. Unsolved homicide." He closed the folder. Then he picked up the glass on the table, held it before my eyes, and turned it upside down. "The Court of Life sentences him to death," he said.

I was flabbergasted. I couldn't believe what I was hearing.

"That's right," he continued. "You have to get back to work again."

"Anything you say, Mr. Hoover," I said slowly. It was like watching an old champ who's been down and pummeled against the ropes coming back to life in the final round and fighting on guts alone.

"You will soon be contacted," he promised and then sat down heavily in the chair. He waved me out of the room and I left him sitting there, breathing with great difficulty but looking satisfied at what he'd done.

For the next six months, I did what I was taught to do in the service: I waited. I was still on full disability pension from the VA—no questions asked about outside sources of income—when Maria received her first Social Security death benefits check. Her name was on the check, but it was referenced to my social security number. According to the United States government, I was dead. I thought it must have been a mistake because lying there, right alongside it in the mailbox, was my PX card with my old military serial number printed out right across the top. But it was no mistake. And it was addressed to me. The death benefits came the next month and the month after that, too. Then all hell broke lose.

I remember watching President Nixon on television, in 1970, the night he revealed that our troops had invaded Cambodia looking for a Viet Cong command post. Sounded like a case of hot pursuit and it seemed logical enough to me. But it went off around the country like a concussion bomb. Nobody wanted to go to Vietnam anyway—that's why people voted for him in the first place because he said he would get us out of the war—and then when he said that he was sending troops into a new battle theater, it was the last card that tips the whole house over. Over the next few days following the speech, when Maria and I would see kids setting buildings on fire, blowing up ROTC buildings, and taking on cops and troops, we knew without saying anything that it was only a matter of time before I'd have another business trip.

College after college seemed to be going up. Even in the high schools, kids seemed to be challenging everything they were being taught. To anyone who had fought in World War II, this was an outrage. Your country was at war—your job is to fight it. But the kids had either not learned something we were taught or knew something we didn't know. Either way, the pressure was building to dangerous levels. You can imagine how Mr. Hoover saw all of this. For him it was a replay of the resistance to World War I and his fears of a fifth column of armed subversives. The Old Man used every means at his disposal to collect as much intelligence as he could while using informants, covert agents, and the Unknowns to infiltrate groups, bring back information, and disrupt activities. But he never ordered a hit, at least he never gave me such an order. Who should be hit? That was the question. Who was behind all of it? That was the answer Mr. Hoover wanted, and it drove him crazy not to have it. He figured that someone somewhere was calling all the shots: push a button on Berkley, throw the switch at Columbia, send the brown shirts over to Madison, Wisconsin. He never figured that it might just be the kids themselves. Then some kids where shot by state troops out in Kent, Ohio, and by the end of that summer, I found myself on a plane to Cleveland.

Who'd ever heard of Kent State University? It was out in the middle of nowhere. But in the spring of 1970, when a small detachment of the Ohio National Guard turned around and fired live rounds into a crowd of college students, people told me that was the only thing Mr. Hoover was talking about. Right after the news reports, the Old Man sent a dispatch of agents out to Ohio. He wanted intelligence, but he had to play by the rules. And you know what came up? Nothing. Everybody was stonewalling everybody else. Nobody could explain why Army reservists had been given permission to load their weapons with live ammo. And nobody could pinpoint who gave the actual authorization to fire weapons. The situation was so illogical, so incompetent, so stupid that the

Old Man didn't buy it. But when he heard from his own people that no federal laws had been broken, he hit the ceiling. In his own gut he believed that either the National Guard had been infiltrated by fifth columnists who were out to incite students by shooting them down and then giving them weapons to fight back with, or by Nazis who were inciting college students just to create enough chaos to influence elections. Either way, he figured it was a conspiracy, the machinations of dark powers bent on destroying the United States. He'd fought spies through two World Wars, the Korean War, the Cold War, and now the Vietnam War and, right or wrong, that's how he saw things. So he turned to the Squad, even though there was no Squad left. In a way, I say to myself when I think about it now, he was living in a past he should never have given up.

That's how I got my marching orders. And I had to run the investigation on the up-and-up, the Old Man said. This was strictly a homework assignment, he gave me to understand. No rough stuff. No slapping college kids around. This wasn't Atlanta. I had to get myself a reason to go to Kent State, find a cover that would give me a reason to ask questions, get the Old Man some names, and get myself out. He'd take it from there.

So I had to get myself a job at the school. I couldn't sling hash like I did in Georgia because I was a little too old for that. Besides, the hash I was slinging then and the hash they were slinging now were two different things, and I wasn't going to push drugs as a cover. But I knew some people in Ohio in the concrete business. They made phone calls to people who themselves made some phone calls, and they found out that a part-time athletic trainer in the physical education department who was supposed to be working at Kent State had decided not to take the job for a few months. I didn't know whether he was taking a vacation, nor did I know whether it was for health reasons or to recover from an accident or to earn more money somewhere else. I didn't ask any questions when a friend of mine from Cleveland called up and said, "Say, Mike, there's a job what's opened up at that college you was asking' about. They need a guy who knows how to work a locker room." Since the Old Man said up-and-up, I didn't ask him about the trainer's reasons for taking the time off. I just figured it was a stroke of the kind of good luck I was familiar with.

I got myself one of those efficiency apartments in an old private house on the outskirts of Kent. Actually, Kent in 1970 was such a small college town, compared to where I came from, that the outskirts and inskirts were really the same thing. My apartment didn't have a kitchen or anything. In fact, it was like the old joke that comics used to tell when they played the hotels in the Catskills: "The room was so small when I opened the door I broke the window."

I began my assignment by doing what I like to do best: making believe I'm the lamppost. That's how I nose around. People talk to one another around lampposts because they think they're alone. I love it. You wouldn't even know I was in the frame unless you had a snapshot and I pointed myself out in the background. After the beating I took in California, I didn't look like a movie star so much anymore—more like an extra. Here I am bagging filthy shit-ass towels in the locker room, acting like I have an IQ of twelve, looking as cock-eyed as an old rummy tank fighter who still hears the birdies, and picking up after a classful of snot-nosed gym students who think they're too good to take a round for the Uncle who's paying their freight. There I am sitting all the way at the end of a bar while these two students in the weekend National Guard brag about how they had the balls to put rounds into the crowd that surrounded them. Over there, I'm setting up an outside volleyball net for some sorority match. This little blonde tells the kid next to her in the middle row that her girlfriend from Long Island was just walking along around the edge of the demonstration late to a class when she was shot from nowhere. Died before she hit the ground. Next, I'm waiting on line in a faculty lunchroom listening to these two investigators from the state attorney general's office talk about how the governor wants them to shut down the inquiry fast.

"Just like the fuckin' Warren Commission," one of them says. "All bullshit."

"Yeah," the other agrees. "You open the book, point a finger at a bunch of Commies, close the book. One of these kids that got shot was a Jew, right? So big shit."

That was how I spent the first few weeks—getting the feel of the place, picking up whatever bits of conversation I could, and putting myself behind people who like to talk. You get your bearings this way. You find out who's supposed to know what about who. Then you make yourself a little scorecard with names and addresses and find reasons to be places where athletic trainers aren't supposed to be. For instance, what's the forty-five-year-old towel boy from the locker room doing out on the parade grounds watching the ROTC cadets throwing their rifles into the air? He wants to see who knows how to handle a rifle, of course, and where that person drinks his three-two beer. Then what's the locker-room towel boy doing sitting behind the ROTC cadet at the Pizza Hut? He's finding out who gives what orders at the platoon level. Specifically, he wants to know what stupid prick issued live rounds to toy shoulders who'd never squeezed off live rounds before in their lives. He wants to know whether the sonovabitches who gave the orders even knew how far live rounds would travel in a straight line if they didn't happen to bounce off some kid's ribs. He hears Joe College tell John College that Sunday Sergeant Steve College told his platoon to chamber the first rounds. If they only knew that lampposts can hear better than anything, I wouldn't have any job.

A few days later, the towel boy manages to sit at the table behind Sergeant Steve in the library. Sergeant Steve takes a piss. The locker-room towel boy looks over at the next urinal in the bathroom and there's Sergeant Steve trying to dig his dick out of his dungarees. He catches up with him at the sink. Says something like "Ain't you the guy I saw on the parade grounds the other day? You sure can handle a rifle." How long do you think it takes for the towel boy to find out that somebody we'll call "Captain Hoecher" issued the orders releasing live rounds to the members of the Steve's unit? "Holy cow," the towel boy says, "you mean a captain was allowed to cut orders like that?" "Naw," Sergeant Steve says, "Hoecher won't even take a shit unless someone tells him to. Orders came from upstairs." "Way upstairs?" he's asked. "What's it to you?" he demands as he stomps out of the bathroom, and the towel boy wipes his hands, shrugs his shoulders, and vanishes. Sergeant Steve has already forgotten what the towel boy looks like.

Captain Hoecher isn't a career soldier. He isn't even a real soldier, I read in his paperwork from the Bureau. He's a little pimply-faced punk who was an ROTC cadet from Ohio State who after two rotations in Vietnam worked his way up to his first lieutenant's bars. He had one year left on active reserve. Then they said to him, "Congratulations, we're bucking you up to captain. All you have to do is sit on your ass in a tent one weekend a month if you give us another five years in the Ohio Guard." It was too good to pass up. How did he know that a bunch of long-haired, bra-burning Commie potheads—you know, these bums, the kinds of hippies who are causing all the problems these days—would try to shut down Kent State? And Hoecher wasn't the only Vietnam vet serving in the Guard back there. There were plenty of other guys who did their time and came home to kids who'd been fucking their girlfriends and laughing at them while they were getting their legs blown off by Viet Cong booby traps.

Hoecher looks at me over a pitcher of beer in a downtown Columbus bar and says, "You were a vet, Mike, you understand. You think I don't go to bed at night with that girl's face in my head? Nobody ever told them to shoot at the kids. They were supposed to fire live ammo into the dirt. But they got scared."

"You cut orders for live ammo?" I ask him, not in an accusatory way but more like one serviceman saying to another, "I didn't know you had the authority."

"No, not me." And I believe him. "Orders were cut by the Commandant of the Guard. Gave his field officers full discretion about when to fire, but the orders to issue live ammo came right from him." Then he looks at me in way which says: "I can't name names but if you don't think he gave the orders, there's only one other person who could, and that's the governor."

"We know it wasn't the governor, Mike," Mr. Hoover said when I got back to New York. "He's either too stupid or not stupid enough. So you're right, it came from the CINC. And he's no medal-winner either," Mr. Hoover continued. "He's a Brigadier General, former Army Colonel in Vietnam appointed to Commander by the governor. A real tweedledee." He could see me turn red. "Nothing you or I are gonna do about that either. But I needed the information." And he pointed to the door.

I put on thirty or so pounds after that, just thinking about a man I'll call General Smith. He's still alive, I think, about sixty-eight, seventy years old. I can find him. Since the shock treatments, I have a pretty short fuse. Sometimes I wake up at four in the morning and I can't sleep. I think about General Smith and the poor girl who was shot dead on her way to class. I see myself in Ohio and I find this general's car and wire a tape-cassette boxful of plastique to the lead wires on his ignition. He goes to work and next thing he knows they're fishing pieces of him out of Lake Erie. I know where he lives. He and Li Chin are on my list. Then the delivery boy tosses my copy of *Newsday* against the front door with a dull thud. I hear it splash into the puddle on the edge of the front grass. I want to plug the paper boy, too. Maybe I won't go to Ohio today.

The Berrigans

Late one night in 1970 two Catholic priests pulled off the single greatest heist in FBI history and sent the Old Man into the most terrible fit I'd ever seen him throw. The priests, Phillip and Daniel Berrigan, actually managed to break into the FBI field office in Media, Pennsylvania, and steal a list of the Bureau's undercover agents running a COINTELPRO against the antiwar protest groups operating in the area. They released the list to the newspapers and revealed that Mr. H. had been running a covert domestic counter intelligence operation in the face of the government's official denials. The Old Man's face was red. He was not only made out to be a liar, but he was humiliated in front of the little pissant puppy dogs who were running around the White House and the CIA, concocting their their own half-baked undercover surveillance schemes, churning stocks, running deals with dope smugglers— "importers" is too nice a word—and laundering bribe money and paybacks in broad daylight. At that point I had been officially retired on my disability pay with a disengaged and spinning U-joint in my head where my memory used to be so I was only what you might call an experienced observer, but to elevate the inept and dangerous *mishigos* that the White House was running by calling them "intelligence" operations was to give them an underserved compliment. There was simply no intelligence about the operations whatsoever. It was more like a bunch of kids who had just seen a rerun of *The Untouchables* and decided they could do it better. Besides, I knew Eliot Ness and he wasn't so smart either—he just had more muscle and more heaters.

The Old Man was getting to be a victim of his own longevity and only the secret files that he kept on the scumbag politicians who had been running the show since Woodrow Wilson were keeping him from being thrown out of the Bureau on his ass. The Kennedys tried to push the Old Man out and he put them in their places. When

Lyndon Johnson had suggested to his aides and to some Senators that Mr. H. take his retirement, Mr. H. just opened the top drawer of his desk and give LBJ a peek at what was inside and Johnson sure changed his tune fast. Besides, all the Old Man had to do was remind Johnson who did what for whom when and Johnson saw the light. Mr. Hoover was given high praise during that administration. Then there was Nixon. Nobody owed Hoover more, with the exception of Johnson, than Richard Nixon. Who gave Nixon his first axe to grind? You think Alger Hiss and Whittaker Chambers happened by accident? Hoover was feeding Nixon under the table, and Nixon paid back the debt while he was Vice President. But now, he wouldn't listen to the Old Man. He had to have his own crew of ex-CIA *gambones* who didn't know a goddamn thing about what they were supposed to do and everything they touched turned to shit. History has borne me out on this one. It was all this group could do just to keep enough cash in the safe behind GW's picture to pay for their own activities. They didn't know the first thing about moving money so nobody knows what you got and where it's at.

Just about the dumbest thing they did—looking back on it now, it was the second dumbest thing they did—was to try to force the Old Man out and turn the FBI into their own private police force. They tried to get him into all sorts of harebrained schemes involving crazy wiretaps anybody's grandmother would have discovered, illegal surveillance that first-year law students would have had used to dismiss cases, and investigations that there was never any hope of ever bringing to conclusion. Do you want to know why they did this? They figured that if they could get him to look stupid enough, he would have to walk away, especially since they were trying to entrap him into breaking the law. The Old Man was too smart for all of 'em. Every time they walked into his office with "Edgar, RMN wants this," or "You can do this for us can't you, Speed?" he would say, "Sure, boys, we can take care of anything. Just have the boss put his John Hancock right on the dotted line here," and that's all it would take. I even heard once that John Mitchell was bounced out of Mr. H.'s office on his ass when he asked him to take care of something for the boss on the q.t. But after the Berrigans had gotten hold of the list of agents in Mr. Hoover's CO-

INTELPRO, the covert operation he was running to gather intelligence on the group and disrupt their operations, the Old Man was held up to ridicule within the Administration that was trying to get rid of him. Even if it was only revenge, he had to show that he wouldn't take it lying down.

No sir, Mr. H. had given his life to the Bureau. He'd held hands with the devil just like everybody else who's had to do business in this world but it was the devil from the Old Country, the devil you knew and trusted. These guys were far worse, and Mr. H. could sense it. That's why he was so frantic about the goings on in this country after 1968. He believed that between the panic in the streets and the panic in the White House, the country was headed for Hell in a handbasket and only a man like J. Edgar Hoover could put a stop to it. On the other hand, he saw the Berrigans as irresponsible criminals hiding behind their clerical collars. He didn't trust Catholics that much anyway because he figured they all took orders from a foreign power. "The Pope's got a Secretary of State don't he?" Mr. H. would say when people asked him why he didn't trust the Kennedys. But when they bragged that they were going to dump LSD in the Washington, DC water supply and blow up the power lines feeding the Washington area, Mr. Hoover just about went crazy. "They can't get away with that," he screamed when he saw me in his hotel room. His eyes were so cloudy I didn't know how he could even see straight. He coughed a lot, too. There was a lot of shit in his lungs. "That's an insurrection. It's high treason." He was as out of control as I'd ever seen anybody. Finally he turned to what was left of the Squad—me—and said, "I want'em dead!" Orders was orders.

When it was in full operation years before, the Squad almost never issued an execution order summarily on its own instigation. When Mr. H. put out a contract for someone to be hit, that was a hit. When the Squad was asked to sit in judgment, that was different. If the distinction between the two doesn't make sense, you had to understand Mr. H. and the way he saw the world. If a guy was a threat, like a Nazi who had crept into the country and was going to cause trouble, or a spy who needed to be rubbed out, Mr. H. would issue a contract for a hit without consulting with anybody. When Gerard Brinkman's number was called, I did him like he was a fly.

Nobody issued any warrant, nobody sat in judgment. A hit's a hit. However, when there was a moral issue, when Mr. Hoover felt that an individual would never be brought to justice for having done something really terrible, he convened his own court: the Court of Life. Maybe there was too much ceremony—I didn't think so at the time—and maybe you might think that it was self-serving since the guy was going to die anyway, but that wasn't true. Mr. Hoover really believed that the man's case should be considered, that people should sit in judgment and look at the man's crime. In the case of the Berrigans and of many, many others, there was no issue about sitting in judgment.

In fact, there was no one around any more who could have sat in judgment. They were all gone: too old, infirm, plain crazy, or dead, except for me, and there were times when I wasn't so sure about myself. In any event, as far as the Berrigans were concerned, there would have been cause in the old days for Mr. H. to have dispatched one of the Unknowns to collect evidence on them and to return with the evidence. If Mr. H. then felt it was a matter for a judgment, he would have asked the Squad. If he felt that he simply needed to put out a contract, he would have done that. It all depended on how it he saw it. But I'll tell you one thing you can bet on—the Old Man was honest with himself. You can bet that he always had a reason and the reason always made sense, even if you didn't agree with it. And that was the case with the Berrigans.

Phillip and Daniel Berrigan ran the East Coast Conspiracy or something that sounded like that. They collected draft cards and burned them. Big shit! But the movement was growing and every week or so somebody would show up with a carton full of draft cards for them to read aloud and burn. It was just like a petition, but instead of people signing their names, they turned in their draft cards and threw their lots in with the Berrigans' group. Technically, the people who donated their draft cards were breaking the law, and that's what got the whole bunch of them into the newspapers. They were holed up in a church in Delaware County, Pennsylvania, which was right near Philadelphia. Infiltrating them was easy. First, I got me some draft cards, thousands of draft cards. I had 'em printed up special for the occasion. They would get me in good with the group. I'd show them that not only was I a sympathizer, I could deliver whatever I was sympathizing about. Next, since I couldn't just show up like Zorro, I had to have some credentials. Nothing special, just a piece of paper that said I wasn't a government plant. That was just as easy. I prevailed upon some of the Good People who still lived in the old neighborhood to ask the bishop to write a letter of introduction for one of their friends who was trying to join a CatholicHoly Name society in Pennsylvania. They said I was just one of the old crowd from the neighborhood who got himself a little shell-shocked in the world war and wanted to straighten out and settle down by doing some maintenance work for a small parish outside of Philly. The bishop was only too happy to oblige.

So we arranged a meeting for me, I hung my head and looked real stupid like some nun had just beaten my brains out with a stick, and the bishop patted me on the head and said, "I wish ya the best of luck, Michael." He wrote a letter of reference in the best handwriting I ever saw, and that was that. When one of the snot-nosed monk types with a bald head, ratty dress, and body odor actually traveled to New York to see the bishop in person, because, as he said, flipping his hand like a *fagela*, "Anybody can write a letter," he received a glowing report on my character. In like Flynn.

You might think that I simply cocked my gun, sat outside the confession box and waited to pop the priests. It was a little trickier than that. I had to contend with a bunch of logistical problems before I could complete this hit so that no fingers obviously pointed at you-know-who. First of all, there were the two priests. They were rarely in the same place at the same time. One of 'em was always running off somewhere: to Washington, DC; to Berkley, California; to jail. It was always something. I saw them together during Mass on Sundays sometimes, but you can't just pull out an automatic and hit two guys praying on an altar in front of a whole congregation. Also, I couldn't hit one, then wait two weeks to hit the other. I would have blown my own cover and alerted the Berrigan who was still alive that there was a contract out on him. So I had to look for an opportunity to wire one of the cars for a bomb or ignite fires in their rooms.

Next, I wanted to find out how these guys were running their operation. If it was the threat that Mr. Hoover believed that it was,

I wanted to have the evidence necessary to back up his fears. So I figured I was in the best position to alert him well in advance to any big plans if the group had decided to cut the power or drug half the capitol with LSD. At the same time, I'd be able to make their operation so that Mr. H. would know what to look for next time. I also wanted to know how much these guys were taking in every week in dough and what they did with it. And, of course, Mr. H. would want to know who else was in the group that he didn't know about, what they were hiding from, and whether they worked for the KGB or some other intelligence organization. A tall order like this can't be filled overnight. You have to spend time, talk to people, blend into the surroundings so that you're just like a church pew. You gotta hold the regular FBI back until you'd gathered everything you were after and gotten out.

Since I'd shown up at their little parish compound as a maintenance worker, they set me to work sweeping floors, cleaning up the kitchen, and mowing the grass. The jobs were menial but they established me as a guy who kept his mouth shut and leaned on his broom. I didn't see much of the Berrigans at all. In fact, these guys acted like a pair of big shots. Any time someone had an order for me, and these college kids really knew how to boss people around, I'd get it from one of the lower-ranking snots. Nobody yelled at me or nothing, they just treated me like I was a personal servant. I had to keep my temper under control and not rub out the first broad who treated me like some piece-of-shit janitor every time she backed up the toilet bowl all over the bathroom floor with a bloody tampex. This was gonna take time, I would tell myself as I leaned over the bubbling mess with a plunger and a snake.

But by the end of the month, I'd been graduated to actually making repairs. The place had obviously been falling apart for years. There was crumbling plaster, peeling paint from the ceilings, busted stairs, hundreds of other problems. Most of the people in this group were so busy stopping the war and saving the human race that they didn't even know how to get on a phone and call a plumber. The simple fact that I could tell one of these guys what to fix and where the pipes were located improved the living conditions at the parish house by two hundred percent by the middle of my second month there. The kids still thought I was an imbecile and called me Lurch when they thought I wasn't around. But, after waking me up the middle of the night for a couple of months to fix this and that, they began treating me like the lamppost. They would think out loud to each other in front of me.

Boy, could these kids think. They didn't just complain about the state of the world, they could quote people who had died ten thousand years ago to prove that things were really as rotten as they said they were. It was like sitting in a room full of Talmudic students at a yeshieva. I wanted to chime in, too, sometimes, but since I had nothing much to say and everything to hear, there was no reason to be a *kibbitzer*.

As the weeks wore on, I was surprised that this group seemed to be exactly what it was—just an organization of college kids. They weren't part of any conspiracy to overthrow anything, but they knew they were being watched, that their mail was being opened, and that their phones were being tapped. They were pretty clever about staying off the phone and using the poor boxes on Sundays to pick up messages from people in other antiwar groups. In fact, I liked the poor-box idea so much, I reminded myself to find a way to tell it to some of the wiseguys that I still knew. They'd get a kick out of it. But I still hadn't said anything to either of the Berrigan brothers even though I heard them talk about raiding draft boards and burning records and stuff like that. I took it all down, of course, and tried to keep track of the draft records they destroyed and the cards they burned so that the Old Man would have a conspiracy case that would stick no matter what happened.

Finally one night I followed the Berrigans to a secluded spot on the grounds of the little parish compound. They were talking, as they usually did, about strategies, tactics, schedules, and money. They had big plans, big ideas. They were going to stop the war and change the world. They actually believed they made a difference, that they had the power to change something. I knew they'd be there for hours, but I didn't know how long they'd be alone so I wasted no time in getting my gun from my room. I screwed on the silencer and got back to the garden where I sat behind a wall, put them in my sights, and listened for as much information as I could wait for before popping them off. It would have been quiet and easy, and I would have been gone within the half hour. But something told me to wait. Other people were still walking around and anybody could have walked into the garden and seen me leaning over a couple of dead priests. So I waited.

I was amazed at how seriously they took each other. Even the toughest, meanest *capos* on the street knew how to laugh. Irish cops who would put you head first through a window and lay off bets on the number of glass fragments you would be picking out of your teeth also knew how to laugh. These guys didn't. They really believed that what they were doing was right. No doubts, no second guesses. I was hoping to hear something incriminating, or maybe even just that they had had a little sex on the side or made some ten-year-old boy give them a blow job, but nothing. They talked about nothing but how fucked up things were in the United States. They were dead wrong, of course. Nothing they said was right. In fact, I'd never heard two people more off-base in my life. You might even say they were stupid, in spite of all the education they wanted you to think they had. But they weren't dangerous. Then, without the least bit of warning, they got up to go to bed. I stuffed my gun away before they passed and they looked right at me like I was a rock or a clod of dirt or a popsicle stick that someone had left on the ground. Didn't say good night, didn't say hello. Just looked at me. Then they went away.

I could have killed them right then and there, and they wouldn't have stopped me. They probably wouldn't even have called for help. They were so dumb they would have thought that that was the way it was supposed to be and took it. But whatever they were, they certainly were no threat. I'd explain it to the Old Man somehow, I said to myself; tell him that we had enough on 'em to put 'em in jail for the next twenty years, but for the first time ever, I couldn't kill somebody just because somebody else wanted 'em dead. Maybe I was getting too old.

I stood there after they left, released the hammer on the gun and popped the clip, and went back to my room. I wrote up where all their files were located, made sure I dated my entries concerning what their plans were and what types of conspiracies they were planning, packed my bags and drove away. In a few days later, the Old Man would be able to get all the indictments he needed to throw these guys in jail and bust up their organization. They would never again toss an FBI office or break into a draft board's files, but at least they would be alive.

I was standing there, looking at the Old Man straight in the eyes when I told him I'd left these guys alive. He started right back at me, mucus clouding up his left eye so badly I wanted to take a piece of toilet paper and clean it up. Then he just sputtered. But I said to him if he was still sitting down at the Court of Life, he'd be asking for a decision. Years ago, he wanted our judgments. He wanted us to say this man lives and this man dies. I was only doing what we'd set out to do. I paid them a visit, listened to what they said to each other when they didn't know I was listening, and made my judgment. I did my job.

He didn't answer me in so many words. He just took my report and nodded, shrugged his shoulders and said they'd go to jail, turned very slowly, and shuffled out of the hotel room. That was the last time I ever saw the Old Man. On Janauary 12 the following year, I heard on tv that the Berrigans were arrested on federal conspiracy charges. The Old Man had listened to me. A few months after that, very early in the morning when my nightmares woke me up and I was reading the paper that the kid had thrown in a puddle, I saw where Mr. Hoover was found dead right in his bedroom. It was as quiet and without ceremony as if a cloud had been blown away from the face of the moon. And that was really the end of the Squad.

The Company

The two black fighters circled each other in the ring at the Nassau Sports Gym where I had my office. I leaned out from my office door to watch them prance, but the ballet was taking too long. They bobbed and weaved in the now classic peek-a-boo style that Cus D'Amato had made famous, alternately grimacing and staring glassy-eyed, throwing occasional pawing jabs at each other's head that fell well short, shrugged their shoulders at the bell, and dragged themselves back to their corners.

"Dhie-rohñ, ju esteeck 'em, ju unnerstañ?" I heard one of the trainers yell at his fighter in the corner. I tried to hear the other corner man bawling out his fighter, sitting bleary-eyed, slack-jawed, and hunched over on his stool, and but it was lost in the clatter of water buckets and talk from ringside.

"Ya called me out to look at this?" I asked Louie Barone, a kind of lookout that I pay off to round up promising ring talent. "Y'ain't workin' for your dough if this is what you consider talent," I said. "Maybe I should get me somebody that knows where to scout."

"Dontcha worry, Mike," Louie said behind a giant ring of cigar smoke. "I toedja I had a kid ya should see and I mean it. Wait 'till these sleepwalkers is finished."

"I got a card to fill for Friday night, Louie," I warned him. "And it's already Wednesday. Every minute that I spend looking at the walking dead is a minute I'm not filling the card."

Louie waved off everything I said and walked me away from the ring as the bell sounded and the next round of you-don't-touch-me-I-don't-touch-you shadow boxing began. "Who in the hell trains these kids?" I asked to no one in particular as Louie walked me around the gym.

I looked at guys who were still seeing stars from their last fight punching out what was left of their arms on the heavy bags, kids dancing and skipping while they tapped away on the speed bag, and real tankers trying to skip rope and falling on their faces because they couldn't keep count anymore. There was gym business going on as well. Promoters just like me were down here trying to fill their cards and scout the young talent that would someday fight at the Garden or at Caesar's Palace in Vegas. Managers and trainers were pushing their kids into our faces: "Give'em a chance, Mike. He's give you two, maybe three rounds. He needs a fight bad." You have to walk away from managers like that. New York State Boxing Commissioner'd be all over my back if he thought I put a kid in a ring just to take a beating for the audience. This wasn't like the old days anymore.

"Mr. Mike," another voice said from over behind the heavy bag. "You been puttin' on the feedbag since I seen you last." I nodded to the guy. Why take offense? He was right. I had blown up to almost a hundred and seventy pounds since I turned fifty. Nothing I tried brought the weight down so I just accepted my new figure and pasted up my old fight pictures all over the basement room. I lost my hair, too. The docs told me that the shock treatments sometimes had that affect on people in later years. They burn the scalp or something.

There were a few more occasional nods from some People standing around the edge of the gym. They sometimes hung out there, too, also checking the local talent that they could recruit. Young, threatening-looking black kids needing quick money were ideal candidates for weekend collection work. They didn't have to do anything except glare at whoever the shylock collector was looking to threaten. "You don't meet your weekly payment, Manny, and Tyrone here gonna pay you." Manny always paid something. He'd hand over a twenty and cry, "No mas, no mas, dos nes' week" but a good collector knew how to take that extra ten away that he was holding back for himself. It'd been a long time since I'd made collections for the downtown sharks. If they needed my services these days, it was more to represent their interests at a sitdown if they stepped on somebody's toes by venturing out of their territories. Then their lives would be in the balance, and it would cost them big to buy their lives back.

I'd represented a shark I had known for years just the other week. We'd gone to a little Spanish place called the Running of the

Bulls over on West Fourteenth Street for a sitdown in the back room. The people he'd crossed made threats. They told him where they were connected. He told them where he was connected. They said, "Prove it," and I showed up. The wiseguys were edgy and acted tight at the sitdown. Nobody wanted trouble. I worked out a deal, the shark promised to cut them in for thirty percent of the vig from the territory he'd intruded upon, and I gave my word. That was as sacred to me now as it was when I started. Our agreement was sealed. Then as we walked out, the shark turned to me and laughed. "You were great, Mike. Just stared them down. Now they won't see a cent and they won't dare cross you." I turned red and lost control. The sonovabitch had just stepped over my word. I turned him around by the neck and dragged him back inside the restaurant. Shoved him down in a seat and gave him back to the wiseguys. "He's yours," I said. That was the last I saw of him, and the People returned the gratitude for the service I had performed for them. Nobody crosses my word. It was one of the few things I had left.

Rumors of the Squad and the People who'd worked the line between the Bureau and the Families were all but faded now. Some of the old timers might have still swapped stories of the days before Hoover died, but most of them were sitting in wheelchairs staring at the passing cars. Now even Nixon was gone as were the maniacs who'd worked for him. Most of the People now were third and even fourth generation. They were kids who'd gone to business schools and worked out percentages on their pocket calculators at sitdowns over lunch at Ivy League clubs. They knew how to figure money and little else. They weighed their money instead of counting it and dealt only with the Columbians and the Taiwanese who'd cut you out as soon as look at you. Maybe I was too old, but it was not my idea of business.

"He's ready, Mike," Louie called from ringside.

A strapping giant of a fighter stepped through the ropes. Big and menacing, he looked 225 pounds if he was an ounce, and he shadow boxed and danced for the crowd that had gathered around to watch the show. He had killer hands, big, meatball fists that looked like they could pummel you into a fog with a flurry of punches. And he had good legs. Thick thighs and a springy stride that could take him out of trouble or carry him in to finish off a guy weaving on the ropes. I liked the looks of him the minute I saw him. I wondered who else was there looking to fill a card and I was glad I had a pocketful of dough I could wave in his face. If he was like most of the kids who crossed my path, he'd go for the legit dough before taking it from promoters who were really recruiting for the sharks. He glared at me from the ring.

"This is Mr. Mike, Henry, the guy I told you about," Louie told him. "You show him your best stuff. Dance and stick. Show him."

Henry put on a show, dancing and skipping, moving around in the Ali shuffle, spinning around the ring while throwing combinations of punches upstairs and downstairs that seemed almost too good to be true. Part of me, the part that was twenty years old, wanted to get into the ring with him and dance him around for eight rounds. Let him punch himself out until he was so tired he could barely stand. Then I'd be working him over myself, building up points, cutting his face into bloody ribbons until his eyes were so puffed he couldn't see. Then I'd test his strength, see if he could still punch. I'd test my strength against his. And if I were lucky, I'd drop him in the tenth round while the crowd bellowed in disbelief that a little runt from the Lower East Side could take on the brute and pound him to the canvas. That's what I did in the Navy.

"Whaddya think, Mike?" Louie asked.

"But can he punch?" I asked back.

"Say what?" the kid growled and balled his huge fist in my face. "Check it out! Where'sa muvafucka I'ma fight. Mess 'em up."

Another giant heavyweight stepped into the ring, clearly older than Henry but just as menacing. Louie had arranged a show for me this afternoon for sure. Henry glared across the ring at him and shook his bandaged fist. He pointed his monster arm at the second fighter, rolled his eyes, and yelled: "I want you! I want you!" Then he danced around the ring, firing off left-right combinations in no particular order, did the Ali shuffle again, and stopped—just like he was in a Road Runner cartoon—inches short of the man's nose. The older fighter didn't flinch, didn't even twitch a muscle. They looked at each other eye to eye, the tips of the hairs on the very edges of their noses just touching like the antennas of two ants telling each other where Little Miss Muffit's picnic basket was spread out. "You ugly," Henry sneered. "Too ugly. I'ma mess you up."

"Yo', blood, iss awright," the older fighter said. "Chi' wout, bruvah. Who be watchin'?"

"Man be watchin'," Henry said, jerking his bandaged fist back in my direction.

The older fighter looked over at me and stared hard. I'd seen him before, although I don't know if he got a good look at me at the time. He was in the dressing room at one of the local arenas when some wiseguys worked over a friend of his for going independent on them instead of following the company policy for that night. This big man tried to voice his opinion but he quieted down real fast when one of the wiseguys shoved the muzzle of a nine millimeter pistol into his mouth, cracking off his front teeth and busting his lip open. I was standing by the door that night, making sure that no one lost his head and hurt somebody. Did he get a look at me? Watching him staring at me from the corner of the ring, I could just about hear the gears cranking around in his head. Why did I look so familiar, where he had seen me before, what was he expected to do for me and for Louie—who he also scanned real quick—and what was in it for him at the end of it? Then his eyes widened as a distant memory flashed between his ears like current through a wire. The gears stopped. He came to a decision. Now I was interested.

"Eveythin' be chill," he whispered softly to Henry like a father talking to an unruly child he was trying to quiet down while at the same time keeping his mind on the more pressing business at hand. Louie nodded to Henry's trainer who dragged him back to a corner and laced on his gloves. The trainer nodded to Louie who nodded to another man holding a stopwatch on the other side of the ring.

"Time!" The man called out, and the two heavyweights bobbed into the center of the ring.

Henry moved out quickly and peppered the older man with a barrage of lightning left jabs to his forehead. His opponent took them like was wearing a helmet, crouched, and came up quickly with a short left hook under the ribs that took Henry's wind away for a moment, but didn't cave him in. Henry was more concerned about not showing that he was hurt than he was about protecting himself from another punch so he never figured out how the punch landed. He only stepped away, flicked off a light show of jabs, and did the Ali shuffle in circles around the older man.

"Time!" The timekeeper called out from the side of the ring, and the two fighters trotted back to their corners and leaned against the ropes.

Both Henry and the older man kept their eyes fixed on me. Louie leaned over and whispered, "I know you're busy, Mike—Henry'll set him down this round and you can go back in your office. I'll set the deal for you." I didn't answer because maybe I knew something that Louie didn't. Henry's opponent looked out over the ring at me and asked in a slow, deliberate voice. "You be hangin' or checkin' out?" I shook my head to tell him it depended on what happened, and he nodded and let a glaze come back over his eyes.

"Time!"

And this time Henry seemed to swarm out of his corner, all lefts and rights, as if was a one-man fireworks show on the Fourth of July. He flailed away at the man in front of him, slipped his long, almost lazy counterpunches, and swept low and in with counterpunches of his own. Henry was technically very well-trained, a real student of the fights he had seen on TV. He knew how to use his shoulders and his legs, knew how to keep his head moving so an opponent couldn't get a bead on it, and understood what Ali meant when he said he "stung like a bee."

A sharp tap on my shoulder took me away from the ring for a second. "Telephone for you, Mike," one of the trainers whispered loud enough for the whole world to hear. I glared at him, and he lowered his voice. "And someone just left this for you." He handed me a padded envelope with no name on it.

"How do you know it's mine?" I asked.

"Guy in a suit just walks up and says give this to Mike Milan. I don't ask no questions—I give it to Mike Milan. Guy drove away in a red Chrysler Fifth Avenue, white vinyl roof and Jersey plates 'case you're interested."

I turned he package over in my hand and quickly slit it open so I could see inside. There was a gold coin inside. I felt my heart stop beating for a second.

"Phone, Mike!"

"Checkin' out," I called to the ring.

Henry's opponent nodded in acknowledgment, stepped away from the flailing heavyweight, circled low and to his left, and threw a murderous left-right uppercut combination to Henry's midsection. Henry stopped in his tracks, dropped his hands as he desperately tried to catch his breath. But, even as Louie screamed, "Get out," the older fighter unloaded a left hook to the side of Henry's head that staggered him, a looping overhand right that crashed over the bridge of Henry's nose, and a second left hook that caught him flush on the jaw. Henry fell forward like a tree in a forest and lay there face down with his legs twitching wildly on the canvas in a stuporous dance.

"Get him to a doctor, fast," I said to Louie as I looked squarely at the older fighter who was standing over him. Even he was surprised that Henry fell so hard. He knew exactly what I was saying and leaned over the unconscious Henry, turned him on his back, and pulled out his mouthpiece before he choked on it and unlaced his headgear.. I pointed at the older fighter, "And set this guy up for Friday," I called out to Louie as I left for the phone receiver that was dangling against the far wall. "And call Artie if I'm not around."

"Yeah?" I said into the phone.

"You get your package?" A voice asked. It did not sound familiar.

"The key fits locker 390 JFK International Terminal. Repeat."

"I don't repeat nuthin'," I said.

"Everything is in the locker. We expect you tomorrow night." The voice hung up.

Maria wasn't going to like my taking another business trip, I knew that without even wasting any time thinking about it, but if whoever sent me the gold piece knew where and when to find me that easily, I had no choice but to follow the instructions. If I didn't like what I found wherever I was going, I'd have to worry about it then and there. This was too close to home and too late in the game for me to walk away like a yo-yo. But Maria let me off easy when I broke the news to her later that evening. I was able to get to the People I needed before midnight so they could watch the house, the car even had gas in it, and the traffic along the Southern State wasn't bumper to bumper. I didn't know what flight I was taking or where my destination was, but I figured it was better to get a jump as close to sunrise as possible.

I hadn't been at the International Terminal for years, but the lockers were in the same place they used to be. There were lots of rent-a-cops, though, and plenty of plain-clothes security wandering around. The terminal was crowded because of the all the early morning flights most international travelers take, and I had all the cover I needed to get into the locker and out. I followed the same drill I'd practiced for the past twenty-eight years and opened the envelope only after I was alone in my stall listening to the shitting and puking taking place on the toilet next to me. I was carrying my plastic .22, not much better than a BB gun for any serious business, but useful in close quarters when the other guy thinks he's got the drop on you. Back in '75, without any rounds in the barrel, you could wear it on your leg and it would pass through the metal detectors like plastic buttons. Back then you could've packed the individual rounds in harmless-looking film canisters and let them pass through the X-ray machines separately. If I'd had a silencer, I could've used it to put the guy next door to me out of his misery. But as it was, I didn't have to spend much more time in the can because the envelope had tickets to an afternoon flight to Detroit from LaGuardia, confirmed hotel reservations for a Ramada Inn near the airport, a reservation card for a rental car, and fifty grand in cash—twice my going rate back in the '60s for a private contract. Inflation wasn't so bad after all, I thought as I folded the money into my pockets.

I still had the morning to stash the money and act as if life were normal, so I drove back to my office at Nassau Sports in Merrick where I locked the dough in my desk safe and had some coffee with the girl who answers the phone. She'd be a good alibi if anybody asked any questions. Then I put together the final card for Friday night, walked around the gym and talked to some of the fighters in training there to establish my whereabouts for the day even further, and grabbed a bagel at a deli where people knew me before driving to LaGuardia airport. After I checked in for the flight, I stood well off to the side of the waiting lounge just in case anybody was to show up to see that I got off. When you don't know who you're dealing with, it always pays to take extra special care. In this case, I figured, I could've been dealing with anybody, and my gut sense told me they were rank amateurs with a lot of dough to spend to make sure somebody didn't wake up in his own bed.

It was after dinner when I landed in Detroit. I got my bag, picked up the car, and drove to the Ramada Inn just off the airport exit ramp from the Interstate where I checked in at the desk and picked up an envelope that was already waiting for me in the room's mailbox. More *govaldin,* I said to myself as I turned the odd-sized, official-looking, sealed brown envelope over and over in my hand. I was hungry because the dinner on the plane was cold and I felt like we were flying most of the time upside down anyway. Worse, we landed so many times along the way, I thought I was on the Long Island Railroad's Babylon local instead of an airplane. So, by the time I recovered from the bouncing plane and smiled my way past the chirping Barbie doll at the car-rental counter, I was tired, ready to eat the bed, and in no mood for a midnight meeting. I folded a ten spot into the bellboy's basketball player's-sized palm and grinned him out the door. Then I stretched full-out on the bed, kicked off my shoes, and looked inside the envelope where I found a typewritten note that said DINNER AT 10—RM 247. It was almost nine but I couldn't wait so I ordered a coffee and danish and told the desk to call me at 9:45. I was asleep before the coffee and danish arrived. By the time the wakeup call came, the coffee on the tray outside the door was cold and the danish smelled of plastic food wrap. I splashed water on my face, put on a tie, and went to dinner feeling every inch like an old, old man.

"I can't tell you how I've looked forward to this meeting, Mike," the gentleman sitting across from me at the dinner table said. "I've heard some of the stories about you from the old Indochina hands at CIA—the way you shut down that whole gold pipeline yourself when you found out the Thais were running heroin back to the States. That took balls, Mike. And then, how you beat up on Li Chin—he's still bellyachin' about it. The Company wanted your head on a platter for years after you shut them down in Hilo. They still do—even after you and the boys saved their collective asses in Dallas! I even heard the stories about the botched shock treatments and the brain cutter who worked you over." He stopped to let the effect of his next remark sink in. "And the way he was flattened out by a hit-and-run driver right in front of the hospital at that hour of the morning. Never even caught the driver. There are those of us at the Company who are very happy that you were pulled out in time. It was the Old Man's doing. He let them bring you in. He got you out."

It had been going on like this for a half an hour. All I wanted to do was eat and find out what the fuck was going on here. All this guy did was fall on his face over stuff that I'd done fifteen years ago. I still didn't know what this was all about, and I was beginning to get very suspicious. He'd only given his name as Mr. Brown, had dodged every question I put, especially the ones about why I was there, and hadn't asked any of his own. He and I were the only two in the room. Either he was stalling for time, which seemed to make no sense, or he was buttering me up. That didn't make any sense either, unless this was a suicide hit. All the buttering up in the world wasn't going to get me involved in a suicide hit because after you pass the downside of fifty, I can tell you that the recliner, a Nathan's frank, and a beer look too good to pass up for a damp coffin no matter how much money they promise your kids.

"Mr. Brown, I understand that you've managed to get some very privileged access to records that should have been destroyed years ago, but what I can't understand is of what possible use they can be to you now," I said in my most businesslike way.

"You underestimate your value, Mike," Brown said.

"Mr. Brown," I answered quickly. "I underestimate nothing. That's how I've stayed alive all these years. Least of all, do I underestimate you. That's why I must ask you again. What possible use can twenty-year-old records hold for you? You can't expect to blackmail me for anything, because I have no money. I can't deliver anybody to you, not only because I won't, but because anyone who would trust me enough to be delivered is dead. I'm afraid you're looking at an antique, Mr. Brown." I figured I'd goad him into revealing something. If that didn't work, I'd go back to ping pong.

"Now you and I both know that's not true," Brown said. "We know that you've undertaken a number of investigations—some of them involving prejudicial terminations of extraneous personnel— for years. In fact you come highly recommended. Your discretion, which I've just spent this past half hour ascertaining, has been more than accurately represented. It is one of your qualifications for this job. The other qualifications, given the types of assignments you've had, are all attested to by the fact that you're here, alive, and in one piece. Blackmail is out of the question. If we thought you were so dangerous to control that blackmail was our only alternative, you'd already be dead. I mean no offense, of course. You've lived with that understanding for years."

"So?" I asked, gratified at least that my goading had some effect on the meeting. But before he could answer, the phone rang. Brown picked up the receiver and grunted "Yes?" into it and nodded as he heard what the voice at the other end said. Then he hung up.

"Actually," Brown continued after putting down the receiver, "there is somebody you and I both know. He instigated this, but for reasons that will become obvious, could not contact you by the usual method. Thus, we had to set this meeting place."

There was a knock at the door and a person I knew all too well walked in. I'm not going to reveal his name because he is one of the few people from my past who is still alive, very active, very public, very society-page hoity-toity, and in a position of great sensitivity. I'll call him Mr. X., although that's not the initial of his last name. It's the best you're gonna get from me. I ran a number of very private investigations for Mr. X.—none of them involving hits— since the 1960s. Although not formally connected, he, like any *Fortune 500* businessman, has had extensive, albeit indirect, dealings with People and may continue to have them to this day. You should know, in case you haven't guessed by now, that since 1960, our national security services, our biggest corporations, and the people who need People all eat at the same table and break bread together. They were the ones who signed my checks. In any event, it was Mr. X. who walked through the door.

"Mike," he said with his usual very broad rich man's smile and very firm rich man's handshake. "Sorry about the charade, but it was necessary. I just couldn't see you in New York. I wanted the chance to talk to you without any interruptions."

"Mr. X.," I said. Actually that's not what I said, but it'll have to do. "Now you've really got my curiosity aroused." And that's all I said. For all this trouble and for all of Mr. X.'s contacts, I knew this meeting had to be about one of two things, neither of which was going to involve me if I had any choice in the matter.

"Circumspect, as usual," he said. And I still don't understand the meaning of the word circumspect enough to know whether to be insulted or not. When I was younger I would get insulted whenever he said it. Now that I was over fifty, I figured I didn't have the time to be insulted so I took it as a compliment. Either way, I'd been circumspect for enough years that the word had lost most of its effect. "I've kept your curiosity aroused long enough," he continued. "I am part of a group of businessmen, a special group, some of whom you've worked for for twenty years now, who need you to do a job for them. You've done this kind of job before, almost."

And he paused to let the almost sink in. I made my face go as blank as a wall. He was getting nothing out of me, even though I knew what the next thing was that he was going to say. And I knew what I was going to say.

"You were in Dallas in 1963 and learned more than you should have," Mr. X. said. "We know that. That's why the CIA picked you up two years later. You know that. And then you spread their best brain cutter all over Third Avenue. There was talk of a sanction meeting after that. Mike, I'll cut to the chase: Ford's been sanctioned. He's got to go. He won't go by himself; we've asked him. We've bloody told him to move out of the way for Nelson. But he wants to get elected. He's made a mess of everything and now he wants to lose the election to make matters worse. Besides, he was part of the same coverup you were—you know that, too."

It was one of the two things all right. In fact, the first thing. And, no, I wasn't going to do it. There was no percentage in it. I just wasn't going to be that stupid.

"You know why we want Nelson in," Mr. X. continued. "You've indirectly worked for him already. I'm not saying Rocky's one of us. We haven't even spoken to him about this. But he would understand if he were in our position."

"I'm supposed to squeeze the trigger?" I said. "Aren't you afraid that I'm a little too old? Besides, it's a suicide hit."

"First of all, you're not too old and you know it. Second of all, you don't have to squeeze any triggers unless you want to. Think of yourself as kind of a general contractor. And last of all it's not a suicide hit," X. said, and that intrigued me most of all.

"For it not to be a suicide hit," I said. "You'd have to have the Secret Service. Without the Service, you ain't got nothing."

"If you're in, you'll know; if not, what you know is a liability."

"Mr. X.," I said. "I didn't ask to be here. I didn't ask to know anything. You told me. If what you said about what I know being a liability is meant to be a threat, I have to tell you, you're in way over your head. The advice I gave you about needing the cooperation of the Service isn't meant to tell you how to do something that can't be done, it's meant to show that you need too many people to do the job. This ain't Dallas. People like this guy."

"Dallas was different," X. said. "It was botched—you saw that for yourself. It was more of an accident than anything else. There were so many people after Kennedy they almost tripped over themselves trying to get to him first."

"And that's exactly what's gonna happen now unless the whole Service has been turned," I said. "And what's the point?"

"Mike," X. broke in. "It's a done deal! We have them. It's over. Now all we need is the shooter. Feel better?"

I knew finally, not to ask why. After all these years, I didn't need to know why anymore. Why was for newspaper reporters. Since I knew I wasn't going to shoot President Ford, there was no purpose in my staying around to share information.

"Mr. X.," I said, swinging back in the chair like I was conducting a meeting. "is there anything I can say to change your mind?"

"No, Mike," he said. "If you turn us down, we have other people. We've already covered the Secret Service so nobody you talk to there will act on the threat. And your friends at the FBI, all dead. There's nobody you can call. Nobody's gonna stop it. You're all alone, Mike—the last brave on the reservation. Let me make it more than worth your while, for old time's sake. Consider it the pension you never got. You'll be a multimillionaire for thirty seconds' work. In or out?"

"Out," I said and stood up to leave.

"Wait a minute," Mr. Brown said and stood up as well. Mr. X. put his hand on Brown's arm and forced him to sit down.

"If he doesn't want to do it, he can't be forced. Let him go," Mr. X. said. "What's he going to do, blow the whistle on himself? He's a player, an accessory before the fact, a co-conspirator. He attended a meeting at which the assassination of the President of the United States was negotiated. He's as guilty as hell. Besides, nobody will believe him."

Mr. X. was right. He knew my hand as if he were reading the cards in a mirror. By the time I'd gotten in the car and was off to the airport, I'd run through an entire list of names to call, and not any of them would have been any help. Most of my contacts were dead and I couldn't go to the police without opening up a giant can of worms. It looked to me in the car as if I'd just have to sit back and watch it happen. I also figured I was being watched and followed so I did nothing but stand around the security gate at the airport to wait for the flight back to New York.

I was as careful in New York as I had been on the way back from Detroit. I didn't immediately check in at the house. Rather, I stayed with friends in the old neighborhood while I looked for a secure enough phone booth to call in my information to Washington. Meanwhile, I had someone I trusted keep an eye on the house and office and report any new cars that seemed to be cruising the area. Nothing was out of the ordinary and nobody was scouting the house. At least Mr. X. was keeping his word. Finally, I called the Secret Service and found that Mr. X. was right about that, too. On three successive occasions, I phoned the White House office and on each of the occasions they asked me my name and address, heard my story, and thanked me for the information. However, when I'd called back, they reported they were unable to confirm any of my facts. Mr. X. was covering his tracks well. I didn't know where the attempt would take place, who would make it, and who was behind it. You see, the way the game was played, for me to stay alive, I couldn't breach Mr. X.'s trust by revealing that he was plotting against the President. But for me to get off the hook legally, so that I was not, myself, an accessory, I had to stop it from happening.

Finally, I made one chance call at an old phone number in Virginia. A strange voice answered the phone, claimed he'd never heard of anyone called Receiver, claimed that there never was any serial number like the one I gave him, and finally hung up before I could go any further. I tried again and this time, I made the connection.

"You're takin' a big chance by doing this," the familiar voice I recognized as Receiver said. "You could get a lot of career people in a heap of trouble by using that number."

"But there's a contract out on Ford," I said.

"So you say," Receiver answered. "Secret Service has been checking up and down since you first called and there's nothing."

"That's 'cause they've been gotten to," I told him. "My information tells me that they're going to stand away. It's inside all the way."

"Nonsense," Receiver said. "We'd know. Who's behind it?"

"You know the rules," I told him. "Just have your people watch the Secret Service, that's all I can say."

"Not good enough, Mike. Give me something else."

"Figure it this way," I told him. "If they contacted me and I said no, they might have contacted others who said no. I'd play the longshot and bet that nobody's agreed to take the contract. If that's true, they gotta go to an amateur. An amateur's gonna make mistakes. They're gonna be easy to spot. That gives you the edge."

"Mike," Receiver said. "Your story doesn't help me as it is, but I'll push it as far as I can. You've done your job on this one. You've reported it. You're in the clear as far as we're concerned. Don't call back!"

And that's as far as it went. I lived out of a suitcase for the next week, staying away from Long Island, and when nobody turned up on my doorstep, I finally came in. I kept my word to Receiver and didn't call back. For all I knew, he could have been one of the deputy directors or not even in the Bureau at all. But, a few months later, it was all over the news that Lynnette Fromme had tried to shoot Ford at close range when he was in Sacremento. And two weeks later, Sarah Jane Moore made another attempt. Mr. X. had done it after all. Fortunately, with the whistle blown, the Secret Service had no choice but to do its job. No doubt whoever was working with Mr. X. had calmly swept everything under the rug. And I assumed that Mr. X. had given up Lynnette Fromme and Sarah Jane Moore when he was told that the FBI was investigating. The girls were easy tokens.

I never heard from Mr. X. after that. I slipped back into my life like putting on an old winter glove just as he slipped back into his life. And whatever Gerry Ford did or didn't know about what was going on around him, that became history as well. He still kept on beaning whoever played golf with him, and the man who was supposed to replace him in the White House was found dead in his girlfriend's arms shortly after he left office. I often wonder who got to him.

The Good People

"So you saved Ford's life after all?" the Marine captain asks me, his eyebrows raised up and his eyes wide with the thought, "Is this what really went on in the old days?"

I sit back in the chair and take my time. He ain't goin' nowhere. My head's still swimming with memories. I walked away from that whole Ford business with my life still in one piece. I sweated off every pound of weight that I'd put on back in those years. Did my roadwork. Worked out on the heavy bag. Even stepped into the ring with some of the kids to build up my hand speed again. It took me years, but I got back into fighting shape. I figured I might have to take it on the lam if what Mr. X. said about the CIA came to pass. Maybe it was coming to pass now.

"I asked," the Marine captain said, even louder, like he was talking to an *alter cocker* who could barely understand what he was saying. "Is this what really happened in the old days?"

I drain my cup in one long, loud, final slurp. The coffee is cold and I'm anxious to get outta here.

"He lives to attack people with golf balls to this very day," I says, but the Marine captain, he don't laugh.

"And you say the Secret Service was in on it?" he asks. "They actually let Squeaky Fromme get into the hollow square and aim the gun?"

Maybe he's asking too many questions and maybe I'm giving too many answers, but I been in the shadows too long to care. I'm figuring as I look at him, maybe people should know what really went on. I was proud of what I did. So what if I was a hitter? I saw what the cops were doing, and the FBI, and the CIA, and plenty of other government agencies with lots of letters that really stand for "Blow their brains out and don't tell nobody." And what Uncle Sam sanctioned for himself, he sanctioned for some pretty big corporations, too. But just because we were poor Jews and Italians from the

Lower East Side who tried to scratch out a living during Depression, we were the "syndicate," the country's official outlaws. I'll tell you something about law and what it means to be inside of it and outside of it. I was both at the same time and you couldn't tell one from the other. Know why? Because law is made by lawyers for lawyers. It ain't made for people. When you wanna take something that's outside the law and bring it inside the law, you simply change the law.

Buying booze was as legal as buying a strawberry phosphate in 1915. But then a bunch of pantywaists got on a bandwagon and they made buying booze a crime. It didn't change anybody's habits, it just made it more expensive to get booze. Then when the government saw that everybody still wanted booze, they made it legal again. They did the same thing with the numbers racket. Arnold Rothstein, Meyer Lansky, and Dutch Schultz invented the numbers game. They figured their percentages and made millions. Then the lawyers wanted a piece of the action and tried to put the numbers syndicates out of business. It didn't change anybody's mind. People still wanted to play their daily number. So the lawyers said, let's call it a "lottery" instead and we'll make all the money for ourselves. It's still gambling, only now it's legal. So don't call anybody an outlaw until you know the whole story. Maybe tomorrow some lawyer will write a law that says that hitting is legal. It already is—if you work for the CIA.

When the CIA wanted to hit Castro, who'd they call? They didn't have anybody who could do a hit worth talking about. They called on the People. When Mr. Hoover was alive, he wouldn't dare send his own agents undercover. He thought they'd get corrupted. He was right. So he sent us. We were already corrupted, he thought deep down in his own mind. Even though I thought there was nobody better than Mr. H., I have to face the truth. In his eyes, I was a hitter and that's all I'd ever be. When the CIA said they were gonna scramble up my brains so I'd be useless to anybody, he went along with it. He apologized in his own way years later, but he let it happen until it ate him up inside that he wasn't being stand-up for the People who were stand-up for him. Who's to say who was more stand-up?

So now I'm sitting here in the commissary at Mitchell Field looking at a guy dressed like a Marine captain and he doesn't know what to make of me. I'm a relic and a threat to his little world at the same time. But when they send him on an errand to find a hitter to snuff out an embarrassing situation, they send him out to find me. Now I'm giving him a history lesson and he's eating it up. But now it's time to wrap it up for today.

"It was the Manson family," I tell him. "They'd been doin' contract hits for dope pushers out on the West Coast for years before that little bitch went to whack Ford. Pathetic. And they were the only people who'd take the contract."

Class dismissed. I'm getting set to leave now and hoping this guy doesn't want to tag along. "Worst part of it was, nobody believed me. If it hadn't been for this one contact who still knew me, I don't how I could've gotten the message through."

"So you walked away," the Marine continues. "Just like that, walk away?"

"I walk away with my life," I says. "I told myself that was the end of it, and I meant it. Still do."

"You know they're not gonna take no for an answer," he's warning me now. "They're gonna wanna know why and they're gonna stay on your ass." He waves the indictment in front of me like a flag. "This is a big one, Mike. A lot of butt is on the line. If they talk, they bring a lot of people down with them. Who knows, maybe they even bring you down."

It was a nice try, but I was having no part of it. I slide the gold piece back across the table. I want no part of it now. I am strictly a retired war veteran trying to stay in shape for my golden years. "Captain," I said. "Even if I wanted to get back in the game, this ain't the kind of job I do. Tell your people, these are my People." I pointed to the names on the indictment. "I never used what I knew from one side to help the other. I never crossed the line."

"That's how you stayed alive all these years?"

"That was the big way. You never cross your friends. For everything else, you have to be a born actor. You have to make yourself over into a new person who's the right fit for each different situation," I explain. "Can't do it for this."

"And that's your final answer?" he asks.

"Final answer," I tell him again. One more time and I'll have to hire a skywriter.

"Then I suggest you find a safe place," he tells me. "It ain't like it was way back when. They don't take no as an answer anymore."

I stand up and reach my hand across the table. "You've already told me what I need to know," I say. And I leave him sitting there in the commisary before he has a chance to answer.

This morning's news is certainly disquieting. You know when you've established a kind of balance to the long view of the rest of your life. You know where you're gonna eat your bagel and cream cheese on a Tuesday, where you're gonna sit and read the paper in the morning, where you're gonna talk on the phone. You accept that either you have to lose some weight or that you're gonna look too heavy for the girls that you're never gonna impress anymore. You make your compromises with your past and your future and you're prepared to live with them. That's how I was before I bumped into the Marine captain. Suddenly, he pushes a gold coin across a table, tells me that some snotnose CIA punk in Washington with spaghetti for a spine wants Jake Littman hit, and now I gotta worry that he might get pissed at me. That's why we had a Court of Life, precisely because the Old Man knew that you had to stare somebody else in the eye and explain why the man who's picture was on the table had to go. Just that simple.

I remember back some twenty-five years ago that the Old Man was once crazed over an appellate judge out in Kansas, who threw out every conviction the local cops could get. Mr. H. knew the judge. Had a file on him. Knew he was bought and paid for. Normally, Mr. H. would say that it's the state's problem. They elected him. They gotta get rid of him. But this judge, he just got on Mr. H.'s mean side. The judge had a real weak spot for little girls, especially little blonde ones. He was buying and selling them like commodities futures. What could you do? The local cops wouldn't touch him. LBJ threw up his hands and told the Old Man the judge would be in office for the rest of his life. "The rest of his life," the Senator said, leaning forward over the big desk in Mr. H.'s office and shaking his big jowly, hound-dog head into Mr. H.'s face. Then he winked. That was all the Old Man needed. He polled each one of us after that meeting. He said, "It's a judge, boys, take your best shots." He didn't like judges on principle because most of 'em couldn't measure up to his standards.

They sent me down to do the hit, but Mr. H. wanted him to experience pain. "He's gonna die anyway, Mike," he said. "Make it special. Make it nice and slow. But let him know that it's only the beginning. The Judge upstairs is really gonna hammer him when you're done."

I have to admit, I hated these "vengeance is mine" hits. They always took too long, left you wide open for people just walking in on you, and unless the guy was a Nazi or Kyoshi Moro, I could't work up the amount of hate necessary for a really good acting job. That's why, if you ask me, I always thought that Method was the way to go in these situations, but Strasberg threw my ass out of the Studio for trying to look down the front of some broad's blouse. So I never learned Method.

Probably for that reason, it always took a lot out of me when I had to work up a good hate for one of Mr. H.'s special assignments. But I gave this Kansas judge his money's worth. He actually thought that not only was I crazier than he was, but that he himself had triggered the apocalypse that was going to take place the minute he breathed his last. I started slow, getting him on my side like Pat O'Brien in *Angels with Dirty Faces:* "You got to set an example for the boys, Rocky," I says. Then I became just like Walter Huston or Lionel Barrymore, eyes rolling, eyebrows going up and down like the King Kong monster, frothing at the mouth, hands around his throat, hand on my lapel—"Don't you touch that girl"— gun goes right in his mouth. Ended up with Cagney in the search-lights, "Top of the world, ma!" I was really playing this part. I had 'em. I was doing *shtick*. I coulda walked out of the storeroom right then and there and he'd never touch a little girl again the rest of his life. Then some janitor bangs open the door with his bucket, scares the character right out of me, and ba-da-boom: the judge's brains are all over the cleaning locker. What a mess. The janitor had to go and stick his head through the door. I belted him across the head so hard that when he woke up I bet he couldn't figure out which brains were his and which were the judge's.

The point of all this is that even Mr. H., who could order a hit over the phone like you'd order a pizza, still wanted to look right into the eyes of one of the Unknowns and ask, "Is this the right thing?" I guarantee you the guy in Washington who put out the contract on Jake Four Eyes didn't ask anybody. He just looked at a printout, matched it with another printout, and ordered an intelligence officer out with the contract. Plug 'em through some keyhole and slink away. Fuck 'em! Not the way I work. What am I— some work-for-hire creep? I was an artist. When I hit a guy, he knew he was gettin' hit. That's why they call it a hit. When they tried to hit Frank Costello, you think they did it like cowards? No! The Chin calls out "Frank, this is for you," 'cause he knows you never shoot a don in the back. *Rispetto! Menschlichkeit!*

I didn't want to spend any more time than I had to at Mitchell Field, especially with this Marine interested in who I know and what I did. So I drive like a bat out of hell into Manhattan. Somehow the old neighborhood is gonna feel good today, I'm thinking. Haven't been there in a while. No reason to go 'cause all the boys are dead. I drive down Houston, over to Ludlow, down Delancey, across Mulberry to Canal. I hate driving these days. I need to get out and walk in the afternoon sun. Lots of Koreans and Japanese on the streets where Italians and Jews used to slug it out over territory. Then we'd join forces and go kick the shit out of the Micks. That's why the cops hated us so much. Maybe we'd go south of Canal and eat some Chinese. The old men'd see us comin' and get out of our way. The Jews moved out to the Island. The Italians moved out to Jersey. Mulberry Street's a shell. Japanese tourists come here on Sunday to laugh at the old waiters just trying to make a buck to keep their kids in school. This is not the way it should've been. Turned out all wrong. We won the war. I heard years ago that Four Eyes was a stand-up guy. Now they want to foreclose? This is dead wrong.

I don't know how long I'm walking, but the shadows are getting long. Maybe Maria's worrying by now. Maybe she figures I just disappeared, put out in a bag with yesterday's chow mein. I dunno what she figures, but I gotta walk. I gotta make it seem right. I see a man I knew years ago sitting by a coffee house where I used to sit. I remember his daughter was roughed up, slapped around by some guy whose father worked out of the District Attorney's office. Cop told the guy to hang himself 'cause it was the only satisfaction he was gonna get. I found the ADA's kid and beat the living shit out of him. Gave him scars he'll never outgrow. Walked into the precinct house where the cop was and faced him down. "You tough guy with little girls, Boyo. You 'n me, outside, see who walks away. Rest of you guys can take numbers." Cop backed down and apologized to the father. DA didn't even lift a finger. I didn't ask for a dime from the father. I wouldn't take money for something like that. Girl wrote me little note from the hospital. Frank Costello told me I did the right thing.

The old gent recognized me now and he nodded just slightly. Never nod too much down here, people might think a car'd be pulling around the corner and you'd wind up over the curb in your own blood. He bows as I walk up. He knows who I am even though he only saw me once. I don't answer, I just bow a little, too. You know how people do it when they don't want to talk? I gotta figure all this out. Then the old man hangs on my sleeve.

"*Buona sera,* Mike the Enforcer," he says. Just like that, "*Buona sera.*" Whaddya think of that? After all those years, too.

Index